ONLY WANNA BE WITH YOU

April 1994: Twelve weeks before the release of their debut album, *cracked rear view*, Hootie & the Blowfish stand on the steps of the South Carolina State House in Columbia. This was the same photo session that yielded the altered and atmospheric images used on the cover of the album. (Photo by Micheal McLaughlin)

ONLY WANNA BE WITH YOU

THE INSIDE STORY OF
HOOTIE & THE BLOWFISH

TIM SOMMER

THE UNIVERSITY OF
SOUTH CAROLINA PRESS

Published by the University of South Carolina Press
Columbia, South Carolina 29208

www.uscpress.com

Manufactured in the United States of America

31 30 29 28 27 26 25 24 23 22
10 9 8 7 6 5 4 3 2 1

Library of Congress Cataloging-in-Publication Data
can be found at http://catalog.loc.gov/.

ISBN 978-1-64336-275-5 (hardcover)
ISBN 978-1-64336-276-2 (ebook)

To the Brouts—Jennifer, Emily, Madeline, and Bo
—with gratitude and love.

CONTENTS

PART III: 1993–1997

The Ultimate Boon

PART IV: 1998-2003
The People They Lend Money To

PART V: 2003-2008
Paying Dividends

PART VI: 2019-2020
The Soundtrack of Your Life

PREFACE

Hootie Is the Name of a Group and Other Textual Notes

First and foremost: Hootie & the Blowfish is Darius Rucker on vocals and guitar, Mark Bryan on guitar, Dean Felber on bass, and Jim "Soni" Sonefeld on drums. Hootie & the Blowfish is the name of a band from Columbia, South Carolina. Darius Rucker is not "Hootie," nor has he ever been.

For the sake of brevity, to avoid repetition, and to occasionally balm the gods of prosody, I frequently refer to "Hootie" instead of using the full name "Hootie & the Blowfish." At each and every one of these instances, I am referring to the band, which comprises Rucker, Bryan, Felber, and Sonefeld (except when discussing events that take place between early 1986 and mid-1989, during which time Hootie & the Blowfish denotes Rucker, Bryan, Felber, and original drummer Brantley Smith). At absolutely no time whatsoever when I refer to "Hootie" am I referring only to Darius Rucker.

This book is built on the words and memories of the band members and their closest associates. It is based on personal interviews with the five present and former band members and many of their friends, musical and studio collaborators, and business associates. I was also granted access to thirty-five years' worth of files, photos, contracts, documents, scrapbooks, and other ephemera. Finally, it is essential to note that I spent an enormous amount of time on the road, in the studio, and in social settings with the band, their organization, and their friends and family between 1993 and 1998, an experience that contributes significantly to this story. This is the reason I sometimes say "we" when talking about the activities and decisions the group made during that time.

Thank you, and it is my pleasure to take you on this remarkable voyage.

INTRODUCTION

On September 16, 1993, I flew from Burbank Airport to Charleston, South Carolina, to see Hootie & the Blowfish for the first time.

It was high noon in the age of grunge.

Major record labels faced off against each other on the bleached fields of Doheny Drive and the echoing canyons of Madison Avenue, firing money and promises at any band that fused punk, metal, self-loathing, and flannel. In the very early 1990s, Nirvana, Soundgarden, Pearl Jam, Green Day, and others hit it big, inspiring a signing frenzy that was surprisingly undiscriminating and almost comically all encompassing. Bands rapidly changed their wardrobes and hairstyles to conform to the new grunge realities, and the labels seemed barely to care who was who and what was "real," as long as the sound and the look was vaguely correct. No one wanted to miss the next Pearl Jam.

A&R people (the in-house label talent scouts who also supervise album production and provide essential career advice) have dreams, too, you see. Regardless of the pressure to find the next Faux-vana (or a replicant of whatever is hitting big at the moment), most A&R people dream of discovery. They dream that they will stumble across The Next Big Thing on a tiny stage in a dark, dripping saloon. Today, you may help them carry their guitars to the their old, beaten-to-hell van; tomorrow, they might be looking out at the sparkling blue lights of a horseshoe-shaped football stadium. Those bragging rights are part of our rock 'n' roll DNA. We've all read about the Beatles in Hamburg, playing their hearts out to hipsters and sex workers for eight hours a night on the Grosse Freiheit. We all think, "If only I was there."

For A&R people, that dream is their bread and butter, and in 1993, you buttered your bread with grunge.

Hootie & the Blowfish could not have had less to do with the grunge movement. No label was chasing them down, not a single one, despite the fact that they wrote monstrously good songs; were playing in front of large audiences; and were selling reams of T-shirts, self-made CDs, and cassettes in the Mid-South. They were a band that had far, far more in common with Bob Seger; Crosby, Stills, & Nash; and Toad the Wet Sprocket than they did with Soundgarden and Stone Temple Pilots.

Yet here I was, on my way to Charleston to see Hootie & the Blowfish. I was an A&R person for Atlantic Records, based out of Los Angeles.

I had to transfer flights in DC, and rain and missed connections meant that I arrived about four hours later than scheduled. I worried that I might not make the gig, but I also knew that the band was playing the next night in their hometown of Columbia, South Carolina. I figured that I would get off the plane, get a cab to the Hampton Inn, buy some potato chips at a nearby gas station, and call it a night. But as soon as I stepped off the plane, an assistant to the band's manager, Rusty Harmon, flagged me down. Since we were running late, we drove straight to the venue, which was located about twenty minutes from the airport, on the eastern end of the historic Charleston peninsula.

The perfect rock saloon is long, low, a little smoky, gold lit at the back and edges, and blue lit on stage. It is as crowded as a subway train during rush hour, and hotter than a sauna. The perfect rock saloon is full of history, lousy and luxurious, crazy and mundane. It has heard the plaintive sobs of moping, blowsy Brits, and the gnarling strut of cover bands playing "Smoke on the Water." It has hosted kings and queens, bikers and brass bands, emo mopers, goth moppets, and tattooed moshers. The perfect rock saloon is sacred and profane, ass deep in history and ankle deep in beer, and the bathrooms are no place for angels. And Myskyns in Charleston was a classic. Tonight it was sardine-packed with about six hundred happy people in various stages of drunkenness, absolutely enraptured by the four gentlemen on stage, all of whom were dressed in the same baggy shorts, long T-shirts, and striped polo shirts as most of the audience.

Rusty Harmon found me immediately. At six feet, eight inches tall, with a face that looks like what would happen if you copied a picture of Nicolas Cage onto Silly Putty and stretched it, Rusty makes quite an impression. He has the kind of Texas-via-North Carolina drawl that turns "Dude" into a four-syllable word. Rusty handed me two shots of Jägermeister—very cold Jägermeister. I threw them down. My throat rebelled, my head felt lighter, and my knees disappeared just a little bit. Rusty handed me a third shot. I would later learn that, basically, you could be friends with anyone in the Hootie & the Blowfish circle if you liked Jägermeister and dogs.

Anybody who has ever been an A&R person will tell you that they have an ingrained habit when they first walk into a venue to see a band: They scan the room to see what other A&R people are there. It's practically a reflex. But I knew, with absolute certitude, that I was the only A&R person at Myskyns that night. It was virtually unheard of to sign a band no other label was looking at. Common wisdom held that if no one else were looking at a band, they could not possibly be worth signing.

If any of my fellow A&R men and women had been there in Charleston—or, for some reason, known I was in there—I state, without hesitation, they would have told me I was barking up the wrong tree. The group on stage, already cracking thirty, had been performing in local clubs and frats for eight years, ignored or dismissed by most every major label. They didn't dress in black or flannel, wear eye shadow, or dye their hair blue or pink. They loved their mothers (and happily told you so onstage) and regularly stopped the set to toast local sports heroes, accept drinks from the audience, or share a joke with one of their fans. Nothing could be further from the nihilism, dissonance, and mosh pits of grunge.

Yet within forty seconds of the first song (it wasn't even an original, but a cover of Bill Withers's "Use Me"), I knew I was going to sign them to Atlantic Records. There was *something* about their weird, groovy energy that reminded me of what happens when you are at a crowded party and the DJ plays "Brown Eyed Girl." Who doesn't want to bottle that feeling and sell it? There was *something* about their absolutely bizarre mixture of college rock Whiteness and deep, primo '70s soul.

A few minutes later, when the band played "Let Her Cry," any lingering doubt that my judgment may have been impaired by travel fatigue and alcohol vanished. In the future, when I was asked why I decided to sign Hootie & the Blowfish on that night, the shortest and most effective way to answer that question was: "What kind of idiot would watch a band play an original song as good as 'Let Her Cry' and *not* sign them?"

After the set, I climbed backstage. (Literally. Accessing the dressing room required engaging a ladder and pulley situation; it occurs to me now that the band may have been playing some kind of joke on me.) I was feeling the effect of the Jägermeister that Rusty had fed me more-or-less continuously, but I still was reasonably certain that I was more sober than the band: back in those pre-Atlantic days, there was a tradition at Hootie shows that audience members would buy rounds of shots and send them to the stage. I'm fairly certain the band rarely, if ever, declined the hospitality.

There were no introductions. There were no pleasantries. I immediately, and excitedly, announced that I wanted to sign them to Atlantic.

A&R people are *not* supposed to do that. A record company president *might* make that kind of spontaneous commitment, but a relatively untested, unproven A&R guy such as I was definitely, absolutely, positively should not say that kind of thing out loud when first meeting a band. *But it felt right.* I had never met this band before. I hadn't spoken to anyone back in Los Angeles. I'd only seen them play half a set. But I stood there and told them I was going to sign them to Atlantic Records. I just knew I wanted to work with them. Their music felt like home. It felt as if they'd ingested all of the guitar-based, sensitive-but-playful college rock I loved and spat it out in an unusually muscular, uniquely soulful fashion.

After the show, the band took me down the street to a brand-new venue that was about to open—a huge, sleek warehouse-like room called the Music Farm. They proudly showed me the size and the airy confines, and announced, "From here on, *this* is where we'll play when we play Charleston." They shot hoops inside the venue. I would soon learn that Hootie had a very weird, almost supernatural skill: Wherever two or more band members stood for more than a few minutes, a basketball hoop would materialize. It wouldn't surprise me at all to learn that there never was a basketball hoop at the Music Farm, and it had just arisen, Brigadoon-like, from the humid South Carolina mists, simply because Hootie & the Blowfish were in the room.

Two days later, I flew back to Los Angeles and began to unpack the reality of telling my boss that I had committed the label to signing and recording Hootie & the Blowfish, an act that no other label was looking at and who played music that was nothing like any of the other acts our label was chasing.

My history with Hootie & the Blowfish started that night in Charleston. What lay ahead was an extraordinary voyage, where we achieved the kind of heights that we most certainly could never have dreamed about (after all, the kinds of bands we idolized sold tens of thousands of records, not hundreds upon hundreds of thousands). But through millions and millions of records sold, and audience numbers that only the biggest stars could equal, one thing remained constant: I had found friends who felt instantly familiar to me, because we had all come of age in the great era of 1980s college rock.

PART I

1983-1989

Let's See If We Know Any of the Same Songs

–1–

MAN, WAS THAT YOU SINGING?

It was the best of times. It was the end of a time.

Sometimes it feels like it didn't happen at all.

We try to imagine an era before we were instantly and constantly accessible. We try to remember when we would wait for friends and not summon them, when we would stand on Five Points corners, under movie theatre marquees, or in front of noisy saloons and tap our Chuck Taylors or our Docs and be *within* time, not chained to it. We burrow deep in memory, and try to recall when time was counted in minutes and hours, not the interminable number of times we checked our phone.

We watched the world, we did not watch a screen watching the world.

It was the best of times. It was the end of a time.

We were teenagers play-acting at adulthood. We were away from home for the first time, we ran down dorm hallways singing Sabbath and Springsteen and everything in between. We tapped on doors and borrowed razors and shaving cream and imagined this is how adults acted. We piled Russian dressing on Bac-Os in loud, low-drop-ceilinged cafeterias, just because we could. We ate rocky road ice cream for breakfast just because we could. We tried black coffee for a day and a half and then resumed milk and two sugars. We gave up rum for Jim Beam because it seemed like something we should do now that we were twenty, now that we were adults. We were unhip hipsters and hip rednecks hiding from reality until the last possible moment. MTV was our stock market. We went fifteen days without putting on long pants. We were as tall as adults but full of a teenager's fear and tenderness. Our hearts were made of glass, and all our love notes were handwritten. Sundays and Wednesdays we called home. We ate chocolate chip cookies as the sun rose and called this freedom. We smoked four Merit Lights twice a week. Four out of seven evenings when the clock struck half past nine, we collected in threes and fours like noisy birds grinning in anticipation of whatever the night and the Coors would bring. We were children in adult skins.

Our hearts were free, and our hearts were looking for locks. It was the time of teenage vulnerabilities stretching into adulthood.

We passed the time until well past midnight in long, narrow, blue-lit barrooms that smelled of beer and bleach, sweat and cigarettes, patchouli and pot and Sure Roll On. Within these brick walls, we borrowed kisses and begged for Life Savers, and begged for kisses and borrowed Visine, and we were begged for kisses and we were begged for chewing gum, and the band played "Mustang Sally."

This was life in a college town in the mid-1980s. Maybe you were in Ithaca, New York. Maybe you were in Northampton, Massachusetts. Maybe you were in Westwood, Los Angeles. Maybe you were in Gainesville, Florida; Ann Arbor, Michigan; Providence, Rhode Island; Burlington, Vermont; or Athens, Georgia. Maybe you were even in Columbia, South Carolina.

It was late on Thursday afternoon in the third week of September 1985. Darius Carlos Rucker, a sophomore at the University of South Carolina, was taking a shower. The showers were, both literally and figuratively, a central part of life on the fifth floor of the Moore residence hall. Although the building was only twenty years old, Moore was generally known as one of the most decrepit and charmless dormitories on the University of South Carolina campus. The "jailhouse showers"—six nozzles, no curtains—were located at the core of the building, so they were a convenient spot to gather to drink beer, listen to music, and make plans for the night ahead.

But this afternoon, Darius was alone. He began to sing.

Darius liked to sing. In fact, he was a prominent member of Carolina Alive, a prestigious campus-sponsored singing group. They were a show choir (that is, they combined fairly precise group vocalization with some limited choreography). Carolina Alive entertained everywhere, from senior citizen homes to halftime at basketball games, to big events at the State House. Darius, with his warm baritone that was full of both power and charm, was a valued member of the group. Earlier that year, he had performed a solo at Ronald Reagan's second inauguration. He had also recently fulfilled a lifelong dream: He had sung onstage in an arena with a rock band, when Carolina Alive joined Foreigner to perform "I Want to Know What Love Is" at the Carolina Coliseum.

On his way into the shower, Darius had noticed that the dorm hallways were completely empty. Late-afternoon classes were still in session, and people were hitting the library or the gym for one last touch of self-improvement before the weekend. This was a rare treat, so Darius figured he could *really* belt it out and take advantage of all that beautiful, bouncy, bright tile that would make his voice snap and ring.

Darius began singing "Honesty" by Billy Joel. He was enjoying it so much (hadn't he read that doo-wop singers loved to practice their harmonies in the bathroom?) that he stayed in the shower a little longer than necessary. In fact, he remained under the water until he had sung the song a full two and a half times, repeating the bridge three times for good measure. Man, he thought, that bridge is *so much* fun to sing.

Darius toweled off. He threw a towel around his waist and put on deodorant. He would finish getting dressed back in his room.

Darius and his best friend, Chris Carney, would be going out that night (after all, in a college town, Thursday is almost Friday). The year 1985 was tough for partying. South Carolina had changed the drinking age to 21, and this made finding alcohol a little challenging. But Darius and Carney had made plans. There were some ROTC guys down at the bottom of South Main who always had a keg going. Even if you didn't know the exact address, all you had to do was look for the house with the water tower on top. Sometimes they even had bands there. Plus, there were *always* some guys in Laborde, the dorm next door, with fully stocked bars in their room.

If Carney and Darius wanted to make the evening really interesting, the Grateful Dead had just played the Coliseum, so there was *a lot* of acid floating around. Darius knew some guys who were basically paying for their entire semester by reselling sheets that they had *found* in the parking lot after the show.

Walking down the hallway to his room, Darius was startled when a tall, thin freshman with curly blond hair popped out of a doorway. Darius had seen him around. He looked like he was entirely made of toothpicks and rubber bands.

"*Man*, was that you singing?" Mark Bryan said.

"Yeah," Darius Rucker answered, stretching the beginning of the word for a long time, as if he was reaching up to pull it out of a ceiling tile. "That was me."

Mark Bryan glowed like a kid who had just been told his favorite baseball player would be signing autographs at the car dealership down the street.

"I play guitar!"

"You do?"

"Let's get together later and see if we know any of the same songs."

It really went just like that.

Darius taped a note to Carney's door saying where he was and walked over to Mark's room. Mark had a Redskins-insignia flask with some Southern Comfort in it. Darius took a sip. "Jesus," he said. "This is what killed Janis Joplin, right? What a horrible way to go."

Thirty-five years later, this is what Mark Bryan remembers of that late afternoon. "Darius would go, 'Hey, you know this song . . . do you know that song . . . do you know this song?' and I would go, 'Yeah! How about this one, how about that one?' That night, the stuff we played was all over the map: Beatles, Simon & Garfunkel, Commodores, and Hank Williams Jr. It *blew my mind* that a Black dude knew the words to Hank Jr. songs."

While they sang, a crowd gathered outside. Darius Rucker and Mark Bryan, singing and playing together for the very first time, already had an audience. Carney showed up, too. He hadn't seen the note, he had just heard the harmonies.

While Mark tuned his guitar, Darius stared at the poster on the wall of Redskins' star John Riggins. Looking at his curly hair and Clark Kent jaw, Darius wondered if the poster was there because Mark was a fan or because Mark wished that that's what he looked like. Because, frankly, Darius thought, Mark looked like a Muppet version of John Riggins. As the tuning continued, Darius's gaze moved downward from the poster to an empty cassette box on the floor, partially obscured by a pair of socks.

It was a mixtape. Darius, scanning the carefully written sleeve, saw that it contained U2's "Wire," R.E.M.'s "Can't Get There From Here," "Downbound Train" by Springsteen, "Miss Gradenko" by The Police, and Squeeze's "Up the Junction." Those were all the titles Darius could read without lifting up one of the socks. Darius knew and liked most of those songs, too.

This was going to be interesting.

-2-

AS SOON AS I SAW THE SLEEVE, I WANTED TO SING ALONG

Some of us dream in music.

We don't just hear the sounds, silly, majestic, dramatic, or sexy. We are *in* there. We are right in there. We are in the story. The myths, the legends, the hundred-times-told tales, the glamour and the grit, these run among the neural networks in our mind, and we place ourselves within these stories. Even though we are sitting in a Long Island bedroom, we feel our Cuban heels on cobblestoned Hamburg and Liverpool streets, our plush creepers on Carnaby Street. Even if we are in a Maryland basement, we smell the cigarette smoke inside the Marquee Club in London. Even if we are in a Charleston living room, we step over winos on the Bowery on the way to imagined gigs, we step out into the spotlight and pretend we are on stadium stages.

When you dream of music, you dream in music. You are right there.

Darius Rucker: "My brothers and sisters only listened to music when they were in the car, or when they were having friends over. But I would sit in the living room for hours and hours just flipping through the A.M. channels, listening to different songs, different genres, soaking it all in. By the time I was five or six, I realized music was *everything* for me. I thought I was different than everyone else. There wasn't anyone else sitting in the living room with me, doing what I was doing. It was always just me. Even before I quite knew what it was or that my passion had a name, it was my thing."

Music—played on one of those enormous multifunction hi-fi systems that were a significant piece of furniture in many American living rooms in the 1960s and '70s—was always a big part of life in the Rucker household. "As a kid, I remember thinking there were a million records in there," Darius says. "I remember investigating that drawer for the first time when I was about six. And I remember flipping past Al Green, Gladys Knight and the Pips, Otis Redding, and all of these other things that, as soon as I saw the sleeve, I wanted instantly to sing along with it. The 45s are scattered about, they aren't really in any one place, they are just amongst the LP sleeves. And I pick up two Beatles 45s, 'She Loves You' and 'I Want to Hold Your Hand.' For a moment I thought, 'Why does my mom have these Beatles 45s?' So I walked into the kitchen and asked, 'Mom, what are you doing with *these*?' And she really didn't have time to answer me, but I went back and put them on and it changed my world. *It was a moment.* I distinctly remember putting those on and thinking, *wow. Wow.* I think I listened to those two songs, and the B-sides, forty times. I am not exaggerating."

"And from the first moment I was *aware* of music," Darius continues, "as a little, *little* kid, I would tell anyone who would listen, 'I am going to be a singer someday.' There was nothing else for me. It was *all* I wanted. There was nothing else, no 'I want to be in the NFL, I want to be in the NBA,' none of those usual kid dreams. It was just 'I want to be a singer.'"

Darius Carlos Rucker was born on May 13, 1966, in Orleans Woods, a neighborhood to the west of historic Charleston. His semi-professional musician father having absented himself at a very early age, his mother and grandmother raised Darius.

"I had five brothers and sisters," Darius told me. "Up until my junior year in high school, my grandmother lived with us. Really small three-bedroom house. My mom worked hard. My mom worked for twenty-five years at the Medical University of South Carolina. And my grandma worked at a cigar factory downtown, until she got too sick to work. We tried to make ends meet. There were times when we were kids when we just didn't eat, but these times were few and far between, but there were times."

"But it was a great time," Darius says, shifting tone, "and I wouldn't change anything about my childhood. We were tight. We had a great neighborhood, it was an all-Black neighborhood. Behind us were the projects. Always had someone to play with, always had friends around. For me, I thought it was just a typical southern single-mother household upbringing. We worked hard and everyone got jobs early. I think I got my first job at thirteen or fourteen. I worked at a pizza place, doing dishes and busing tables. Then, after six or seven months, they told me I could make pizzas, so I did that, too."

Although Orleans Wood was virtually entirely African American, Darius did attend integrated schools. Darius's high school classmates remember him as funny, charming, and popular. He was a valued member of his high school choir, The Middleton Singers. Darius also took a significant role in the school's more exclusive vocal group, Razor Backs Live.

"Darius always had a very distinct voice," recalls a Middleton classmate, Kelly Ann Sharpe. "When we were at parties, he and a girl who played the piano would always sing 'The Rose' together. So we were always singing. Another one of our friends, Gigi, would holler down the hallway at him and say, 'Hey Darius, sing some Kenny,' and he'd start bellowing out Kenny Rogers down the hallway. He always had a smile, and he was always singing."

Darius Rucker: "I have always liked what I liked. I wasn't one of those kids who was listening to Kurtis Blow exclusively. I was listening to Journey and Boston and Kansas—and if you are a Black kid in high school in the '80s, you're not supposed to be listening to that shit."

Darius becomes a little more animated and remembers a band that really had an impact on him. "I went through a massive Kiss phase. *Massive.* It was all I listened to for probably two years. I just thought it was the greatest thing I had ever heard. I remember being in my living room, and I got three—was it three? Yes, three—cans of vegetables, probably corn, out of the cupboard, and I got a flashlight that had a magnet and put it on top of those, and *that* was my microphone. And I would get a broom, and that would be my guitar. And I would sing all of *KISS ALIVE II*. The whole fucking record. And I remember, about six songs in, my mom, who was in the kitchen doing dishes, finished the dishes and she was *done* listening to Kiss, and she came in and said, 'All right, honey, sit down and I am going to play some music.' So she would then play me all the songs she wanted me to hear. That moment always makes me laugh when I think about it. At our house, someone was *always* putting a record on."

"In high school," Darius continues, "I couldn't get enough of music. I was suspended, just for a day, because I pulled into the parking lot one morning playing Boston at about volume twelve. I had my windows down. The assistant principal walked up to my car—I didn't see him walking up because I was too into the music—and he said, 'Darius, you can go home now, you're suspended for the day, that music is too loud, Darius, get out of here.'"

-3-

THE WOLF BROTHERS

Almost nightly throughout the autumn of 1985, Darius and Mark met in Mark's room to strum, sing, harmonize, argue about sports, drink, review the relative plausibility of each other's fake IDs, fiercely debate who was the best member of KISS, *really* get into it about whether they should try a Led Zeppelin song, talk about girls, curse the drinking age, discuss whether they should test their fake IDs at the 7-Eleven across from the Laborde dorm, curse the 7-Eleven across from Laborde for rejecting Darius's fake ID, applaud the 7-Eleven across from Laborde for accepting Mark's fake ID, and discover a mutual love for R.E.M. that was, more than anything else, the glue between them.

Almost immediately, these informal dorm room sing-outs became virtually a public performance and a regular part of social life on the fifth floor of the Moore residence hall. Word about the duo spread to other floors of the dorm, too.

"It was just a rectangular hallway," says Chris Carney, a firsthand witness to the formation of this formidable musical pairing. "They would set up in Mark's room strumming and singing. They would figure out some songs they both knew, and they would entertain us. It was a regular part of something that would happen when we were sitting around the dorm figuring out what we were going to do that night. It wasn't just two guys playing and everybody staring at them—if you knew the words, you would be singing right along with them."

The Moore residence hall was tucked into the southwest corner of the University of South Carolina campus, right off of Main

Street. Immediately on the other side of Main Street—at the corner of Blossom—there was a little wings and beer joint called Pappy's.

"Pappy was an ex-Marine," remembers Mark. "The place was jacked out in Marine posters and memorabilia. He had a big screen projection TV and he would play these classic movies, especially soldier movies. And everyone would go there and eat chicken wings and drink cheap draft beer."

Barely two weeks after they first met, Darius got the idea to ask Pappy if he and Mark could play a few songs there. Things were going so well on the fifth floor, why not take the act some place that actually served beer?

For Darius, it wasn't a big deal. In his mind, there was little separation between what he and Mark were doing on the fifth floor of Moore and what they were going to do at the wing joint across the street.

"There was *no* difference," Darius remembers. "Our rehearsals were us just sitting around in the hallway drinking and everyone would listen to us play. We just took that and went down to Pappy's and did the same thing."

On Friday, October 12, 1985, Darius Rucker and Mark Bryan performed outside of the dorm for the very first time.

Mark Bryan: "Our first set at Pappy's wasn't any different, really, from playing parties in our hallway. People would look at us and say, 'Hey, you guys know this?' and we'd look at each other and go, sure, we can play that. If I didn't know a song Darius or someone else suggested, I'd play a few chords and realize, 'Yeah, I can figure that out,' so it's highly doubtful we played everything correctly. We determined our first set list by jamming with everyone on the dorm floor and figuring out what songs we actually both knew, as opposed to approaching this as a deliberate process."

Because of the casual nature of the gig, Darius and Mark hadn't given any thought to naming their duo. "There was this guy on our hall from Barbados named Steven Adderley," Mark recalls. "His nickname was 'The Wolf.' And he said, 'Hey, I really want to introduce you guys tonight.' So before we went on that very first time, he said, 'Ladies and Gentlemen, here are my very talented friends Darius and Mark, the Wolf Brothers!' So he named us after *himself*, in the moment, on the mic. It was never discussed beforehand. We just kept the name, and became a band."

Darius Rucker and Mark Bryan, both still in their teens, had performed publicly together for the very first time.

The opening song of the Wolf Brothers first set was the Eagles' "Take It Easy." That evening at Pappy's, they also played "The 59th Street Bridge Song (Feelin' Groovy)" by Simon & Garfunkel, "Sultans of Swing" by Dire Straits, "Sail On" by the Commodores, and "Family Tradition" by Hank Williams Jr.

Time and the significant amounts of beer that very young men can consume without considering limit, reason, or repercussions, has fogged memories of whatever else Darius and Mark played that night. Pictures of the event show multiple people gathered around Darius and Mark, joining them on the tiny stage and singing along, just as they did on the fifth floor of Moore.

"That first night at Pappy's . . . it was not impressive," remembers Paul Graham, later to become a very close associate of Hootie & the Blowfish. "Everyone was yelling, and all their friends were onstage singing with them, and everybody was so drunk, there was no actual attention on the performance. *But it was so much fun*. It wasn't, however, like seeing this band and thinking, oh man, they are killing it, and they're going to be famous."

From the very beginning, Mark and Darius were drawing large and vocal audiences. "Our first show, Pappy's was packed!" Darius enthuses. "We had friends, and people who had heard us in the hallway knew we could play, and the people who were seeing us for the first time would go, oh, these guys can play, and that dude can sing. So next time we would play, more people would come out. In Columbia we had a following, as soon as we started playing."

That first night (and at subsequent Pappy's shows), Mark and Darius were paid with a keg of Stroh's, which they rolled back to the dorm, where the party—and the singing—would continue.

There were a few more Wolf Brothers shows before winter break, and in the meantime, Mark and Darius continued to work on their craft, usually in the slightly more sober environment of Mark's dorm room. An important step was teaching Darius how to play guitar. "I would show him where to put his fingers," Mark says, "and he would say, 'It hurts.' and I would say, 'Press harder.'"

In return, Darius taught Mark how to sing harmonies, which allowed the young duo to expand their repertoire and appeal.

The Wolf Brothers *only* played at Pappy's (with one exception, a frat-sponsored show at the Russell House student union). At the end of the 1985 fall semester, Darius and Mark realized they wanted to move beyond leading sing-alongs on their dorm floor and in the wing joint. Darius and Mark wanted to turn their duo into a band.

-4-

I'LL PLAY BASS UNTIL YOU FIND SOMEONE ELSE

Mark Bryan had known Dean Felber for as long as he could remember.

"I was in Dean's basement, when we were just little kids," Mark says, "and on the wall was a picture of the 1958 varsity basketball team for Bethesda–Chevy Chase High School. And there's Dean's dad and my dad standing next to each other in the picture. So we were always sort of around each other. But around when we were twelve or thirteen, we were hanging out at his house watching a Redskins game, and I noticed he had a bass rig in the corner. I had just started to play guitar, so I got excited that he played bass."

Soon, the teenagers were playing in a high school cover band called Missing in Action. Missing in Action had a very effective built-in marketing plan: Half the band (Dean and Mark) attended Seneca Valley High School, and the other half (guitar player Mark Johnson and drummer Gary Jenkins) were from another area high school, Gaithersburg. This earned them a fairly avid following relatively quickly.

Missing in Action broke up the last day of senior year. Both Dean and Mark ended up at the University of South Carolina, although they claim this was a total coincidence. Naturally, when Mark and Darius wanted to expand their duo and create a full band, Mark's first choice to fill the bass spot was Dean.

Dean, of course, said no.

Mark asked again.

And Dean said no again.

"I had told Mark before we left for USC [University of South Carolina] that I was going to give music the semester off," states Dean Felber. Dean had initially come to the University of South Carolina to study computer science but had relatively quickly shifted to a double major in marketing and finance. "I was burnt out," he says. "All the time in high school I had done orchestra, I had done jazz ensemble, I had done the pit in plays, I had been in bands. I had been playing bass nonstop since eighth grade, and I was just *burnt*. So my intention was to give music a rest for a semester."

But Mark Bryan had his mind set on Dean and kept at it.

"I kept on saying no," Dean says. "It wasn't that I didn't want to play with them personally, it was that I didn't want to be in a cover band. If I was going to get back into music, after that little hiatus, I wanted it to be creative, I wanted to start from scratch and have some fun. But they wanted to do the free-beer-and-make-people-happy kind of music thing."

This resistance didn't mean he wasn't a fan of Mark's new project. "After all that time with all those terrible singers back in Maryland, my God, it was certainly nice to hear Mark play with someone who could actually sing," says Dean. "Darius also had a much softer palette with music than we did; he was into more pop and more quieter and melodic stuff than we had been into. It all showcased his voice so well and brought out something interesting and wonderful in Mark."

Mark and Darius kept on asking, and Dean finally gave in. But there was still one piece missing from Wolf Brothers + Dean.

Dean Felber: "At the beginning of the second semester of freshman year, I had more or less decided I would give in and play with them, though there was still no drummer. But my first roommate told me about this drummer named Brantley Smith. So I got in touch with Brantley, and then I told Darius and Mark, now that I have found you a drummer, I'll play bass with you until you find someone else."

Thirty-five years later, Dean is still waiting for Darius and Mark to find someone else.

Brantley Smith, the original drummer in Hootie & the Blowfish, is from Taylors, South Carolina, a suburb of Greenville, about a hundred miles northwest of Columbia. He grew up in a family that was active in the Baptist church and encouraged him to experience and perform music from an early age. After coming to the University of South Carolina (where he majored in political science and minored in music), Brantley played cello with the University Symphony, the University Choir, and multiple ensembles both officially and unofficially linked to the school.

Shortly before Christmas break, 1985, Dean and Mark formally invited Brantley to join their new group, still known as the Wolf Brothers.

At the beginning of 1986, Darius, Mark, Dean, and Brantley began rehearsing in Brantley's dorm room in nearby Douglas. The change in locale was logical: It was easier for Dean and Mark to haul their amps to Douglas than it was for Brantley to bring his drums to Moore.

Dean and Darius were now roommates (on the fifth floor of Moore, same as Mark) and would remain roommates for the next ten years, forming the tightest bond of any two members in Hootie & the Blowfish. "We were like the brothers," Dean says. "There's no way to describe how much time Darius and I spent together, from '86 on. We could be around each other for days on end, say so few words, and have this great sense of quiet acceptance; we didn't have to talk, yet we would be in the same brain wave. That was so great to have, because I didn't have brothers growing up. It also really helped with the band, because the two of us were always on the same page, even if we didn't start that way, because we were able to talk things through before in a really good way. I don't think, honestly, two people could be closer."

"There has never been anyone in my life that was my everything more than Dean was," Darius Rucker says. "We were inseparable, and we loved it that way. Our idea of a date back then was, 'Hey, Dean and I are going out, you can meet us at the bar.'"

"I don't think either one of us is afraid of silence," Dean says, thoughtfully, about the foundation of their relationship. "I was surprised as I got older how many people need something constantly happening. We didn't."

"God, that's perfect," Darius says. "Dean and I could sit in a room, forever, and not talk, and yet we would *feel* like we've had a conversation. We were always together, and we loved it. It didn't occur to us to *not* be together. For me, it's a rare thing to have a friendship like that."

This sense of closeness also allowed them to explore—and expand—each other's musical tastes.

Dean Felber: "We also had the odd ability to really like each other's opinions on music we hadn't heard before. I think that goes for everyone in the band, but Darius and I had this ability to sit down for hours upon hours and listen to each other's music, and it was never contentious . . . well, Zeppelin gave Darius some fits, but for the most part, if I didn't go all classic rock on him, it was all good. We shared common passions, whether it was video games, music, or beer."

Darius has one special memory of a music-bonding moment with Dean. "One of my absolute favorite moments is, well, we would like to take acid and listen to *Abbey Road*. So we are laying on the floor listening to *Abbey Road*, and *Abbey Road* ends, and I say to Dean, 'Hey, man, can I play a record for you? I'm not going to tell you what it is, I am just going to put it on.' So I put on this record, and we listen to the whole thing, and it ends. And we are laying there, and Dean turns to me, and he says, '*Fuck you, man*,' and I'm, like, 'Why?' and he goes, 'Because you just made me *love* George Michael.'"

WE HAVE TO NAME THE BAND

Once Darius, Mark, Dean, and Brantley committed to the idea of a full, electric band, it became apparent that the Wolf Brothers was no longer an appropriate name for the ensemble.

Before there was a band called Hootie & the Blowfish, there were two young men whom Darius Rucker had nicknamed Hootie and the Blowfish. Their names are Ervin Harris and Donald Feaster.

This decisive event in our story takes place at a holiday party that Dr. Richard Conant, the much-loved director of the Carolina Alive, threw for the choir members in December of 1985. Conant would regularly host parties for the group at his house.

Kevin Oliver was there. "We were sitting around in Dr. Conant's living room, and Darius was saying 'We have a gig, we have to name the band!' So Darius, and everyone else, starts throwing names around. Ervin and Donald walk in the door together. Wherever one of them was, you saw the other one. And Darius looks up and he says, 'Hey, it's Hootie and the Blowfish!' And he literally slaps his head and says, 'My God, that's it!' You hear about moments like that, and you think, 'Oh, it probably didn't *really* happen like that'—but in this case, it happened *exactly* like that."

At the next band rehearsal, Darius brought the potential new name to Dean, Mark, and Brantley.

Dean Felber: "The funny thing is, the other names we discussed were *so bad* that Hootie & the Blowfish was the only viable name on the whole list. So we decided, we will use this name until we can come up with something better. Which never happened. We are still waiting."

Even when I pushed him, Dean flat-out refused to tell me what other names the band considered. They were *so* bad that he prefers they remain consigned to the dung heap of history But Jim "Soni" Sonefeld (who was to replace drummer Brantley Smith in late 1989) *did* tell me. When Soni became a member of the group, the secret horror of (some of) these rejected names was revealed to him.

First among them, Black and Blue. "If that's not bad enough," Soni told me, "the *reason* they almost named the band Black and Blue was because there were three guys with blue eyes and one black guy. Isn't that *horrible?*"

Just to wrap up the story of the band's name, another factor has created a degree of confusion regarding the origin of the Hootie & the Blowfish moniker. In 1988, a film called *Satisfaction* was released (and flopped). It starred Justine Bateman as the leader of an all-girl band called The Mystery, and it details the fictional group's struggle for success (the bassist in the group is played by a then-unknown Julia Roberts, making her major film debut). A key plot point of this obscure movie is a battle of the bands, where The Mystery's main opponent is—wait for it—a group called the Blowfish. What makes this even more complicated is that the film was shot largely in South Carolina, and the fictional Blowfish were portrayed by a *real* band from Charleston called The Killer Whales.

However, since the Hootie & the Blowfish name was in use two years before the film was released, we can be 100 percent certain that Darius, Dean, Mark, and Brantley did *not* take their name from the movie. However, it is entirely possible (perhaps even likely) that the filmmakers did name *their* Blowfish after *our* Blowfish, since local fans and musicians knew Hootie by the time the film was shot.

Now that Mark, Darius, Brantley, and Dean had a name for their band, they enthusiastically rehearsed and explored their expanded new sound and embraced the four-piece group's ability to perform in places not necessarily suitable for an acoustic duo.

In early 1986, one thing hadn't changed: They were still rehearsing in dorm rooms. But rehearsing in the middle of a dormitory was a terrific way to provide easy and enthusiastic publicity for the new group, much as it had when Darius and Mark were still the Wolf Brothers, working on their craft in the Moore dorm.

"Of course, when you rehearse in a dorm room, *that* becomes a party," Mark says. "As soon as people hear you playing, they come to watch and hang out and drink beer. So a lot of our early gigs were actually these dorm room rehearsal-slash-parties. Every now and then, we'd go to the downstairs communal area to rehearse, and of course, every time you start playing music people would start gathering around, so *that* would become a party, too."

This overlap between rehearsal, party, and gig provided the band with vital experience and confidence when they did move into local venues such as Greenstreets, Rockafellas, and Group Therapy. Even though Mark, Dean, Darius, and Brantley were doing sets made up almost entirely of covers, they rapidly began to attract a large and loyal audience. Hootie & the Blowfish were one of those rare bands that people seemed to like virtually from the very beginning.

"We played the *right* songs," Mark Bryan explains. "We were right in the pulse of what people were listening to at that time. We leaned towards learning the cooler tracks—R.E.M. and U2, the college hits. In fact, 'I Go Blind' dates to that time, we were covering that nearly from the beginning. We did 'I Go Wild' by The Three O'Clock, we did 'In the City' by The Jam. Darius loved singing that one. We even did some Ramones back then. We did 'Add It Up' by the Violent Femmes, which we still pull out sometimes."

Dean Felber: "When you ask me what we played in those early days, the first thing that comes to mind is *a lot* of R.E.M. We were doing, basically, half of *Murmur*, half of *Reckoning*, and then when *Fables* [*of the Reconstruction*] came out, we were doing half of *Fables*."

Brantley underlines this. "Any time a new R.E.M. album would come out, we devoured it, and then we'd play it immediately. We would also get our hands into a lot of what may have been at the time fairly underground music, like Dumptruck or The Reivers. We prided ourselves on discovering hidden gems."

Only a year earlier, Darius was singing as part of the Carolina Alive ensemble. Now, he was fronting a rock band.

"I always thought I'd just be a singer," Darius says. "Then, my senior year in high school, *Purple Rain* came out. I'll never forget this moment as long as I live. You go watch *Purple Rain*, and Prince and the Revolution are awesome, of course, but I will never forget the first moment Morris Day and The Time hits the stage in that movie! I thought to myself, *oh my God, I want to be in a band so bad*. I had never been even *close* to being in a band. Then I get to college and Mark comes along!"

But did he think, in 1986 or '87, huh, this band might actually become something?

"Oh, at first we were just playing to meet some girls," Darius answers, without hesitation.

Nearly everyone who saw the band between 1986 and 1989 remarks on what a skilled musician Brantley was, and how well he harmonized with Darius.

"Great player, and he was a great singer," Mark remembers. "He could sing all these harmonies with Darius. With him on board, we were on our way, and didn't stop for three straight years. On top of that, Brantley was studying cello and piano—he really was a great musician who had this depth of knowledge of music that went way past rock 'n' roll. He was by far the best musician in the band, probably the best musician who was ever in this band."

Brantley would also sing lead for at least one song every set (most notably, the Beatles' "Blackbird," usually performed just with Mark on acoustic guitar and Brantley on vocals), and handled the counter-lead "answer" vocal in "I Go Blind," a part that Dean took over when Brantley left the band. Brantley would even occasionally pull out his cello and played it with Hootie onstage when they covered "Eleanor Rigby" and U2's "MLK."

"Soni and Brantley were very different," Darius notes. "Brantley was like Stuart Copeland [the famously adept drummer for The Police]. That's how he played. With Brantley, we were as close to being a punk band as we ever would be, because we played everything so fucking fast! His talent level as a drummer was *sick*. And that kid's voice—when we sang together—man, that kid could sing."

By 1987 and '88, Hootie & the Blowfish were beginning to significantly build an audience and had begun to play three or even four times a week. In a region where the marketplace for party bands, frat bands, and cover bands was very competitive, the relatively new group were earning a reputation for their left-of-the-dial repertoire, high-energy but loose and unpredictable performances, and a uniquely powerful African American lead singer.

With the increased gigging schedule came the band's first foray into original songs. "The first original we wrote and played as Hootie & the Blowfish was this terrible song called 'Calendar Girl,'" Mark Bryan remembers. "Not long after 'Calendar Girl,' we wrote another really bad song called 'I'm After You.' If you heard those, you'd understand why we were doing mostly covers."

"'Calendar Girl' wasn't *that* bad," Brantley remembers. "Maybe it was, actually, but it was fun to play. It kind of had a reggae feel to it. Mark and I were pretty heavily influenced by The Police at that time, so we loved putting that feel into an original song, and then it ended on a more driving groove. Regardless of what Mark says, we had a lot of fun with that song."

Mark, Darius, and Brantley all agree that the first truly good original song the band wrote and performed was called "George Harrison." But like "Calendar Girl" and "I'm After You," "George Harrison" did not survive into the Soni-era of the band. The only familiar Hootie & the Blowfish song that dates from Brantley's time in the group is "Look Away," which they never performed live but worked on during rehearsal.

Darius departed from the University of South Carolina in the spring of 1988. Mark, Dean, and Brantley were ending their junior year. Although still primarily a cover band, Hootie & the Blowfish not only had a full gigging calendar at Columbia nightclubs and University of South Carolina frats, but for the first time, they were also beginning to perform out of town.

A talented, charismatic, hard-working cover band—even one who did a few originals—could get a lot of work in the Mid-South and the Atlantic Coast college towns and make some real money. These acts worked a circuit that included regular stops in Gainesville, Florida; Athens, Georgia; Columbia, Charleston, Clemson, Rock Hill, and, of course, the beach towns in South Carolina; Charlotte and Raleigh/Durham/Chapel Hill, North Carolina; and Charlottesville, Virginia. The more successful acts could work steadily from Wednesday through Saturday, thirty-six to forty-eight weeks of the year, and might venture as far west as New Orleans or Houston and as far north as Boston, Buffalo, and Burlington, Vermont.

There were a great many of these acts in the region, all of which had their own image, their own specialty, and their own gimmick. These included the Groovy Cools, the Hollywood Squares, Impulse Ride, the Vectors, the Root Doctors, the Agents, Johnny Quest (who play a big part in this story), and also from Columbia, Tootie and the Jones, who featured drummer Soni Sonefeld. In the days before DJ culture really exploded, who better to entertain your college-age drunken revelries or frat parties than a high-energy, highly entertaining cover band that snuck in an original song every now and then? Many of these acts made a couple of thousand dollars a night.

By early 1989, Hootie & the Blowfish were on the precipice of becoming a band that could work steadily and play away from their home base. They were also beginning to explore their abilities as songwriters. Something that had begun in dorm rooms now had the possibility of taking on a whole new life.

In the spring of 1989, the band played their biggest out-of-town show yet. It was an outdoor show at West Virginia University in Morgantown, set in a natural amphitheater. The band performed for well over a thousand people, and for the first time, they tasted what it might feel like to be *real* rock stars.

But the show was a turning point for Brantley, who had already been wrestling with the escalating popularity of Hootie & the Blowfish. "There was a lot of debauchery at that West Virginia show," Dean recalls, "and the three of us were very into that, and Brantley was very *not* into it. I think that event made it clear he was the odd man out. I can only imagine—he was sober and watching three idiots have a very hedonistic time."

"We were starting to throw in these bigger out-of-town shows," Mark adds. "We realized, oh shit, we are graduating this May, and we were starting to get these offers in Charleston, and DC, and these other out-of-town places. We realized that *this was getting serious*, and that was great! And that spring Brantley looked at it, looked at the sort of things we were booking and where we were going, and I think he just thought, 'I don't want to do that. That's not who I am, that's not who I want to be, I love playing with you guys, but I'm not into making these big road trips and skipping class.' He decided not to be in a touring secular band, and this is clearly where we were heading. He was real honest with us: 'If that's where you guys are headed, that's great for you, this isn't for me.'"

Dean echoes this and also honors and applauds the way Brantley handled the change. "Brantley was way up front with us. He told us he was following his faith, that this wasn't in his master plan. He was really cool about it, and gave us plenty of time to find a new drummer, and he indicated he would play with us until we did."

Brantley Smith: "Very simply, God had a different path for me. This was not an easy decision. I loved the band, I loved those guys, I sought out God, and I prayed, and I asked him, God, what's next for me? And it wasn't like it was a huge revelation of, '*oh, this is it.*' It was just a little bit at a time: 'This is where I want you, Brantley. I want you to trust me in this.' And so for me, that meant leaving the band."

"My leaving the band was not something that I was doing out of any negativity towards anybody," Brantley continues. "It was more of what I felt was stirring in me, in my relationship with God. I considered these guys my friends—they were my friends and they *are* my friends—and I wanted to say, hey this is not about you guys. This is more about me and what I feel like God is leading me to do."

Since leaving Hootie & the Blowfish, Brantley Smith has spent his entire adulthood committed to faith, music, and ministry. "I was thrilled for the success the band attained. And there was a part of me, of course, that would've loved to be a part of what they have experienced. And yet, I really felt, as much as that would've been something I loved to have been a part of, I really felt at peace about where I was and what I was doing."

Brantley Smith's last official performance as the drummer of Hootie & the Blowfish was at Rockafellas in Columbia on September 1, 1989.

There was never any question of stopping. "As strongly as we felt about Brantley," Mark says, "there was no turning back at that point."

PART II

1989–1993

Four Guys Who Wanted to Shoot for the Moon

-6-

BEACH MUSIC AND THE CHARISMATIC QUIRK

Before this train really gets rolling, let's take a moment to discuss the musical legacy of South Carolina, and what it may have contributed to the sound and character of Hootie & the Blowfish.

Although a lot of famous musicians were born in South Carolina —James Brown, Chubby Checker, Eartha Kitt, Peabo Bryson, and Nick Ashford, to name just a few—the state isn't generally associated with many well-known recording artists. Name any state on the entire Eastern seaboard, and even the casual music fan can throw out the names of the famous artists linked to the place. Even teeny-tiny Rhode Island has the Talking Heads, Throwing Muses, and the Cowsills. But South Carolina? Generally, people can cite Hootie & the Blowfish and the Marshall Tucker Band, and that's about it.

However, the state is associated with a genre of music. For generations, beach music played a big role in the musical, social, and romantic education of young people, of all races, in North and South Carolina. And to be clear, the beach music of the Carolinas has no stylistic connection whatsoever to Southern California beach music. Different ocean, different sound, different dances.

So what's Carolina beach music?

If I had to describe the beach music sound, I would say this. Draw a line between these four points: The tick-a-ticka tick-a-ticka shuffle of classic New Orleans rock 'n' roll; the slightly sobbing, soulful melodicism of Motown; the skanking, weeded-up sway/nod of Jamaican blue beat and ska; and the light, hopping, horny proto-disco of Philadelphia soul. Now, put down your pencil. Somewhere in that peculiar rhombus, you might find beach music.

In *Step It Up and Go*, his groundbreaking book on the music of North Carolina, journalist David Menconi notes, "Beach isn't actually a specific style so much as a catch-all label for a tradition that's as much about lifestyle as music. Ask any beach-music fan to define it and answers might range from old R&B groups like Hank Ballard and the Midnighters to latter-day cover bands like The Embers, or just dance music paced at that ideal shag-tempo heartbeat in 4/4 time. It's a big tent that also has room for the likes of Texas roadhouse-blues singer Delbert McClinton, twenty-first-century electro-soul duo Gnarls Barkley, and even the occasional old Piedmont blues tune like Sonny Terry and Brownie McGhee's shuffling 'Gonna Move Across the River.'"

By the 1980s and '90s, beach music was still very much a part of the musical ambience of South Carolina, so it was bound to seep into the sound of South Carolina's most famous band. The skipping, shagging "She Crawls Away" (from *Fairweather Johnson*) is probably Hootie's most deliberate and aware homage to beach music. You can hear a little beach music in "Let It Breathe" on *Fairweather*. There are also (likely deliberate) traces of it in *Kootchypop*'s "Sorry's Not Enough," and "What Do You Want From Me Now" on *Musical Chairs*.

One other southern band—and another nearby regional scene— was to have a much more obvious impact on the music and personality of Hootie & the Blowfish.

You cannot talk about the Beatles without discussing Little Richard, Chuck Berry, Buddy Holly, or the Everly Brothers. Those four artists are essential to the foundation of the Beatles' style. This is true, too: In the early stages of his career, Bob Dylan's debt to the work of Woody Guthrie and Ramblin' Jack Elliott was so ferocious that many initially dismissed him as a mere copy of those artists. Likewise, you can't seriously examine, say, Green Day without citing The Clash or Stiff Little Fingers, the British punk acts they borrowed their rhythms, chording styles, and accents from. Almost everything in pop and rock, even the stuff that knocks us on our ass and carries us to the heavens, is built on things that came before.

Darius Rucker: "I remember it like it was yesterday. I was in high school, and I am sitting on my mom's bed watching MTV. We were stealing cable, and I am watching on this little TV. MTV is still a pretty new thing—and I am watching it every day, all day. And 'South Central Rain' by R.E.M. comes on. And it was a *moment* for me. It ends and they back-announce it and I am writing down the name of the band and the song. That very same day, I went to every one of my relatives in the neighborhood and asked for a dollar so I could get enough money to go buy that R.E.M. cassette. And I bought the cassette, and it blew my mind. It changed the way I heard music. After that, my ears were different, I was different. That band instantly became everything I wanted to be, everything I wanted to hear, from that moment forward there was nothing more important in my life than R.E.M."

We cannot underestimate R.E.M.'s importance not only to Darius and Hootie but also to an entire generation of musicians and listeners who came of age in the 1980s. On that first night I saw Hootie perform at Myskyns, I could tell, literally within a minute or two, that Darius, Mark, Dean, and Soni were, like me, children of R.E.M. And that means a lot. It's like saying, *hello, friend. I know you.*

"A new R.E.M. record would come out on Tuesday," Darius remembers, looking back at the early days of Hootie, "and by Friday two or three of those songs would be in our set. When a new R.E.M. record came out, and if I couldn't get it—which is to say, couldn't afford it— the day it came out, if I was at your house and you put it on, I would leave—because I wanted to, *needed* to, listen to that whole record by myself in my room before I heard *any* of it. R.E.M. were part of *us.* We were basically an R.E.M. cover band. At one point, we were playing twelve R.E.M. songs in our set."

R.E.M.'s sense of charismatic quirk, their distillation of virtually all extant elements of college rock into one charmed package, set the template for much of guitar-based pop for the next thirty years, from Hootie & the Blowfish to Nirvana, from Radiohead to Arcade Fire. Each of these acts is profoundly stamped by the R.E.M. imprimatur. R.E.M. reset guitar pop's *emotional* core. It was R.E.M. that hung up a sign saying, "Sensitive Souls, Freaks and Geeks, welcome here." One of the prime functions of pop and rock is that it enables outsiders to find their tribe. We were Tribe R.E.M.

According to R.E.M. co-founder and bassist Mike Mills (who was later to become close friends with Hootie), "Basically what R.E.M. did was to create a template for people in the sense that you don't have to sign with a major, you don't have to have funny haircuts and space age clothes. Basically, you can defy any of the rules you want to. That was one of the templates we set, and Hootie followed that, to a point. We were happy to blaze a trail, as it were. And if someone chose to follow it, I would hope that it worked out for them, and it certainly did with Hootie & the Blowfish."

Significantly, both R.E.M. and Hootie & the Blowfish were influenced by the pioneering indie and alt-rock that developed in the 1970s and '80s in North Carolina. In the mid-1970s, a small group of musicians from Winston-Salem absorbed the jangly, poppy influences of the Beatles, Big Star, The Hollies, The Searchers, Badfinger, The Byrds, and so forth, gulping them down like they were beer, bread, water, and air. The (very) young Winston-Salem-ites condensed these influences, simplified them, and infused them with an energy that anticipated and paralleled punk rock. Out of these seeds, there emerged a small family of local musicians and bands who produced highly melodic and energetic power pop, released on independent labels long before doing so was trendy. These musicians represent a veritable who's who of Mid-South power pop heroes, many of whom were to come into direct contact with both R.E.M. and Hootie. The list includes Mitch Easter, Will Rigby, Don Dixon, and Peter Holsapple, and (among) the bands they formed were The dBs, the H-Bombs, Sneakers, Arrogance, and Let's Active. These artists affected Mid-South power pop and alternative guitar-based music in ways that cannot be calculated.

"Those guys are the pioneers, as far as I'm concerned," notes North Carolina–based musician, actor, and comedian Jon Wurster. "Mitch and Chris Stamey and Peter and Will and Don and all those guys are, to me, ground zero for all the music that came in its wake. I think it was impossible to live around here during that time period and not be impacted by it."

-7-

JIM SONEFELD DREAMED OF PLAYING SOCCER

Some people dream in music from a very early age.

Mark Bryan, Darius Rucker, and Dean Felber had dreamed in music, dreamed in the arc of pop. They dreamed of standing on stages, riding in buses, sitting in deep studio couches. This was especially true of Darius, who felt that music, his all-consuming passion, might be the only way to lift his family out of poverty.

But Jim Sonefeld was different.

What were the fantasies that manifested in scribbles on the back of Soni's notebooks and in the margin of his math textbooks? What were the idle thoughts that danced around his head when he looked out the classroom window, on days sunny and snowy?

Soni dreamed of playing soccer.

He also loved music. Growing up in Napierville, Illinois, music was all around him, and he took up drums, avidly, at a fairly early age. But unlike Mark and Dean, Soni did not play in a high school band. He played sports, and a lot of them. As he ran, jumped, and kicked his way toward the end of high school, Soni was eager to attend a university that had a Division I soccer team.

"Soccer was my first and last priority," Soni remembers. "For me—and I know this now to be true after sending three kids to college and being part of that process—all a kid has to do is stand in that one place where it *feels* like it's the *right* place for him or her. Where he can say, Oh, I can see myself here. And I couldn't do that anywhere, until we made a trip down to Columbia, South Carolina, in the spring of my senior year. I figured I probably did not have a fighting chance of making the soccer team, but that didn't stop me from picturing myself on the campus, even on the team. That self-picture, that desire, was stronger than odds and stronger than logic."

Then as now, making a Division I team (in any sport) as a "walk-on" is rare. But that wouldn't keep Soni from leaving Illinois for the University of South Carolina.

"Somehow," Soni states, firmly, "I was always able to look at this opportunity—even if it was something that was a desperate long shot —and I was able to say, here's my goal, I am able to focus on this, I am going to fight for this. Taking a long shot at a soccer team in another state without much of a backup plan didn't faze me. I just thought, that's where I threw the dart, that's where I am going, and I'll do my best."

Soni arrived at the University of South Carolina in the autumn of 1983 (he is the oldest member of Hootie & the Blowfish, two-and-a-half years older than Mark and Dean and a year older than Darius). Against great odds, in his freshman year, he made the soccer team.

"He was clearly a good athlete," remembers Mark Berson, who has coached the University of South Carolina's men's soccer team for over forty years and is one of the most respected coaches in college athletics. "He had a tremendous energy. He could run forever. He's still, to this day, one of our top scorers in our athletic testing. Athletically, there was no question of his skill. He came in, and was an outstanding player for us for four years, not only earning a spot on the team, but becoming a starter. When Jim came to South Carolina, soccer was his identity. He emerged as a musician later, but his primary focus when he came here was to play soccer, and he had a really notable focus on and commitment to that goal. Good technical player, good passer, able to score goals, very good in the air—that is, a player who could win challenges in the air—a really *sound* player."

Somewhere in his Columbia journey, Soni started taking the drums a bit more seriously and joined a few bands. "It is often misconstrued by people, even by people who knew me at the time, that I quit soccer to join Hootie & the Blowfish," Soni states. "And that would be a great story if it was true. The truth is, after three years of soccer, I took a gap year to join a reasonably average but interesting alternative band and work at the state mental hospital."

That "reasonably average but interesting alternative band" was Bachelors of Art, who Soni joined in 1986. In fact, Bachelors of Art were a damn sight better than "reasonably average." Here's a funny thing about Bachelors of Art. As a former A&R person, I believe that if Bachelors of Art had been working in New York, Los Angeles, or Seattle instead of Columbia, South Carolina, they would have been signed to a major label. Bachelors of Art were not your typical Columbia band: They were an accomplished, dynamic goth/postpunk band with a charismatic and attractive female vocalist who had an unusual and powerful contralto voice (the lowest female vocal range; think of Cher, Sade, or Annie Lennox). Clearly influenced by Bauhaus, Siouxsie and the Banshees, The Mission, and Sisters of Mercy, Bachelors of Art were positively dripping with cobwebs, eyeliner, kudzu, drama, and attitude.

"That was like jumping into a new hemisphere for me," says Soni, recalling the switch from jock to goth. "First, I had three years behind me of Division I sports and academia, but I had a calling to get out and do something a little different and ended up in Bachelors of Art. That was the first real band I had ever drummed with, written songs with, or played in front of people with. So that was a big adjustment. But they were also towards the outer edge of anything I had ever listened to. I had grown up on classic rock and country and some weird Frank Zappa stuff, but alternative music was not in my collection. Suddenly I was being exposed to bands I had never heard of—Echo & the Bunnymen, Bauhaus, Simple Minds, Cabaret Voltaire. It was outside of anything I had ever experienced and I thought, well, this shit is kind of cool. It also led me to watch the movie *Eraserhead* on acid for the first time, and I thought, Ooooh, this is what being in an alternative band is all about! So suddenly I was in this new world, which I actually quite liked and found fascinating, and it opened my mind: What do you people listen to, and why is your hair dyed purple? Honestly, it was a lovely experience, and I was looking for something like that. Soccer and college sports, out of necessity, can be a little conformist, and I was itching to jump outside of those guidelines."

After his gap year ended, Soni returned to University of South

Carolina soccer in the autumn of 1987 for his last year of sports eligibility. Then, shortly before graduation, Soni joined a popular Columbia cover band called Tootie and the Jones, whose repertoire leaned a little more toward classic rock than the college radio-leaning Hootie.

The strange similarity in names between Soni's second band, Tootie and the Jones, and his third, Hootie & the Blowfish, appears to be genuinely coincidental (the Tootie and the Jones name came first; they had been gigging for at least a year before Darius and Mark even met). However, that similarity was what initially brought Soni's future band to his attention.

"I distinctly remember being thrilled when I turned a corner on the campus and I saw a flyer that said, 'Hootie & the Blowfish, Friday Night, $2.' And I thought, 'Damn, I am not the only one cursed with the stupidest fucking name of a band ever,'" says Soni.

Tootie and the Jones were doing quite well, but Soni was ready to move on. He was eager to join a group that would allow him to write and perform original music.

There was one song in particular that Soni was especially proud of. "I was struggling to find a voice and put together words that weren't just pain-based, and all about *my feelings*. When I wrote 'Hold My Hand' I thought, wow, that's got a verse, and I am singing it confidently, and the chorus is overt, and gosh, harmonies will sound real good on it, wow, I have just written an actual good song. I was very proud that it didn't suck."

Of course, it's not just the melody and chord framework of "Hold My Hand" that makes it so appealing, so universal, an object so very, very many people want to bring into their life. It's the lyrics and the sentiment, too.

"I had worked a number of jobs in the community," Soni explains, "and seen a little bit of life outside the college bubble. I had this awareness that there's some ugly, painful things out there. I was thinking of that stuff, I was thinking of the pain and suffering in the world, and the main thing motivating the song was that I didn't like to see people hurting. Although Darius has occasionally referred to it as a protest song, to me it was a song of compassion or empathy, saying 'We're all hurting, why don't we get together and help each other through it?'"

Soni played it for Tootie and the Jones. They turned it down.

-8-

FIFTEEN R.E.M. SONGS AND A PROMISE

It was the beginning of May 1989. In South Carolina, spring is not the time of cool, refreshing breezes and weather fit for skipping across new, dewy grass. In South Carolina, spring is the opening credits for a horror movie called summer. In this first week of May, the bright, white, wet washcloth of summer had already wrapped itself around the University of South Carolina. It would remain in place, both happy and angry, until at least the middle of October. Sometimes it would break for bursts of rain so thick it was as if the world had turned as gray as the screen of a turned-off TV set. Mostly, it would be just bright, white, brighter, whiter, and so hot that collars, even on polo shirts, were unthinkable.

But that was okay. Everyone except northerners knew that came with the territory.

Soni Sonefeld and Mark Bryan had stopped to chat in the sunlight in front of the Carolina Coliseum on the southwest corner of the University of South Carolina campus. They were not going to a concert or a sporting event; they were in the same media arts class, which was held in a classroom on the ground floor. Soni does not know it, but he is about to find out what he's going to do with his life.

Mark and Soni weren't really friends and they had never really hung out, but Mark knew that Soni was a drummer looking for a band, and Soni knew that Mark was in a band looking for a drummer.

Relatively quickly in the conversation, it emerged that Soni was frustrated being in a cover band and also that Mark's band had just started doing originals and wanted to move further in that direction. The next time the media arts class met, Mark gave Soni a cassette.

"It was very straightforward," Soni says, looking back on the audition. "Mark said, 'Learn these and we'll do an audition.' I was very eager, too, I remember spending a good amount of time studying the tape. I didn't necessarily want to learn fifteen R.E.M. songs, but there was a promise that came with it: They promised that we would be doing original material, too. So, we went to a self-storage unit near campus where a lot of bands rented space. Really plain room with concrete floor, and metal roof and doors. In other words, the worst place to make music ever. But twenty-five bucks a month for an eight-by-fourteen room, can't beat that. I must have done a diligent job in learning the songs because I recall the rehearsal going really well, and at the end I remember us all going, 'Well, let's do this thing.'"

The night after the audition, Soni and Mark met up at Mark's house at 2203 College Street, off campus in Five Points, to have a beer, or two, or eight, and sit down with their guitars and play a few songs.

Mark Bryan remembers. "Soni played 'Hold My Hand.' It was already fully written, almost exactly the way you hear it now. I distinctly recall sitting on my couch listening to him play it. My first thought was, wow, that is so simple, just three chords, and it's so perfect, what can I add to that? What do you do? So I played along with him, and came up with that little riff you hear at the top, that little lick you hear right over the intro. I wrote that in the room, that day."

"At first I thought, huh, that is *definitely* something poppier than what I would write," Mark continues. "And I *still* think that about all of Soni's music, every time he brings in a song—like, that is *so* poppy —but it is also really good, really catchy, and different from anything I would do stylistically. The next time we played it, it was with Darius and Dean, in our practice space. It was already there, written, complete. Darius picked up on it right away, added some ad-libbed bits and some soul to it, and it *took off.* We had ten or so other originals we were working on at that time, so the timing was perfect."

Darius Rucker: "I cannot describe to you the feeling I had when I first heard 'Hold My Hand.' We were trying out new drummers, and Soni came in. And I did not like him, because my college girlfriend was in love with him, but what the heck, I'll listen to the guy play. A little earlier that year, my girlfriend made me take a picture of her—this is before we started dating, in fact this is how I met her—she wrote in the volleyball sand, 'I Love Soni' and asked me to take a picture of her standing over this. That's how I met her. True story. My girlfriend in college was madly in love with him, and she made no bones about it. So I *hated* this guy. Didn't know him. Just hated him. Honestly, I told Mark and Dean, there's no chance he's going to be in the band, but we will let him play, I'll listen to him play."

Soni Sonefeld: "I knew this girl, apparently she liked me, but at that age, I wasn't very good at reading signs. So I never saw it, we never kissed, though we did hang out and get drunk a few times and I think I even walked her back to her dorm one night. So nothing ever happened, *except* if you are in Darius's shoes, and you found out that some other guy from another band walked a girl home that you really liked, or were even dating."

"But when we heard 'Hold My Hand' for the first time," Darius says, "we are looking at each other going, 'Holy shit. . . .' And we *had* to put him in the band, no matter what my initial objections were. I mean, that song says, 'You're in the band.'"

History is written in disappearing ink, so we must note that the key participants have slightly different recollections of these events. Soni remembers that the girl's name was Jenna, whereas Darius is fairly certain it was Deb. Also, Darius recalls Soni playing "Hold My Hand" at the very first audition, although both Soni and Mark remember it being at a second rehearsal.

In any event, in "Hold My Hand" Hootie had found their true sound, the mixture of emotion, simplicity, depth, and soul that would lie in the DNA of nearly everything to follow. After "Hold My Hand" was revealed, there was no question that Hootie & the Blowfish would never again be "just" a cover band. There was too much at stake. They had this one grand, beautiful, majestic, and utterly simple song, and they would need to write more and more to equal it, frame it, contextualize it, and even beat it.

Dean says that it wasn't just "Hold My Hand" that made Soni the absolute *right* guy for Hootie & the Blowfish's future. It was his experience and his temperament, too. "Because we knew that Soni had been in a hard-working band, we knew he could handle it. Some of the other people we auditioned had been drummers in high school bands, and were quite good, but it's different if you know you are going to be going on the road. It's not luxurious, it's not clean, and a couple of the people who auditioned, I remember thinking right away, they're not going to last a month on the road, because it's pretty brutal. It's a lot of foot an' ass, and a lot of people in your space, and we had been around each other for a while and were quite comfortable with each other, so throwing someone else into the mix isn't the easiest thing. But knowing that Soni had been with Tootie and the Jones, we realized he could probably handle this, at least part time. He could at least be a weekend warrior. And then once we heard the songs he had already written, it was slam-dunk. Once he tried out, once he played us the songs he had been working on, we were done. We weren't going to consider anyone else."

Soni also felt an instant sense of community with Dean, Mark, and Darius, an immediate sense that they were all on the same page.

Soni Sonefeld: "If there's anything I felt, it was that here were four guys, including myself, who really wanted to shoot for the moon. I felt that nothing in any of our lives was going to be allowed to get in the way of us working hard and moving forward. Who knows where forward goes and where forward ends. None of us had a job we really liked that took precedence, none of us had a serious girlfriend. There was this unified, singular desire to play music, write music, have fun. We came from three different distinct paths—Darius being out of school and scrambling to pay off student loans, me taking six fucking years to graduate, and Mark and Dean on a fairly straightforward four-year college plan—we all came together at the same time, looking at the same signpost. We have all arrived here with the same idea: To do this thing we enjoyed doing and do it very diligently. I don't think we could have gone wrong, because each of us put our hand in and said, Go Team. Let's go for this."

Darius Rucker: "What I will always say about Soni—it's like the Beatles said about Ringo—we weren't Hootie & the Blowfish until Soni got into the band. Simple as that."

-9-

GO TEAM

When you turn on the TV to watch a football game, it's pretty clear that a team isn't just the ballplayers on the field. And when you watch a film, all those credits that roll and roll and roll after the movie is over testify to the fact that a bunch of actors didn't just wander into a field where some cameras happen to be and that the whole thing did not get packaged magically and slapped on Netflix.

The same is absolutely true for a working musician, *any* working musician. A band, after all, is just the visible part of a whole organization, the "storefront" for an entire business. Even, if these people never write a song or play an instrument, they are as fundamental a part of the story as any band member.

It is highly unlikely that Hootie & the Blowfish would have achieved the things they did without the assistance, hard work, and wisdom of manager Rusty Harmon and attorney Richard "Gus" Gusler. It is equally unlikely that the band would have ever gotten to Rusty or Gus if it wasn't for Dick Hodgin, an extremely respected music industry figure in the Carolinas who was also Hootie & the Blowfish's first producer.

As so many of these things do, it began when someone was handed a cassette.

For a hopeful young band in the very late 1980s, a cassette didn't just hold a few songs. It wasn't even an audio resume, although it certainly had that function, too. Any musician who ever handed a cassette to a stranger will tell you what it really was—a dream catcher: Here is my hope. Will you help me catch my dreams?

One evening in the autumn of 1989 after a gig at one of the band's favorite Columbia venues, Greenstreets, Hootie & the Blowfish asked the club's live soundman, Charlie Merritt, to make a live recording of five of their original songs. It was an extremely primitive session, but if they ran into anyone who could help them out, at least now they would have something to give them.

A few days after recording and copying their demo cassette, Hootie & the Blowfish appeared at the 4808 Club in Charlotte, North Carolina. The 4808 was a particularly grim venue; from the outside, it looked like a cheap buffet restaurant that had been converted into a porno video store, and on the inside, it wasn't much better. It was also near legendary on the hardcore punk, hardcore metal, and death metal circuit. Hootie, a fairly nontypical booking for the place, were opening for another band who also didn't quite fit into the venue's mold: The Accelerators, a band from Raleigh who played a rockabilly/roots-tinged variation of the North Carolina Mitch Easter/Peter Holsapple jangle sound.

The manager of The Accelerators, Dick Hodgin, was at the show. After Hootie's set—which, to be honest, Dick hadn't paid much attention to—Mark gave Dick one of the new Hootie & the Blowfish demo cassettes.

Dick, of course, refused to listen to the cassette (at first, anyway) because the name was so bloody stupid. When you were one of the hardest working and most respected producers and band managers in the entire Mid-South, as Dick was, you really didn't have time for bands who gave themselves ridiculous names. But his assistant, Rusty Harmon, listened to the cassette. And Rusty told Dick, you *have to* listen to this band.

Rusty Harmon was born on Shepherds Air Force base in Wichita Falls, Texas. He moved around a lot, rarely living in any one place for more than a year, but he spent most of high school in different cities in North Carolina. He only applied to one college, and it accepted him: North Carolina State University (NC State) in Raleigh. He soon discovered two things that were to change his life: weed, and college radio. He says the former created a distraction so significant it would lead to him losing his scholarship and almost flunking out, but the latter opened up not only a whole world of new music but also the potential for a career in the music industry.

Toward the end of his time at NC State (Rusty, like Soni, took some time off on the road to graduation), Rusty began hosting Triangle Live, a music interview show on WKNC, the NC State college radio station. "I'm getting every good band from the area," Rusty remembers. "And every single time I needed to get in touch with a band, everybody would say, 'You have to call Dick Hodgin. Dick Hodgin knows all the bands.' So you would call Dick, and he would give you whatever phone number you needed. Eventually I met him at some gigs, and we just hit it off. Next thing I know, I am interning for Dick, at his office on Western Boulevard in Raleigh."

Since 1984, Dick had been running a company called M80 Management. M80 handled some of the top artists in the region. These included The Accelerators (who were signed to Profile Records), Flat Duo Jets (who had a deal with Doggone, a label run by then-R.E.M. manager Jefferson Holt), an extremely popular local act called Johnny Quest (who played a Red Hot Chili Peppers/Beastie Boys–type rap/punk/funk). At the time, the Raleigh/Durham/Chapel Hill area—"the Triangle," as locals refer to it—was one of the most fertile and fascinating areas in the country for independent music of all genres, and Dick was the man right at the center of the action.

Rusty Harmon: "Dick Hodgin wasn't just a manager, he was also a producer. He worked at this place called Jag Studios, and any band that could come up with five hundred dollars or a thousand dollars, he would do a really first-rate demo for you. If you were in that region and you had reached the stage where you were together enough to record a demo, a single, or an EP, Dick was your guy."

"He was definitely part of the state's music-industry establishment," remembers journalist David Menconi, who has documented multiple generations of music and musicians in the Triangle. "He was also an experienced & reputable producer, with enough connections to where he could get you a hearing from the industry. Definitely one of North Carolina's gatekeepers—get his attention, and that could be step one. So bands beat a path to his door."

"He was a one-man operation," emphasizes Rusty. "Then I came to the office, and it became a two-man operation. He was booking every show himself and doing the contracts himself—so eventually, that meant I was booking and doing contracts, too. We were keeping a database of everyone we thought might want to go to gigs in the area and sending out concert calendars, and in those days, that meant putting it all on a floppy disc, bringing the floppy disc to Kinko's, printing out mailing labels, and putting them on thousands and thousands of postcards. Dick taught me how to do *everything*. And I mean everything: getting registration on vans, and changing the oil, and doing band's taxes, everything."

Between all the different hats he was wearing, it makes sense that when Dick was handed a cassette by an unknown band with a distinctly uninviting name, he hands it off to his office assistant. "He couldn't record everyone he wanted to or everyone who asked, because he simply didn't have enough time," says Rusty. "So he would give me a box of cassettes—literally a box—every weekend, to take home and listen to and tell him what bands he ought to consider producing. So me and my friends would sit around, get stoned, and listen to twenty or thirty cassettes. One of these cassettes is from a band called Hootie & the Blowfish. The letter says, 'We apologize for the way this sounds, but we just got through playing a show at Greenstreets and we had to wait until everyone cleared out of the room, then we ran five songs through the board, so this is a live recording made at the end of a long night.'"

"I called the number on the cassette," Rusty continues, "and Mark Bryan picked up. I said, 'I have a question for you: This letter says you started recording after the gig?' And he says, 'Yeah, about two or three, closer to three o'clock.' And I said, 'Wait—y'all stayed sober the whole night?' And he said, 'Yessir, we stayed sober and then we ran these songs.' And I thought, wow, that's really impressive, I better talk to Dick about this band. Obviously, they mean business if they stayed sober a whole night just to make this tape. In addition, there were a whole bunch of really good songs caught my ear right away—'Hold My Hand,' 'They Don't Understand,' and this fake ID song that I really liked. So, on Monday, I walked into the office and told Dick,

'Dude, you really need to listen to this.' And he literally picked it up, saw that it was Hootie & the Blowfish, and said 'Rusty, I am not going to waste my time with a band whose name is that stupid.' But I hung in there and made him play it. We listened to three songs and he said, 'Alright, alright, I hear what you're saying. Go ahead and book a session.' So I booked a session, and they came to Raleigh."

In mid-February of 1990, Darius, Dean, Soni, and Mark made the three-and-a-half-hour drive from Columbia. Hootie & the Blowfish would be spending five days at Jag Studios, working in a real recording studio for the first time.

Dick was immediately impressed by the band's attitude. "When you bring young bands in, they're all concerned with their individual thing. What are my drums gonna sound like? What's my bass going sound like? Is he gonna be able to capture my guitar tone? What's my voice gonna sound like? Young, novice musicians tend to be centered on what the individual does. And one of the things I remember about Hootie is they were more concerned with what the overall sum was gonna be at the end of the project, and they let me lead them in that direction. They wanted the whole thing to really be the sum of the parts. And they really shined."

Listening to *Hootie & the Blowfish* (as the debut cassette would be titled) over thirty years later, I say without reservation that Dick kicked ass. Tight, brisk, bright, this first studio recording reflects the spring-wound energy of the band's first four years while also having a depth of tone and songcraft that looks forward to the band's future. To those only familiar with Hootie's later recordings, you'll notice a couple of things about *Hootie & the Blowfish* right away. First and foremost, everything is so fast. The band performs with a hyperactive hop and strum that recalls both (very) early R.E.M. and The Feelies, not to mention the early work of stylistically similar guitar-based bands like The Smiths and Orange Juice. Multiple observers (and the bandmates themselves) note that the band played considerably faster in the Brantley days, and it's worth remembering that this recording was made barely half a year after Brantley left.

Second, less than half a year after the group committed themselves fully to performing (mostly) original material, they are already writing songs of great depth, texture, and skill. For instance, "Little Girl," is arguably as good and deep as any song that made it onto *cracked rear view*, even if Mark, Dean, Soni, and Darius play it like they have a firecracker up their ass. (Please note: I always identify the debut album by Hootie & the Blowfish as *cracked rear view*, written entirely in lowercase. This is how the name appears on the original album cover. The use of lowercase was an intentional decision of the art director, the band, and the management, and I honor this choice throughout this book, regardless of how odd it may look.)

Perhaps most surprisingly, here at the literal dawn of their recording career, Hootie & the Blowfish have made what is almost without a doubt the tightest and most precise studio recording they would ever make. The five tracks on the debut cassette contain absolutely none of the loose ends, slightly weedy tempos, or loosey-goosey rhythms that were to mark *Kootchypop* or any of Hootie's major label albums. These five tracks sound virtually nailed to a wall.

I won't disguise my enthusiasm: I *love* Hootie & the Blowfish's first cassette release, and it is my favorite of their pre-Atlantic recordings. Also, unlike the second cassette (*Time*, recorded exactly a year later) or *Kootchypop*, this first release does not feel like a preview of *cracked rear view*. This cassette documents a completely unique stage in the band's development. This is the "college-rock" Hootie.

Dean Felber: "We *wanted* to sound like R.E.M., we *wanted* to sound like The Smithereens, there were a lot of bands we *wanted* to sound like, but we just couldn't, even when we tried, even when we played the same notes, the same parts. At first that was kind of upsetting to us, but eventually, when you *see* how the audience catches it, and that they get what you're doing and they are responding to you and your particular combination of players, no matter what song you're playing, you realize you have your own sound."

Of course, Hootie's first cassette features the recorded debut of "Hold My Hand." The arrangement is virtually identical to the (two) later recordings of the song (on *Kootchypop* and *cracked rear view*), but as with all the material on this first cassette, the performance is strident and a bit rushed. It's also worth noting that Gerald Duncan of

The Accelerators performs the high harmony bit in the chorus (a role filled by David Crosby on the *cracked rear view* recording).

There were two high-impact aftershocks to the initial February 1990 recording session in Raleigh. One of these was that the band's association with a credible and established figure like Dick Hodgin significantly boosted their standing and visibility in the region. The second enormous benefit from the sessions in Raleigh was the immediate bond Mark, Soni, Darius, and Dean established with Rusty Harmon, who hosted them, showed them the town, and took them drinking and clubbing during the band's five days in Raleigh. This relationship with Dick's second in command was to really blossom a little later, in late April of 1990.

Rusty Harmon: "After they left Raleigh and went back to Columbia, I didn't talk to them much for six or eight weeks. Then the cassette came out, and I asked them, who is shopping your cassette, who is helping you get it around? And they didn't even seem to really understand what that meant. So I asked them who was booking the band. And Soni said, well, whoever can, sometimes it's me, sometimes it's Darius, sometimes it's whoever feels like making the call. And I was, like, No, no, no! It's got to be one voice, one person. And you have got to be able to answer the phone every time it rings. So after that, once a week we would talk, and I'd give them advice like that, and after three or four weeks of these conversations they said—I think it was Soni—Dude, why don't you just be our manager?"

Rusty said no. And he said no the next time they asked him, too.

"I kept saying no, because I was *finally* about to graduate," Rusty says, "and I had a line on a *real* job. I was going to do production for NC State football games, for WPTF, 680 A.M. I was going to be the guy who held the parabolic microphone on the sidelines. Which seemed like a good job at the time. But the band wouldn't give up. Finally, they said, 'We are going to a buddy's house by a lake in South Carolina, why don't you come down and spend the weekend with us?' I had a DJ gig on Friday night, so I drove all through the night after I finished and got to the lake house just as the sun was rising. And the only person still awake was Darius. And they had *just* written the song 'Time.' So Darius was sitting on a hammock, drunk as he could be, playing the song 'Time.' And, honestly, as soon as I pulled up and saw Darius on that hammock with the sun rising singing that song, I *knew* I was going to be their manager. And when I left on Sunday, we had started a management company. But every time for the next ten years, whenever we saw someone on the sidelines of a football game holding a parabolic microphone, Darius would go, 'Rusty, that could have been you.'"

-10-

THE JOHNNY QUEST PLAYBOOK ... AND BEYOND

LAWYERS, CASSETTES, AND GOOD AND BAD TIMES AT THE FRATS

By the summer of 1990, Hootie & the Blowfish were decidedly no longer a cover band that played a few originals, but a band that played originals and *also* did some fun and quirky covers.

By early 1991, the band you would have seen at any one of two or three dozen venues in the Mid-South and the Atlantic Coast states would have been totally recognizable as the Hootie & the Blowfish who blew up big in the mid-1990s. The shows were out of control but in control; and on stage you saw great friends—a brotherhood— capable of playing serious music but apparently mostly interested in having a good time with each other and with their audience. They sang of their audiences' hopes, dreams, romances and flirtations, but remarkably, they did so in a way that said, "We are only up here on stage so you can see us better, not because we are better than you."

Hootie & the Blowfish emerged from a unique environment for live rock music. Unlike better publicized scenes in New York, Los Angeles, or Seattle, bands in the Mid-South weren't competing for a record deal; they were competing for the attention, applause, and the repeat patronage of real, paying fans. Hootie came from a culture (fairly unique to the Mid-South and the Atlantic Coast states in the 1980s and '90s) where people who wanted to drink, dance, meet someone, and be entertained sought out (largely local) live bands, instead of "just" listening to a DJ or waiting for a national act to roll through town.

This was a sink-or-swim culture. You had to be good, then you had to be better. You had to get the job done, no matter how drunk the audience was or how much they wanted to hear covers and not your original songs. And Hootie succeeded in this milieu (as did Dave Matthews Band, the other breakout from the early 1990s Mid-South live music circuit).

One of the reasons this all came together was because Rusty Harmon and Hootie & the Blowfish followed the Johnny Quest Playbook.

Johnny Quest, who formed in Raleigh in the late 1980s, played a mega-sweaty, brittle, gnashing, grinning punk funk, equal parts Red Hot Chili Peppers, Black Flag, and Beastie Boys. They were silly, sexy, self-mocking crowd pleasers, perhaps *the* ideal band for an audience full of sorority girls blitzed on Long Island iced teas. The Johnny Quest Playbook was a strategy used by the band and manager Dick Hodgin to build Johnny Quest into one of the most successful indie acts working in the United States. The Johnny Quest Playbook—that's what Dick, Rusty, the Hootie guys, and others in the region actually called it at the time—took advantage of the unique infrastructure of the live music scene in the Mid-South to create a pathway to financial security, provided a band was good enough, appealing enough, and willing to put in the mileage.

In the simplest terms, this was the Johnny Quest Playbook: To start, you need a new or unknown act but one who can potentially appeal to the kind of audiences that would attend frat or sorority parties. It is essential that your act is willing to work hard enough (and have enough material) to play multiple sets in one evening.

- First, you approach a frat or sorority. You explain that they can have your band for free, all they need to do is supply the public address (PA) system.
- Second: Your band does such a terrific job and puts on such a great show that the frat or sorority says, "We want you back for a big party in three weeks, and we will pay you lots of money!" (Frats and sororities traditionally have large entertainment budgets.)

- Third: After playing an area frat or sorority two or three times to enthusiastic audiences, you call the local rock club and book yourself a gig. Because of the audience you built up playing the frat/sorority and making fans there, you *pack* the club. You can then book *another* gig in that same club, possibly even on a weekend, and get a very good guarantee (money a club is committed to paying you, regardless of how many people show up).

- Next, you expand your base. Since frats and sororities are generally part of a national organization, you call one of the brother frats or sister sororities at another college in another town, and you say, "We did so well at your house in Columbia, why not book us up there in Charlottesville? Pick up the phone right now and call your brothers/sisters in Columbia, they'll tell you how much they loved us."

- You then repeat the earlier step: After having played this out-of-town frat or sorority a couple of times, you go to the local rock club in *that* town, book yourself a show, and sell it out because of the following you built in the new market.

- Before long, you can pack any club in the region. Then you can flip the formula by working mostly club shows, which you occasionally supplement with high-paying frat/sorority shows.

- Repeat this formula throughout the whole Mid-South, Atlantic Coast, Southeast, and even out to the Midwest and up all the way to Vermont.

Et voilà, the Johnny Quest Playbook!

It takes time, effort, enormous stamina, and a lot of changed tires, but by following the Johnny Quest Playbook, the right band, willing to put in the miles and put up with a lot of boredom and bullshit, can earn a very good living. At their peak playing the Mid-South/Atlantic Coast circuit, Johnny Quest and Hootie were regularly making between five and ten grand a show.

"You could create a circuit of frats in ten university towns," Rusty Harmon explains. "Durham for Duke, Chapel Hill for UNC, Raleigh for NC State, Wilmington for UNC Wilmington, James Madison up in Virginia, Virginia Tech in Blacksburg, Spartanburg for Presbyterian, Clemson, and so on. The first set would be all originals, the second set would be half covers/half originals, and the third set would be all covers. But Hootie & the Blowfish did it bigger, better, and faster than Johnny Quest."

Within a relatively short space of time, Hootie & the Blowfish were working every weekend (that is, Thursday night through Saturday night, and sometimes Wednesday, too), all across the region.

In the early 1990s, according to Chip Latham, who first saw the band at Bar 101 in Rock Hill, South Carolina, "Every show was a party. There were shots before every show, and then on stage, too, usually Jägermeister. It was just crazy. People just drinking and going crazy, and in Rock Hill, it was even a bigger crowd than it was in Columbia. They were just having fun, and Mark would strip down to his underwear sometimes. He'd start pulling off clothes. Someone else would take off his shirt, but Mark would sometimes go all the way down to his underwear."

"It was such a party atmosphere on stage. They went up there and had fun. And Mark has always done that Pete Townshend kind of thing, windmill his arm, jumping around. I always thought Mark had a really cool style. Everybody talks about Darius and his unique voice, but Hootie's not anything without Mark."

Nearly thirty years later, Mark can still rattle off the names of the venues the band played in those days when they were putting a lot of miles on the van, spending too little time in the shower, and building a following. "Rockafellas and Greenstreets in Columbia were both kickass," he says. "Every six weeks we would play one of them. Greenstreets was significant for us because it was a real venue, with a real stage and sound system, and real national acts came through and played there. Playing there gave us relevance and credibility at a time when we were still drawing in people with covers, but we were trying to keep them coming back with originals. This was also true of Rockafellas on the other side of Five Points, but it had a smaller capacity and was more divey."

"In Charleston, it was Myskins," Mark continues, "and the Windjammer out on the Isle of Palms, out on the Beach. Hilton Head, it was the Old Post Office. In Myrtle Beach, it was the Purple Gator—not the kind of place you would think you would see us—it was a cheesy beach disco pick-up–type place—but we would draw two thousand people. So who cares what kind of place it is, there are two thousand people there! In DC, we were playing the Grog and Tankard, which was great for us, then we were able to move up to the Bayou. These were our favorites, though, of course there were a bunch of spots in Maryland, North Carolina, and Virginia. We got as far north as Boston—played the Rat, played the Muse in Nantucket, the Paradise. We got as far north in those early days as Burlington, Vermont."

They had also grown out of Mark's beat-to-shit Ford Fairmont station wagon and moved into their own Econoline van. Even though it was a step up from the Fairmont, it was still not for the faint of heart.

"The nickname of the van was Foot-n-Ass," Rusty says, bluntly. "And it had that name for a reason."

"They would roll up in a van and open the door and it would smell like feet and bud," Chip Latham recalls.

Rusty Harmon: "There was one row of bench seats, and then captain's chairs in the front, and all the other seats had been taken out. We had a pretty good system of loading up the equipment so that there was a barricade, so the big stuff was closer to the front of the van, and the smaller stuff was in the back. That way, when you stopped short, there was some sort of barrier so that the guitar cases or whatnot wouldn't come flying forward and take your head off."

"We would get one hotel room with two double beds," Rusty adds. "Now, if you got a bed, you didn't get a comforter, because the person who slept on the floor would get the comforter. And then one person could sleep in the van, and there was a Styrofoam pad for that purpose. Keep in mind that the person sleeping in the van was the only one who had privacy, so sleeping in the van was actually desirable if you wanted to hook up."

In this manner, Hootie & the Blowfish spent most of their weekends between 1990 and 1994 moving between the greater and lesser cities of the Mid-South and the Atlantic Coast states, hitting every club, frat, and sorority that would have them.

Around this time, another important member of the team came onboard.

Usually, musicians only hire an attorney when they have a specific deal to negotiate or, more likely, if they feel that a well-known music attorney might be able to help them get the attention of a major record label or publisher. Music business attorneys, traditionally, are not part of the social, creative, or emotional inner circle of a band but rather someone who helps them make a key contact.

Hootie & the Blowfish's relationship with Richard "Gus" Gusler was (and is) very, very different. He was part of the inner circle. He was one of the six people who, for all intents and purposes, were Hootie & the Blowfish in the 1990s.

As early as mid-1990, the group recognized that they wanted to approach their band as a real business and not as a casual hobby or something they did for fun. They were young professionals, and they wanted to do this right. Therefore, they went looking for someone just like Gus Gusler.

"We started to get some good gigs," Rusty Harmon says, "and started to make some real money. We already had a few thousand dollars in the bank account. I knew we needed to get insurance on the van and our property, and we needed to incorporate so we could properly insure everything. I went to Dick Hodgin—I didn't make a move in those days without asking Dick's advice—and he recommended an attorney in Raleigh named Gus Gusler. I called Gus and he kept on saying no, he wasn't interested in doing any bands."

Finally, the whole band just showed up at Gus's office.

Gus Gusler: "Rusty called me three times and I refused to meet with him. I kept on saying, 'I don't do that anymore, I'm just doing criminal work.' And finally on the fourth time, they were downstairs, Rusty was on a pay phone. He said, 'We're down here on the street, give us fifteen minutes, we've just got some questions.' And I went in the conference room with them, and they sat down, and I really didn't wanna be there. I was tired of dealing with musicians, especially ones from Chapel Hill who only cared about the music and didn't give a fuck about the business. But they sat down and Dean Felber starts talking, and Dean says, 'The van is in Soni's name. We want to set up a corporation, move the van into the corporate name, get insurance so that he's not personally liable if something happens on the road. We want to set up a retirement plan and health insurance.' I honestly looked up and said, 'Are you guys really fucking musicians?' I was just stunned. I had never heard an artist who sat there and wanted to talk about the *business* side of things. I was blown away."

"That night they were playing at Lake Boone Country Club," Gus continues, "and it was packed. And they knew every word of every friggin' song. I couldn't hear the band, 'cause it was like eleven hundred people in there and they were singing along with every single song. I had sworn to the firm I worked for that I wouldn't be doing any music stuff anymore, but I was like, this is amazing, so I agreed to start working with them."

By enlisting Gus Gusler, Hootie & the Blowfish weren't taking on just any local attorney. Gus had a long, diverse, and credible history in the region, encompassing high-profile work in concert promotion, criminal law, and politics. In addition, he had a powerful background in the civil rights movement. Going all the way back to high school in Burlington, North Carolina, Gus was making friends (and enemies) by his willingness to bring integrated bands in to play at the high school dances. After high school, he continued to follow an adamantly socially conscious path in his work, first as a roadie for integrated bands playing in the South when it still was shadowed by Jim Crow, then as a concert promoter, and later as a criminal attorney, representing unpopular clients facing unfair narcotics laws.

After that evening at Lake Boone Country Club, Gus joined a family, creating a unique, seamless partnership between the four band members and their two closest associates.

Meanwhile, Hootie had made their very first appearance on vinyl: In early 1991, "I Don't Understand" was one of sixteen tracks that appeared on a compilation LP called *Snickers New Music Search 1990– 1991 Presented By Campus Voice Semi Finalists*. This was vinyl evidence that (even before the *Time* cassette) the band was already popular enough to make it to the final stages of a nationwide, corporate "battle of the bands" competition (which, alas, they did not win).

The band's second cassette, *Time*, was recorded in February 1991 and released that spring. The four original tracks are a rather astounding step forward from the wonderful, frenzied, overexcited R.E.M./Feelies/dB's-based college rock of Hootie's debut cassette. It indicates that the year between *Hootie & the Blowfish* and *Time* was probably the most crucial for creative growth in the band's entire career. Dick Hodgin's production remains snug and compact, but the songs themselves now expand, breathe, and are filled with a wide palette of emotions. Unlike the earlier self-titled cassette, we are now hearing a direct preview of the band that would conquer America on *cracked rear view.*

In just one year, Hootie & the Blowfish made enormous growths in musical and lyrical complexity: "Running From an Angel" sounds like the kind of song the Eagles or The Band might write, with a loose but muscular confidence and courage of subject and tempo. "Let Her Cry" is the sort of truly classic mid-tempo rock ballad *any* first-rank band in America would sell their soul to write; it is startling to consider that it comes from a band who had only been focusing on original material for about eighteen months. A song like "Drowning," with its tricky pick-ups, double-stops, and serpentine guitar tag would have been unthinkable a year earlier (arguably, the band wouldn't write a song as complex for another half decade, until the *Fairweather* sessions).

"Drowning" often gets singled out because of its strong political content (more on this later). However, even at this relatively early stage of Hootie's career, "Drowning" was not the first song the band recorded or performed that addressed race. No less than three of the five songs on their 1990 self-titled debut cassette deal with race in a fairly direct way (and that's *not* counting "Hold My Hand"). On "I Don't Understand," Darius even goes so far as to note that there are places he can't go because his skin is "the wrong color."

Which is all to say that, even as Hootie & the Blowfish were becoming major players on the fun, loud, and lucrative frat and club circuit in the Mid-South and the Atlantic Coast, there were still constant reminders that their lead singer was Black, working in a milieu that was overwhelmingly White, and that the gigs themselves were not immune from the racial tension that Darius wrote about in these songs.

"There were certainly a few racial incidents at these frats," Rusty Harmon recalls, "but honestly, not as many as you might suspect. Make no mistake, when it did happen, it would piss us off greatly. Soni almost got in a fight one time. I almost got in a fight one time. It was at a frat house in Clemson that we had the worst incident. I was standing out in the crowd watching the band, as I always did, and this drunk kid standing beside me said, pretty loudly, 'That band is pretty good for a n----- lead singer, huh?' And I turned to him and said, 'Dude, you have got to watch you damn mouth.' And that started a whole thing. Darius was the one who stayed the calmest, he was just saying, okay, let's leave, but Soni really wanted to get into it."

Even back in the early 1990s, Darius Rucker wanted to let his lyrics speak for themselves and not react to the racism around him in any other form. He admits that his feelings about race (and his desire to avoid confrontation, apart from the stance he takes in his lyrics) is something he rarely discusses with his band, despite how close they all are.

"That stuff is hard to talk about," Darius says firmly. "For me, it's *real* hard. Y'know, with what's going on in the world today [in 2020], people want me to get out and take a stand—it's not that I don't care, it's just *hard for me to talk about*."

"Y'know, Tim, this is something you can put in the book," Darius Rucker said to me, with great emphasis. "Tim, if I were to stop being friends with everybody in my life who I know, deep down, called someone a n----- at some point, I'd lose at least half my friends, if not more. I have chosen this life and I live this life, but I have never felt like my bandmates would fully understand, so I have never really talked to them about it. I still don't think they would understand. They have lived and played with me for years, and I still don't think they would understand."

-11-

CROSSING THE
FIRST THRESHOLD

A funny thing happened on the way to Hootie & the Blowfish getting signed by Atlantic Records in 1993.

They were signed by another record label in 1992.

This peculiar chapter in Hootie's career starts with Chip Latham, a fan of the band from Rock Hill, South Carolina. He had first seen the group shortly after Soni joined and immediately was taken by their power, potential, skill, and charm. Unlike most of Hootie's early fans, Latham also had legitimate music business experience and significant industry contacts. In the late 1980s, Latham had worked as a long-distance assistant and talent scout for Henry Neuman, who helped manage Rod Stewart, Prince, and others in the Stiefel Phillips Entertainment company. In 1990, Henry Neuman left Stiefel Phillips to begin his own company, Waterfront Artist Management. He asked Chip Latham to join him in the new venture. Naturally, Latham was very eager to introduce Neuman to the local act he had become so enamored of, Hootie & the Blowfish.

On March 21, 1991, Latham set up a showcase for Neuman to see the band at Bar 101 in Rock Hill, South Carolina. Henry Neuman liked what he saw and immediately expressed an eagerness to work with Hootie & the Blowfish. That evening, Neuman, Latham, Rusty, and the group discussed a deal where Rusty would stay in place as Hootie's day-to-day manager, but Neuman and Latham would help the band make some of the bigger music industry contacts that Rusty and Gus might find elusive. For Darius, Mark, Soni, and Dean, there would be relatively little change in their day-to-day business and their increasingly busy (and lucrative) gigging schedule. But now, ideally, someone would be working to help them secure a record deal, a publishing deal, and other opportunities outside the Mid-South.

During the Henry Neuman era, the band would have relatively little direct contact with Neuman. Rusty remained more or less in charge (there was certainly enough work locally to keep him busy), with Chip Latham as a liaison between Rusty and Neuman. Virtually everyone who had any contact with the band during this time is surprised to find that the band had another manager, apart from Rusty.

Neuman and Latham's industry contacts appeared to show some quick dividends. They set up a label showcase for Hootie & the Blowfish at Centre Stage in Atlanta on June 14th, 1991. On that night, the band played for reps from Gasoline Alley (the MCA-distributed label affiliated with Stiefel Phillips), MCA Nashville, Capitol, Geffen, and a new label called JRS.

JRS was based in Burbank, California, and helmed by two reputable industry vets, Artie Mogull and Stephen Swid. Mogull was a legendary music industry figure who had worked closely with everyone from Bob Dylan, Laura Nyro, and Kenny Rogers to Electric Light Orchestra, John Lennon, and Deep Purple. Swid had been the "S" in SBK, another major label–affiliated company that Mogull had also recently worked for. On the basis of Mogull and Swid's reputation, JRS had secured major label distribution via RCA Records.

Stan Shuster was the young A&R rep that JRS sent to the Atlanta showcase. He had just joined the fledgling company. He fell for Hootie right away. Darius Rucker, and the band's independent, hardworking spirit especially impressed him.

"I was leaning against the bar drinking my Jägermeister shots," Shuster remembers, "I wasn't even looking at the stage at that point, and I look up and I see this kid, and it's Darius. And I go 'oh my gosh, this is one of the greatest voices I've ever heard.' I said 'Geez, I gotta sign you guys. I gotta work with you guys.' Not only were they absolutely incredible, but they were already touring and had this whole self-sufficient thing and already selling cassettes and T-shirts. I thought to myself, 'This is an easy one.'"

Shuster flew back to Los Angeles and told Artie Mogull that he wanted to sign the band. Mogull agreed and offered the band a fairly large deal—approximately $250,000 (roughly four times what they would later get from Atlantic), with at least $100,000 set aside to record an album.

Now, where was the wise and usually outspoken Gus Gusler in the midst of all this?

"The JRS deal was done against my legal advice," Gus says, dryly and cautiously. "That whole thing, all that stuff was . . ." Gus trails off with frustration. "The JRS deal and the management thing with Henry Neuman were probably the only two times the band have chosen not to listen to me, at least in regard to anything of any substance. I just felt like they needed to be patient. That something else better was going to happen."

In the second week of September 1991, Dean, Darius, Mark, Soni, Rusty, and aide-de-camp/roadie/friend-for-life/factotum Jeff Poland made the drive from Columbia to Los Angeles to sign the JRS deal and meet their new label. This would be the band's first-ever visit to Los Angeles. As usual, Hootie's memories of any event, no matter how momentous, are bookmarked by sporting events.

"We watched the Cowboys play the Eagles," Rusty immediately responds, when I ask him about the group's first cross-country trip. "It was Troy Aikman's rookie year, and the Eagles sacked Aikman eleven times that game, setting an NFL record."

Uh, Rusty . . . do you remember anything else?

"We drove for eighteen straight hours, stayed at my mom's house, saw the Cowboys game, spent the night, showered, loaded up on peanut butter and jelly sandwiches and vodka, and drove until we hit somewhere in Arizona—there was a country band called Diamond Rio staying at the same hotel, and we hung out with them and they had their own bus, and that seemed like a really big deal to us—and we got up the next day and drove straight to L.A."

In Los Angeles, the band played a showcase for their new label and signed their record deal. Curiously, Chip Latham says that before actually putting their names on the contract, Gasoline Alley (a significantly more established major-distribution label, who were about to have a big hit with Sublime) not only offered to sign Hootie but also was willing to equal the generous financial terms of the JRS contract. However, Latham says Rusty not only turned down that deal but also declined to inform the band about it, under the (very Hootie-ish) principle that they had already shaken hands on the JRS deal. This is an especially interesting footnote, because if the group had signed to Gasoline Alley instead of JRS, this entire story may have been very, very different. There is every conceivable reason to believe that Hootie & the Blowfish could have succeeded on Gasoline Alley.

After the showcase and the JRS signing, the band returned to South Carolina and began to make plans to record their big-budget debut album. Quickly, Mark, Darius, Dean, and Soni agreed on a record producer: Don Dixon.

"We all knew who Don Dixon was when we were in school," Mark Bryan remembers. "We had great admiration for him, because he coproduced the first two R.E.M. albums. *Murmur* and *Reckoning* were gospel for us at the time. He also did Love Tractor and Guadalcanal Diary and Marti Jones and The Smithereens, and the *Positively Dumptruck* album that literally blew our minds. He did all of these incredible records between '85 and '89. That output right there made us think he was *the* best rock producer of the indie rock scene we were so devoted to, and the obvious choice for us. When we got the budget from JRS and asked him, he said yes."

Reflections Studios in Charlotte, North Carolina, was booked for March and April of 1992 for the recording. Meanwhile in Los Angeles, there were problems.

Stan Shuster: "So, I bring them out to Los Angeles to do a showcase. I get a phone call a couple of weeks later from [JRS co-partner] Stephen Swid, and basically he said to me, 'They're nothing but a shitty cover band.' But I really loved the band, so I disregarded that, and moved forward. I was fighting with Stephen, but definitely not Artie, because Artie loved Hootie."

As the March 1992 start date for the recording sessions approached, Reflections Studios awaited the thirty-thousand-dollar deposit they needed from JRS to confirm the session booking. According to Shuster, Swid made it clear that he wanted to pull the plug, without one note being recorded. But Shuster fought hard for the band and was able to eke a little money out of JRS—two payments of five thousand dollars—to send to Reflections. This amount ensured that Reflections didn't cancel the session outright but just postponed it.

Mark Bryan: "It was this gradual thing where the studio was waiting for the deposit check, and it wasn't coming in, and Rusty was, like, guys, the label still hasn't paid the studio deposit, but they say it's coming, they say it's coming! And all of a sudden, three days before the actual start date of the recording, they were like . . . yeah . . . the money isn't coming."

Stan Shuster: "I thought I was going to be able to pull this off, I really did. I thought I would be able to weather the storm with Stephen Swid and get this thing made. But then he just pulled the plug. He said, 'We're out of this one, we just cut them from the label and, by the way, you're fired.'"

According to Shuster, the decision to drop Hootie was not made because of any financial problems at the label (this is the story that has gained some traction in the years since). Rather, it was because Swid had it in for Hootie (Swid passed in October 2019, very shortly before the interviews commenced for this book, so we are unable to hear his side of the story).

"I think Darius and the rest of them thought it was me," says Shuster, who now owns high-end cigar bars in New York and Los Angeles. "I don't know if they ever knew I got fired. I did everything that I could do to save that band because I thought they were incredible."

Hootie had lost their record deal, without having recorded a note.

With the gravely disappointing end of the JRS deal, another relationship came to an end. Rusty and the band had minimal contact with Henry Neuman and Chip Latham after the collapse of the JRS deal. Nevertheless, Latham continued to assume that he and Neuman were involved with Hootie & the Blowfish, and he was very surprised when *Kootchypop* was released in the spring of 1993, with Neuman's name nowhere to be found in the credits.

Rusty Harmon: "Before we put out *Kootchypop*, we had a call with Henry, and we said, 'Sorry it didn't work out,' and he said, 'I'm sorry too, good luck.' Henry *went away*. And we did not hear another word from him for three or four years until we got a lawsuit from him that said he was the original manager of Hootie & the Blowfish and we *forced* him out."

This difference in perception (did Neuman jump, was he pushed, or had he never actually legally stopped being the manager of Hootie & the Blowfish?) ended up being bit of a big deal. Between 1995 and 1997, Henry Neuman and Fishco (the legal name of the corporate entity that included Darius, Dean, Mark, Soni, and Rusty, and also the name of the band's management company) exchanged a whole forest full of legal paperwork before reaching an out-of-court settlement. (Henry Neuman is unable to comment, having passed in March of 2015.)

-12-

THE BILL CLINTON OF ROCK BANDS

The collapse of the JRS deal had brought Hootie & the Blowfish to a fork in the road. If you are in a band that's been around for seven or eight years and your record deal disintegrates, it might be a sign that it's time to consider taking that job holding the parabolic microphone on the sidelines of college football games.

"We were crushed when the JRS thing didn't happen," Darius remembers. "I look back and think, we were such fucking idiots. They give us a record deal, and we have to drive ourselves cross-country to fucking sign it? That right there makes zero sense. But we thought we had this record deal, and we thought we would get to make this record and be big rock stars. It was very disappointing."

But the band didn't stay down for long.

"But it was disappointing *quickly*," Darius continues. "We were very briefly disappointed. That's because then you go out and play four nights in a row to these clubs that are packed with people, and you go, okay, I can keep doing this!"

Mark echoes this. "There was a giant sense of discouragement. Not only did we *not* get to go into the studio when we thought we were going to, and not only did we *not* get to work with Don Dixon, on top of that, we had not booked six weeks' worth of shows because we thought we were going to go to be in the studio doing a full-length album. We were making a living at that time, playing those shows. All of a sudden, there was no recording, no Don Dixon, no shows, and no money from the shows that we didn't play. We were furious, and broke, and it sucked. But we hung in there, got a little bit of money out of JRS, and rescheduled the recording session."

Gus Gusler squeezed a fifteen-thousand-dollar settlement out of JRS. In the autumn of 1992, Hootie & the Blowfish used that money to book time at Reflections Studios, where they had planned to record their JRS album. Since Hootie no longer had the budget to record a full album with the producer of their choice, they instead did five songs with Mark Williams, one of Don Dixon's prime engineers. The result was the *Kootchypop* EP, released (after some delay) in July of 1993.

But before *Kootchypop* could come out, the Hootie family was rocked by a formative tragedy.

On November 1, 1992, Carolyn Rucker passed suddenly at age 51. Darius Rucker has always remained relatively private about how the loss of his mother affected him. He virtually never spoke about it in public and rarely discussed it with his bandmates. The busy Hootie & the Blowfish gig schedule was unaffected; Darius insisted on performing without cancelling a single show. However, much as he did when it came to the subject of race, Darius expressed his feelings about this profound event through his lyrics.

On *cracked rear view*, "I'm Going Home" and "Not Even the Trees" would directly address Carolyn Rucker's passing, and the tragedy also led to the inclusion of the album's final, "hidden" track, "Motherless Child." The event also recasts the mood and the meaning of three of the songs written before Carolyn Rucker's death: "Running from an Angel," "Time," and "Goodbye." What emerges is the remarkable idea that one of the most successful albums of all time, one very rarely noted for its depth, gravity, or darkness, is, in fact, a concept album about loss and race.

But back to 1993.

The *Kootchypop* EP features three songs that would become very familiar to Hootie fans in the years to come: "The Old Man and Me," "Only Wanna Be With You," and "Hold My Hand" (the latter, of course, had also appeared, in a different version, on the band's first cassette release in 1990).

"Only Wanna Be With You" looms very large in the Hootie story. After a series of shows with the band Dillon Fence, Mark noted that the guitarist, Greg Humphries, frequently used capos, small bars you attach to the neck of the guitar over the strings to voice chords in different ways. "I thought, well, I want to try that! So I put the capo on the second fret, and I liked the way it sounded, but I wanted it to be faster, so I used one of my favorite strumming patterns, which is 'Pinball Wizard.' So I went for that, and the 'Only Wanna Be with You' riff came out. This is all happening both subconsciously and consciously, this homage to 'Pinball Wizard' with the fast energy of my right strumming hand, and the homage to Dillon Fence with my left chording hand. I liked what I came up with, so I made a demo of it. It didn't have any lyrics or melody, but the arrangement was almost exactly what you hear now."

The *Kootchypop* EP includes two additional original tracks, neither of which would appear on future Hootie albums. "If You're Going My Way" is a light, funky song, mostly composed by Soni. "Sorry's Not Enough," which emerged from a Mark/Soni jam, is languid and soul scented, and fairly clearly influenced by Bill Withers's "Use Me" (which was a staple of the band's performances at the time and remains in their live set to this day).

Kootchypop is far from a perfect record. The tracks lack the crisp, wound-up tightness of Dick Hodgin's productions, the mixes live inside an ever-so-slight weed haze of reverb, and Darius's vocals sometimes sound a little lazy and occasionally lean flat. Regardless, the world—or at least the Carolinas—responded to the disc quickly and enthusiastically. The EP blew up fast, creating a true regional hit and rapidly selling over twenty-five thousand copies, enough to make *Kootchypop* one of the very top-selling records—indie or major label—in the region. *Kootchypop* achieved all this while being a *true* independent record; the band wasn't on some already existing small label. The entire manufacturing, distribution, and promotion system was coming out of Fishco.

Now, about that title. One night, the members of Hootie & the Blowfish were watching actor and comedian Shirley Hemphill on a talk show. She told a story about her sister announcing that she had purchased a revealing thong bikini. Hemphill explained that after her sister tried the bikini on, Hemphill informed her sister that if she was going to insist on wearing it in public, she was going to need to shave her "cootchie pop." This figuratively murdered the boys, slayed them, made them retch with joy and shudder with giggles, left them laughing so hard they were gasping for air and dribbling beer from at least two orifices. They knew that, with a slight alteration in spelling, they had the title for their forthcoming EP.

Here's a strange fact: Among all the CDs, vinyl LPs, cassettes, and DVDs the band ever released, *Kootchypop* is the only Hootie & the Blowfish release that credits the band as Hootie *and* the Blowfish, with "*and*" spelled out. The band members have no idea why. The most logical explanation, suggested by Rusty Harmon, is that this was an arbitrary decision of the sleeve designer, a University of South Carolina art professor named Mana Hewitt. None of the band members (or Brantley Smith) recall why they opted to use the ampersand in the first place, when the group was initially named in 1986, either. In fact, thirty-four years later, neither Soni nor Mark knew that the name was exclusively spelled with an ampersand. "Why we what?" Soni said, when I brought this issue to his attention. "I always write 'and.' Huh. Is *cracked rear view* like that?"

I assured Soni that it was, as were all of the band's releases, except for *Kootchypop*.

Even before the release of *Kootchypop*, the band was coming to a major reckoning about their future as working musicians, and they had reached the point where they were making enough from shows and touring to quit their other jobs. Mark had been working at channel 57, the Fox TV affiliate in Columbia, editing commercials into reruns and classic movies and transferring one-inch videotapes into the three-quarter-inch format that the station used. Soni worked for Instructional Services Center, the University of South Carolina's in-house video production team, which shot footage of sporting events, lectures, and other university events. Dean was working at JD Stickys, a popular local tavern where the band hung out regularly.

Darius sometimes filled in at JD Stickys, too, but his primary job was working at a popular local record store, Sounds Familiar (where he worked for nearly six years).

Gus Gusler estimates that, in 1993, the band made somewhere between $300,000 and $500,000 (that's about $500,000 to $900,000 in 2022 money). The unsigned Hootie & the Blowfish were making more money than some relatively successful mid-level major label acts. They were certainly putting a lot of wear on the tires of their legendary Econoline van. In the first three months of 1993 alone (before the release of *Kootchypop*), Darius, Dean, Mark, and Soni played forty-seven(!) shows in eight states (always accompanied by road manager Paul Graham and soundman Billy "Squirrel" Huelin; Billy remains in that position today).

No matter how many gigs were on the calendar, the band always made time on the road for golf and other athletic diversions (not a euphemism). "When we would go on the road," remembers Paul Graham, "we realized we would have some time here and there, so we started taking our clubs with us. Next thing you know, I am building shelves in the trailer so we can hang the clubs up. We would also go to the local YMCA—the five of us, Billy didn't play basketball—and look for pick-up games, and we would be pretty good: Darius and I would be very solid, sometimes very hot, from the outside, Dean is an incredibly good defender, and Mark and Soni are just crazy-good athletes. I remember at a YMCA in Wilmington, these dudes who were like the kings of the court there, took a look at us and thought, 'oh, man, we are going to *smoke* these guys,' and we ended up taking two in a row from them."

In April of 1993, Hootie & the Blowfish turned it up a notch and played even more gigs than they had the previous month. They kept up this pace for the rest of the year.

North Carolina–based actor, comedian, and musician Jon Wurster notes that, because of all this time spent working the road, Hootie & the Blowfish earned the respect of other local artists, both in the pre-Atlantic days and after they became a nationally known act. "The average person thinks Hootie & the Blowfish kinda exploded on this first record, first time out of the gate, and that was it," Wurster says.

"But we always *understood* what got them to that place. The rest of the country might have been different, but here in the Carolinas, we knew they had paid their dues."

Jim DeRogatis, one of this country's most well-respected music journalists, states that even someone who didn't like Hootie had to appreciate the way they did business. "Hootie didn't just provide a true alternative to the major label industry; they made their own music industry. They had made it on their own, they had created their own infrastructure."

For a good part of the 1990s, Peter Shapiro ran Wetlands Preserve, a downtown Manhattan music venue. Hootie & the Blowfish played their first New York City gigs at Wetlands in 1993 (and after they became big, they frequently returned for unannounced shows). The bread and butter of Wetlands were bands committed to playing original, "uncool," slightly tie-dyed music and having a good time with their fans.

"Today," Shapiro notes, "you press a button and 'like' a Billie Eilish, or any other new act that suddenly appears. But in the van era, you had to put your time in. A band that put their time in could do very well. A band such as Hootie & the Blowfish could play two hundred gigs in a year. They would spend all that time in a van together, and the way they behaved onstage, it was clear that they got along. They played clubs, they played spring break, they played the fraternities, they hung out, they made friends across the country. Hootie & the Blowfish were a bar band, and I say that as a compliment. That's as good as it gets. Fun, not too serious."

"In the 1990s," Shapiro continues, "you needed that network of people rooting for you. It was like retail politics almost, and I don't say that as a negative. Hootie & the Blowfish went around and they touched every hand. They were the fucking Bill Clinton of rock bands."

The first posed shot of Hootie & the Blowfish, March 1986 (*left* to *right*: Mark Bryan, Brantley Smith, Darius Rucker, Dean Felber). The band was photographed in the very same communal showers at Moore Residence Hall where Mark first heard Darius sing, only half a year earlier. (Photo by Jeffrey S. Rutstein, courtesy Brantley Smith)

Hootie & the Blowfish in 1986, on stage at Pappy's, the bar in Columbia where Darius and Mark had debuted as the Wolf Brothers the year before. Brantley Smith believes the band is likely playing Cheap Trick's "Surrender." (Photo by Jeffrey S. Rutstein, courtesy Brantley Smith)

Hootie perform at Greenstreets in Columbia, 1987. Original drummer, Brantley Smith: "We would often do our Ramones medley, which sometimes featured Mark, Dean, and Darius taking turns stage diving while I kept the beat driving. Then Mark and Darius would fight over who got to play drums while I went stage diving." (Photo by Jeffrey S. Rutstein)

Hootie & the Blowfish (*left* to *right*: Brantley Smith, Dean Felber, Darius Rucker, Mark Bryan) in the studios of WUSC, the University of South Carolina college radio station, doing one of their very first radio interviews, 1986. (Photo by Chuck Denton)

Mark and Soni onstage (with Darius and Dean just visible behind) in 1991 at The Attic at East Carolina University in Greeneville, NC, one of the band's regular stops in their club days (though at this gig, they were billed as "Hooty and the Blowfish," and you could buy a 32-ounce draft beer for $2.00). (Photo courtesy Paul Graham)

A sleepy Darius Rucker in the back of the Hootie touring van, nicknamed Foot-n-Ass, 1993. (Photo courtesy Paul Graham)

ATLANTIC
RECORDING
CORPORATION

75
ROCKEFELLER
PLAZA
NEW YORK,
N.Y. 10019
TELEPHONE:
(212) 484-6000

July 28, 1993

Rusty Harmon
Fishco Management
P.O. Box 5656
Columbia, SC 29250

Dear Rusty:

We have reviewed the material by the band HOOTIE
AND THE BLOWFISH.

We appreciate the time and effort that has been
put into the completion of the project. However,
after careful consideration, the A&R staff has
decided to pass.

In the interest of replying as quickly as
possible to all who submit material, it is often
difficult to offer a personal review of every
tape or record we receive. Please do not feel
that this is a reflection of the band's work.

Thank you for submitting material to Atlantic
Records and best wishes for future endeavors.

Cordially,

A&R DEPARTMENT
ATLANTIC RECORDS

A beautiful artifact of historical irony: On July 28, 1993, a nameless person in Atlantic Records A&R department sent Rusty Harmon and Hootie & the Blowfish this standard rejection. Less than two weeks later Scott Schiff, the junior man in Atlantic's Retail Information Services department, would stumble on *Kootchypop*'s enormous sales figures in the mid-South, starting the chain that would lead to me seeing the band in Charleston and deciding to sign them. Neither Scott nor I were aware that Atlantic had just sent the band a rejection letter. (Courtesy Rusty Harmon)

Busy indie days: This was Hootie & the Blowfish's crowded gig calendar in September 1993, as kept by road manager Paul Graham. The September 16th show, where I would see the band for the first time, led directly to their being signed by Atlantic Records. (Courtesy Paul Graham)

The band in back of the trailer, holding their gear on their first major post–*cracked rear view* tour, late summer 1994. *Left* to *right*: Soni Sonefeld; Gary Greene (who was not yet performing onstage with the band, as he would in later years); Dean Felber; long-time road and office associate, Ricky Wright; an unidentified local Atlantic label rep; Mark Bryan; front-of-house soundman, Billy Huelin. *Back*: Paul Graham (standing in front of guitar tech, Ford McCabe) and Darius Rucker. (Photo courtesy Paul Graham)

Atlantic Records Product Manager Kim Kaiman and Darius Rucker, 1995. Kaiman played a fundamental role in formulating and executing the strategy that allowed Hootie & the Blowfish to capitalize on their popularity in the mid-South and Atlantic Coast states. (Photo courtesy Kim Kaiman)

In their dressing room at the Shrine Auditorium in Los Angeles, a visibly nervous Dean, Mark, and Darius wait to perform "The Lady is a Tramp," at Frank Sinatra's 80th birthday celebration, November 19, 1995. (Photo courtesy Paul Graham)

Darius and Dean on stage in Tuzla, Bosnia, 1996, in front of an audience largely composed of members of the armed forces, during Hootie & the Blowfish's first USO tour. (Photo courtesy Rusty Harmon)

Hootie & the Blowfish chatting with Jay Leno on *The Tonight Show*, October 15, 1998, late in the promotion cycle for their third album, *Musical Chairs*. They would appear on Leno's *Tonight Show* eight times. (Photo by NBC/ Getty Images)

Mark Bryan serenading the gallery at the April 2006 Monday After the Masters (MAM) Celebrity Pro-Am golf tournament. Along with the Homegrown concerts, it is one of the highest profile annual charity events directly linked to Hootie & the Blowfish and run by the Hootie & the Blowfish Foundation, which had a five-million-dollar endowment as of 2021. The band first participated in MAM in 1994, before *cracked rear view* was even released. (Photo by ZUMA/Alamy Stock Photo)

Darius Rucker on stage with Hootie & the Blowfish on September 20, 2019, during the band's 25th-anniversary Group Therapy tour. On their remarkable comeback tour, the band would play in front of over 650,000 people and gross over forty-two million dollars. (Photo by Denise Truscello/Getty Images)

PART III

1993-1997

The Ultimate Boon

-13-

HACKY SACK MUSIC IN THE AGE OF FLANNEL

The debut album by Hootie & the Blowfish, *cracked rear view*, is the ninth biggest selling album of all time. All time is a long, long time; it encompasses the swingin' sixties when the Stones were built, and the Bronze Age when Stonehenge was built. It includes the 1970s, when Elvis Presley ruled from his throne in Memphis, Tennessee, and the twenty-seventh century B.C.E., when Sneferu ruled from his Throne in Memphis, Egypt (Sneferu? Yes, Sneferu). As I write this, *cracked rear view* has sold over twenty-three million copies, roughly one copy for every ten adults in the United States.

The sheer weight of these figures makes it very difficult to believe that, in 1993, just a year before *cracked rear view* was released and two years before it stomped all over the charts, it was nearly impossible for Hootie & the Blowfish to attract the attention of any major labels. But in 1993, the record industry had its head very, very far up its own ass. It was high noon in the time of grunge, and Hootie & the Blowfish were playing hacky sack music in the age of flannel.

If you haven't been inside the weird, artificial, terrified, fiercely competitive, backstabbing, crazy circus of the music business, it may be difficult to understand why the industry occasionally goes completely berserk and chases down one genre of music while ignoring so many other acts of great artistic quality and commercial potential.

By and large, the executives at major labels (and the people who work underneath them who generally follow their lead) are not innovators.

Their business is detecting a trend and jumping on it, not necessarily leading that trend. Of course, there are true innovators, those who detect an artist who might create a landmark moment in music and then invest in them. But for every pioneer, there are legions of others who rabidly follow the paths these trendsetters create, often burning out the marketplace while overlooking commercial acts who don't fit the mold.

Danny Goldberg, who joined Atlantic in 1992: "That's just the nature of the business: To be 90–95 percent risk averse. It is risk avoidance and trying to focus on audiences that are visible, *audiences for people that are currently popular and currently selling records.* Always, 90 percent of the business is trying to fit into existing lanes. Maybe 95 or 98 percent of the business."

The upside-down anti-wisdom that sometimes infects the music business was in full throttle in 1992 and 1993, a time when major label A&R departments were chasing grunge acts to the exclusion of virtually all other genres of music. The origin of this madness was the fact that most of the majors had completely and utterly been caught off guard by the neo-punk and grunge explosion that had burst in the early 1990s. As grunge prepared to dominate the charts, many labels—including Atlantic—were still chasing down the glam metal bands that had dominated the mid- and late 1980s, regardless of the fact that these acts were no longer selling at the numbers they once did.

In 1992, Atlantic co-chairman Doug Morris hired Danny Goldberg to change all that. Goldberg had impeccable credentials: Not only was he the co-manager of Nirvana and Sonic Youth, but he also had a vast range of music industry experience, from being a day-to-day manager for Led Zeppelin in the 1970s to managing Bonnie Raitt's comeback in the 1980s. Goldberg moved into Atlantic's Los Angeles office (previously a relatively inconsequential outpost), intent on bringing the company into the 1990s. In March of 1992, Danny hired me, and I left my job at VH-1 in New York City and my apartment in Hoboken for the sunshine, hills, riots and rattling earth of Los Angeles.

As Danny and I arrived in Los Angeles in early 1992, grunge mania had driven the industry absolutely bonkers. All compasses—and plane tickets—pointed north to Seattle. When Nirvana's *Nevermind*, Pearl Jam's *Ten*, and Soundgarden's *Badmotorfinger* became enormous mainstream hits in late 1991 (with Alice in Chains and Temple of the Dog just a few months ahead), the labels went into a literal panic. A&R people (myself included) were dispatched to Seattle with instructions —and this is almost not an exaggeration—to sign anything that burped nihilistic phrases and wore flannel. Most of the labels had missed the boat on grunge, big time, and were doing everything they could to catch up. We were discouraged from looking at anything that didn't wear flannel and didn't sing about living in a cocoon of sadness. So, in 1992 and 1993, we found ourselves in the throes of a major label madness that would largely ignore a potentially successful yet-to-be-signed act like Hootie & the Blowfish (or, for that matter, Dave Matthews Band, Jewel, or Alanis Morissette).

"The kind of rock 'n' roll that Hootie was making, superficially to the ear of the conventional A&R person, might've sounded dated," Danny says, "like something that grunge had replaced. The major companies, then as now, are businesses, and the people who work there don't want to get fired."

With all that going on, to bring a hacky sack band into the hate-myself era, a few stars had to align fairly precisely.

-14-

A GROUP THE RESEARCH PROVED WOULD SELL

By the middle of 1993, thanks to all that Waffle House food, hand-shaking, and tire changing, Hootie & the Blowfish were beginning to reach a new level of success. At shows and at record stores through-out the Mid-South and Atlantic Coast states, *Kootchypop* had sold as many copies as many of the hit records on major labels.

But now it's time to tell the story of someone who got a copy for free.

In 1993, twenty-three-year-old Scott Schiff was working in the New York offices of Atlantic Records. He was the junior man in a three-person department called Retail Information Services. The entire department was Scott and his bosses, Dick Vanderbilt and Nick Casinelli. Scott's office at Atlantic was, literally, a storage closet with a desk wedged into it.

Retail Information Services had a few important tasks. These included being in active contact with over five thousand record stores in the United States, asking not only about how Atlantic product was performing but also about local market trends and hot selling indie and regional product. Retail Information Services was the corporate equivalent of that guy who wanders into a record store in a strange town and says, "Hey, what's happening tonight that I might want to check out?"

On August 12, 1993, Hootie & the Blowfish played at the Covered Dish in Gainesville, Florida. Exactly 1,003 miles to the north in a repurposed storage closet, the band's life was about to change dramatically. Scott Schiff remembers August 12, 1993, well, because it was his twenty-fourth birthday. But he ended up being late for his own party, because he got stuck on the phone.

Scott Schiff: "While running down my store list and making my calls to South Carolina, I had a conversation with a store manager in Columbia. After getting all the information on the groups we were currently working, I asked if there was anything interesting going on locally that we should know about."

The manager responded by saying, "Nothing. Nothing at all."

If Scott had hung up then, this whole story would probably be very, very different. I might not even be writing it. But for some reason that Scott couldn't quite figure out—maybe it was a weird hunch, or perhaps it was unseen blue electricity that the universe shoots out when it needs to underline the utter randomness of things—Scott stayed on the damn phone.

"Are you sure there's nothing you're not thinking of?" Scott said. "Something you've overlooked?"

"Well, there's a group called Hootie & the Blowfish," the record store manager replied, stopping the conversation briefly to direct a patron to Depeche Mode's *Faith and Devotion*. "They're a local college band that has been around for a while. Everyone knows about them, and they're really popular around here. No big companies seem interested in them, so I figured you guys probably already knew about them and passed."

Scott's friends were waiting to celebrate his birthday at a pub in Gramercy Park called the Old Town Bar. They could continue to wait. Scott's interest had been piqued, so he asked the manager every question he could think of.

How many people come in asking for Hootie product? If your store had new Hootie product, how many do you think you could sell weekly? Where would this rank in sales for your store? Would this be a recurring sale item or just a one-time thing? Who's in the group? What do they sound like? Have they been played on the radio? Do they have a CD out already? Do you have any contact information for them?

By the time he hung up the phone, Scott was very intrigued. Continuing to ignore the shots and backslaps that awaited him downtown, he kept on working the phone in his windowless little office. He called every other retail store in the Carolinas and then widened the scope to hit up a few radio stations and local venues. Before he put down the phone that night and climbed into a cab, he had spoken to stores, clubs, and radio stations all the way to Raleigh.

"At some point a very clear picture emerged," remembers Scott, who had been trained to interpret precisely the sort of data he was gathering from the Carolinas. "It was clear that Hootie & the Blowfish was a group that would be number one in the region, and not just for one week. They were popular and people wanted their product."

The next morning, Scott came in to the office just a shade late, and just a shade-and-a-half hungover. The first thing he did was call a number that had been passed on to him by one of the people he had spoken to the evening before.

On the other end, Rusty Harmon picked up the phone.

"Is this Rusty Harmon?"

"Yessir," Rusty answered, with a long drawl that didn't seem to end the sentence, just hint that it would one day disappear over the horizon.

"This is Scott Schiff, and I work in Retail Information Services for Atlantic Records. You manage Hootie & the Blowfish, correct?"

"That's right," Rusty answered dryly. Scott was used to people sounding at least a little excited when they realized a major label was on the other end of the line, but this guy seemed completely disinterested.

"Our department does research into local unsigned acts who are doing impressive numbers," Scott explained, "and your band came across our radar in a truly significant way. Can you please send me some further information on the band? The current CD and whatever else you might have, plus bio, pictures, and even a video if you have one?"

"Why should I?" Rusty barked, shocking Scott. "Every label passed on us, including Atlantic, and we are doing just fine on our own. I don't need to get everyone's hopes up, and frankly, it's not worth my walk to the post office. Would you, Steve—"

"It's Scott."

"Scott, sorry, would *you*, Scott, want to walk to the post office when it's ninety-five degrees and 98 percent humidity, just to have some jackass in New York tell you that you don't sound enough like Pearl Jam? No. We don't need, that, we are doing just fine, thank you, goodbye."

"Listen. Please," Scott said before Rusty could hang up. "Let me be honest. I'm nobody. I am a lackey in a research department. I work, basically, in a broom closet. I am not in A&R, and I do not have the ability to offer any contracts, and I cannot make you any promises, *except* for this one: I'm doing research on Hootie, and I am very goddamn impressed, and I have the power to put my positive report plus anything you send me directly into Doug Morris's hands. Doug Morris is the chairman of the company."

"I know that," said Rusty.

"I can't guarantee *anything* except that Doug Morris will personally get what I give him, I'll personally put it in his hands, and it will not be filtered through anyone else, and he will pay attention to it. I can promise you that, full stop."

Rusty sent the material to New York.

"I continued to research the group," Scott remembers, "and I put together a comprehensive report. Someone asked if I personally liked the group's music. I did, but that was irrelevant. It did not matter whether I liked it or not; this was a group that the research proved would sell. It wasn't about taste; it was about fact. We would be idiots if we didn't sign them. The research was incontrovertible."

It's time to say a few words about how I ended up playing such a significant role in the Hootie & the Blowfish story.

I, too, dreamt in music. But from an early age, I did not necessarily imagine myself behind a guitar. I loved *thinking* about music, reading about bands, discovering new artists, and trying to make sense of how everything I was taking in—from the Beatles to The Kinks to the Sex Pistols—related to each other.

I grew up on Long Island, about a thirty-minute train ride from New York City. Neither bullied nor especially social, I read a lot, took copious notes on my favorite TV shows and records, and always suspected that life began after high school. When I had just turned sixteen in 1978, I cold-called my favorite rock magazine, *Trouser Press*, a New York City–based publication that specialized in British rock and American underground music. I asked them if they needed an office boy. Amazingly, they said yes, and that summer I began working in their small office in the heart of Times Square. They took a liking to me, and before I returned to high school in the autumn, I had been made a columnist for the magazine. I soon decided to ditch most of my senior year and returned to my daily job at *Trouser Press*. Over forty years later, I am still writing about music, although along the way I also attended New York University, DJ'd at a pile of downtown New York City nightclubs, worked at MTV and VH-1, and played in a few peculiar bands.

In many ways, I was an unlikely character to become the A&R person who signed a mainstream leviathan such as Hootie & the Blowfish. As a working musician, journalist, and DJ, I had spent most of my adult life embedded in the world of far-left alternative and avant-garde music. In 1993, if anyone knew who I was, they likely knew me from my work as a member of a pair of very out-there musical groups, the Glenn Branca Ensemble and Hugo Largo, or for the time I had spent in my late teens as the host of a popular New York City–area punk and hardcore punk radio show, "Noise the Show." Nothing indicated that I would ever be involved in anything that might impact the American charts, much less something that had the potential to reach the *top* of the charts. Yet in other ways, it made sense that I would find myself playing this crucial role in the Hootie & the Blowfish story. Before I came to Atlantic, I had a reputation for being "early" on groups—that is, finding out about them and promoting their interests before most other people had heard of them. I had been the first American to interview U2 (for *Trouser Press* magazine on December 6, 1980). I had literally booked the first public gig the Beastie Boys ever performed (in the autumn of 1981) and was the first person to play them on the radio. Also, I had (very) early associations, both personal and professional, with Sonic Youth, the Swans, R.E.M., and the Misfits, among others.

I had also long understood that the Carolinas and the Mid-South were powerful and fertile scenes for bands playing original, guitar-based music. This certainly made me far more open to what Hootie & the Blowfish were doing. In fact, in 1989, while working for MTV, I shot a special report on the Raleigh-Durham indie rock scene; in addition, during a briefly held gig as an A&R person at another major label in 1990, I had signed a Chapel Hill act called Snatches of Pink.

On Wednesday, September 8, 1993, I was sitting in my office at Atlantic Records, on the eighth floor of a building on the north side of Sunset Boulevard, exactly at the point where West Hollywood ends and Beverly Hills begins. The whole south side of my office wall was a window. If I looked to my left, I could see the sushi gardens, video and liquor stores, and nightclubs of the Sunset Strip. If I looked to my right, I could see the parsley-bushed green trees of Beverly Hills. And if I looked directly in front of me, I could see my boss, Danny Goldberg, who walked into my office, unannounced and seemingly by teleportation.

Unceremoniously, with a voice that communicated neither gravity nor warmth, he placed a package on my desk. "This is from Doug, and I need you to listen to it, and tell me if it's anything. Research says it's blowing up in the Carolinas."

Danny, who was not the type for small talk and who often avoided even saying hello or goodbye in any given conversation, was out of my office before I could even say a word.

So, here we are. Scott Schiff had gotten this package from Rusty Harmon. Scott and his boss, Dick Vanderbilt, had given it to the head honcho, Doug Morris. Doug Morris had sent it to Danny Goldberg. Danny had just placed it in front of me.

I would be absolutely delighted to say that Danny had given me the *Kootchypop* disc and promo material because he positively, certainly, absolutely knew that I, Tim Sommer, was the only person on the entire Atlantic staff who would "get" the band.

Alas, that was not the case.

"I gave it to you because you were the only A&R person I'd hired," Danny recalls. "I didn't trust anybody else. Jason Flom [then a senior vice president in New York and head of the A&R department] and I were both hoping to be president of the label. We were competitive. There was an air of competition that Doug created in the company.

I was still turf-conscious, and in case this thing actually blew up, I wanted it to come from 'one of my people' and not from one of Jason's people. Which believe me, Jason was well aware of, which is why he was so hostile to it when you first brought the record to him. [Spoiler alert!] I'm not proud of that whole lame competitiveness I was part of, but that was the reality of the company at the time. Today, I have all the respect in the world for Jason."

Danny (who had not yet listened to the group, or even opened the package) understood that local sales action alone wouldn't be enough to sign a band on. It was essential to have someone he trusted investigate a little further. "It was important for you to go down there and see them and meet them," he says. "If these guys are all in their fifties, it's a lot less interesting. By seeing them, you could find out if this is somebody with a future, or [if it's] a bar band that built up a following and has already peaked. And you wanna make sure they're not crazy."

After Danny left my office, I sat for a few moments. Actually, maybe more than a few moments; it was, after all, September, and the baseball pennant races were in full swing, so I turned the television on to ESPN to check the scores of the afternoon games. Once I was satisfied that the Mets, who were having a miserable season, were probably going to lose again, I opened the large, off-white envelope Danny had given me.

Even though twenty-seven years have passed, I can fairly clearly recall my initial impressions: The name is awful. One of the worst I have ever heard. "Hootie & the Blowfish" was like a jam band name invented by someone who hated jam bands. Can we change that, or are they already too big?

Regardless of the lemon of a name, even before listening to any music I was intrigued. Although I had long been a fan of independent guitar rock from the Carolinas, I also knew that there were a lot of bands on that scene who were just crowd pleasers and could rack up big numbers based solely on their ability to entertain frats, drunks, and dancers. In other words, you don't sign a band just because they can make a room full of intoxicated people go "Whooooo!" This was all going through my head before I put the CD in. So, I will confess that before I even heard the music, I thought, "There's about a 50 percent chance I am going to be able to immediately dismiss this and tell Danny that it's just a crowd-pleasing bar band."

I put the *Kootchypop* CD on.

The earth did not move. But I liked what I heard, and I immediately sensed that *something* was going on here: It jangled, and it had a fluid, open, airy spring over a solid rhythm section, much like early/mid-period R.E.M. It also had a little bit of a marching-band–type thing, an acoustic/electric thrum-thump that you heard in Seger and Mellencamp. "This is a bit like a college-rock Mellencamp or E Street Band," I thought (*honestly*). And I recall being impressed by the vocalist, although I also remember thinking his baritone growl sounded a bit like Eddie Vedder's. Something in me said, "Huh, Eddie Vedder plus *Life's Rich Pageant*-era R.E.M., yup, huh, that's kind of interesting."

I picked up the phone and called the manager's number listed on the package. I learned that over the next ten days, Hootie & the Blowfish were playing eight shows. (Impressively busy, I thought. Deli, sushi, or pizza for dinner tonight? I also thought.) Rusty and I decided that the most logical time to see and meet the band would be on Thursday, September 16, in Charleston. I could see them at a venue called Myskyns. The following night, they would play Rockafellas in their hometown of Columbia, so I would see them there, too.

Now, I've already told the next part of the story. But to sum up:

1. I was late. Not my fault. Blame it on the rain.

2. As soon as I walked into Myskyns, Rusty handed me two shots of Jägermeister. I was soon to learn that Jägermeister was Hootie's version of a handshake. But in Hootie-world, this gesture had multiple meanings. Being handed a Jägermeister could also signify:

- "That was a great show!"
- "Wow, I can't believe Marino completed that pass!"
- "Isn't that a pretty sunset?"
- "These mozzarella sticks are well above average!"
- "Can you believe Dean is going to go on stage wearing that T-shirt?"
- "Of *course* Marino completed that pass!"

- "You should have seen how badly Paul Graham hit off the tee yesterday."
- "Rusty is passed out in the hallway, try not to step on him on your way out."
- "Rusty is passed out in the hallway, make sure you step on him on your way out."

See, if the Inuit have a hundred words for snow, Hootie & the Blowfish had a hundred phrases that could be implied merely by handing someone a shot of Jägermeister.

3. That night at Myskyns, I knew, literally within thirty seconds, I was going to sign this band. I had *zero* doubt. I did not even consider what anyone back at Atlantic would say. Did I have *any* idea that they would sell millions and millions of records, or even a hundred thousand records? Absolutely not. I just knew I was deeply engaged, hugely charmed by the tight-but-loose warmth and movement, roar and chime, coming off the stage, by the way they seemed to effortlessly communicate with their audience, and how they had the ability to simultaneously entertain them and be *a part* of them. Hootie & the Blowfish seemed so very, very at home under those blue lights. They seemed to be, simultaneously, a manifestation of the audience's wishes and the natural result of a dozen or so years studying the warmer, richer, and user-friendlier ends of college rock. They were clearly not an art rock band, but they clearly knew the name of some art rock bands. I loved them, right away.

By the way, the Inuit do *not* have a hundred words for snow. This is just a myth. However, anyone in the Hootie circle will confirm that the bandmates and their friends do have one hundred phrases, exclamations, salutations, and ideas that need not be spoken but can be communicated merely by handing someone a shot of Jägermeister.

Speaking of, well, alcohol, I can't write about the experience of meeting Hootie & the Blowfish in Columbia, South Carolina, in September of 1993—or hanging out with them down there for much of the rest of the decade—without saying something about this: *All those freaking mini-bottles.*

If you come from South Carolina or have spent time there (and you're over the age of thirty-six), you'll know what I am talking about. If not, let me explain, because as someone coming from out of state, this was an enormous culture shock.

If you bought a drink anywhere in South Carolina between 1973 and 2006, it was poured out of one of these silly little mini-bottles, like you get on airplanes. And when you walked into any restaurant, tavern, or nightclub, behind the bar, you saw *thousands and thousands of those ridiculous tiny little bottles*. The origin of this practice was relatively simple. It was due to a law that greatly simplified the taxation of alcohol and ensured that every single time you ordered a drink in the Palmetto State, you got exactly 1.7 ounces of alcohol (by contrast, studies found that a "free-pour" drink contained an average of 1.2 ounces of alcoholic beverage).

"It actually was from the idea that people wanted to make sure that they got what they were supposed to get in their drinks," says Nikki Haley, former South Carolina governor and United Nations ambassador. "The mini-bottle was proof that if you bought a drink, you were getting *that much* alcohol in it, and no one was gonna skimp you on it. It was really old school from that standpoint. But it was terrible, because we would have tourists come down here, and if they wanted to get a Long Island iced tea, we were charging astronomical prices because you had to put so many mini-bottles in it."

But if you wanted to get blitzed, there was an upside, according to Kevin Oliver, who was in Carolina Alive with Darius. "People who came to South Carolina, they'd find that the drinks were considerably stronger. That's because the bartender would *have to* put the entire mini-bottle in. Does that mean we were consistently drunker down here? I don't know. But we never thought anything of it, until you'd be at a show or at a bar in another state and you'd walk in, and there'd be all these huge bottles behind the bar, and you'd go, 'Oh, what the hell is *that*?'"

In 2006, Haley was in the South Carolina legislature, representing District 87, not far from Columbia. She takes great pride in having been fundamental in the movement to get the mini-bottle law overturned.

"Believe it or not it was quite contentious. But the mini-bottles finally went away! I was a big supporter of the move from mini-bottles to the big bottles. But really, tourism is what changed that, because you couldn't sit there and sell South Carolina to the world and tell people to have a great time here, and then also have them pay fifteen dollars for a drink because it required so many mini-bottles to make it. Tourism won out in the end, and South Carolina is better for it. However, my husband still complains that drinks aren't as strong since we got rid of the mini-bottles."

Here's how Rusty remembers September 16, 1993, the first night I met Hootie & the Blowfish: "It was a hundred degrees and you were wearing a jean jacket, and you had this kinda artsy look to you, so I figured you probably wouldn't like us. And on that night, we were *killing it* in merch, and Jeff Poland wasn't keeping up with the demand because there was a girl there he was trying to hook up with, so I was furious. Finally, I jumped behind the counter and started selling it myself. And I was mad at him that I had to spend time doing that while you were there. But later on, you said how you were super impressed that the manager would roll up his sleeves and sell merch, so I guess it worked out."

Darius Rucker: "I remember meeting you. And I remember you telling us, right away, that you were going to sign us. And when you said it, it went in one ear and out the other because I was still so bitter about the collapse of the other record deal. We were—'jaded' is not the word—we were so affected by the other record deal that even though we knew you were coming, even though you were clearly excited, we didn't expect anything."

Darius's cautious pessimism was warranted. There was still a long, long way to go between my handshake and the release of Hootie & the Blowfish's first Atlantic album.

-15-

ADVANCE? JUST PAY FOR THE RECORD!

In October of 1993, even with the Atlantic deal looming, it was still business as usual for Darius Rucker, Dean Felber, Mark Bryan, Jim Sonefeld, Paul Graham, and Billy Huelin (and sometimes Jeff Poland). That month, the band performed sixteen shows in eight states, including visits to Buffalo, Boston, and New York City. On October 13, at NC State in Raleigh, Hootie played one of their very last frat gigs. But for Rusty Harmon and attorney Gus Gusler, October presented an entirely new set of challenges. They had to negotiate a contract.

In 1993, major labels were generally throwing *stupid* money at new bands. With half a dozen major labels chasing after the same relatively small pool of grunge bands, completely illogical bidding wars broke out. Circa 1993, the low-average major record label deal was approximately $250,000. If you did have a few labels chasing after you and an A-level music business attorney representing you, that number could go up *fast*. Before you knew it, bands were being offered half a million, a million, two million dollars.

There were a lot of reasons Rusty Harmon thought it was a bad idea for Hootie & the Blowfish to sign a big-money deal, even if it was a possibility (which it probably wasn't).

Rusty Harmon: "When I was starting to learn what record contracts were all about—remember, this is not a world I lived in at the time—I did some research. And I heard about this band that had gotten involved in this bidding war, and they had literally gotten a million-dollar advance. Of course, this was not uncommon at the time. And this band put out their first single, and it didn't sell. And apparently, by this point the label had spent an *additional* million dollars on expenses and promoting the single. So by now, their debt was two million dollars. So, the head of the label says, y'know, we are never making our money back at this point, let's cut our losses and drop this act. We're done here."

From my vantage point on Sunset Boulevard, I can confirm that this sort of thing happened every day. Record labels, having overspent to begin with, would readily decide not to throw good money after bad. At the major labels, one hit will pay for thirty flops. A record company can afford to make a few dozen mistakes, because just one big hit record will pay for all of them and more. This is also why you frequently hear about bands signing contracts, making records, and the records never coming out. This happens for exactly the reason Rusty outlined: "Huh," the label will think, "we've spent six hundred grand making this record and signing this band, we probably won't make that back, so why spend a dollar more?"

"We got the first draft of the contract," Rusty continues, "and it was incredibly small, I was like, *whatever*. We already have three hundred thousand dollars in the bank at this point. I didn't give a shit how small the deal was. We didn't need the money. The Atlantic attorney, Michael Reinert, said something about an advance. And I was, like, '*Advance?* Just pay for the record.' And they were a bit stunned. I mean, seriously stunned. *No one* turned down an advance. And I said, 'Look, we don't need your money. We don't want any of your money.' We just needed the label to pay to make the record. I didn't discuss this with the band, but what was there to discuss?"

Regardless of Rusty's certainty, Gus found himself completely blindsided. On Monday, October 4, Gus got a call from Michael Reinert at Atlantic legal, whom he had not yet spoken to. Gus jumped onto the call eagerly and began to explain that he had a list of contract points he wanted to work through. Gus began by noting that the seventy-five thousand dollars the band had been offered was, in Gus's words, "ridiculous." But the next thing Reinert said almost knocked the Raleigh-based attorney off his chair.

Reinert explained that the dollar amount had already been agreed to.

Needless to say, Gus's next phone call was to Rusty.

"What's this I hear about you telling the label we don't need an advance?"

"Yes, Gus. We do not need an advance."

Gus paused, searching for the right words to convey his outrage. "Rusty," Gus stated, "That's the stupidest thing I've ever heard."

"Gus, don't we have to pay that money back? Isn't that money that we have to make back before we see any money?"

"Yes, of course you do," Gus answered.

"Well, Gus, if we take that money and this project isn't working, or is slow to get out of the gate, they are going to look at that and say, well, we gave you a bunch of money up front, and we are never going to make it back, so we are going to stop spending money on you right now. Isn't that correct, Gus?"

Gus agreed.

"We are sitting on three hundred thousand dollars in the bank," Rusty continued, "and each of us are making thirty grand or forty grand a year, and we have health insurance. *We don't need their money, Gus.* And we don't need to take money from them that we just have to earn back."

That logic had made sense to Darius, Dean, Mark, and Soni, and now it made sense to Gus Gusler.

"The deal didn't matter to me," Rusty says, adamantly. "It was always about getting to record two. That's all we cared about, selling just enough to be able to make a second record for the label."

This was something we had talked about a lot—getting to album two. Many of the band's heroes—from R.E.M. to Talking Heads to the Clash—had come out of the gate with relatively low-selling records that sold *just* enough to keep the record company engaged. Then, with every subsequent release, these bands would build their sales base a little more until, by album three, four, or five, they had gold or platinum records.

Rusty Harmon: "That was our mantra: Get to record two, get to record two. So we signed a low-ball deal, knowing we had the infrastructure to do a lot of the work on our own. That was the right thing to do. I figured if we could get Atlantic to pay for a *good* recording, even if the label doesn't do anything with it, *we* can do something with it. We knew how. I can use the same networks that allowed us to sell fifty thousand CDs and tapes already. I can turn fifty thousand into one hundred thousand without Atlantic kicking in at all, and as long as we hadn't cost the label very much money, we could make it to album two."

Hootie & the Blowfish signed a seven-album record deal with Atlantic on October 31, 1993. All the band had to do now was make an album. And not get dropped from their label.

–16–

THE BONES WERE THERE

Although Hootie & the Blowfish signed their contract on the very last day of October 1993, the recording session for the Atlantic debut album did not begin for another six months. This sort of delay is not uncommon. Once a contract is signed, all sorts of i's have to be dotted and t's have to be crossed. A producer has to be selected and their schedule has to be cleared. Budgets have to written, ripped up, rewritten and finalized. A studio has to be picked and time blocked out on their calendar. Housing has to be found, travel arranged, and on and on.

The most important thing I had to do during this period was choose a producer.

In the music industry, a producer is the man or woman who directly supervises the artist in the studio and ensures that every creative, technical, and logistical aspect of the project operates at maximum efficiency and meets its greatest commercial or creative potential. It can be helpful to think of a record producer as the equivalent of a movie director. The record producer will literally *direct* the action and the technical and creative flow of activity in the studio. The producer is a traffic cop who seeks to get the best out of the artist. The best producer is completely invisible yet totally responsible.

I only seriously considered one person to produce Hootie & the Blowfish's debut album: Don Gehman. Don had produced virtually all of John Mellencamp's big records, and in 1986, he had done a beautiful yet tight and commercial album for R.E.M., *Life's Rich*

Pageant. This body of work mixed acoustic and electric, ballad and rocker, barroom and slow dance, art school and factory floor. Sonically and conceptually, it was the pocket Hootie & the Blowfish already lived in.

I had a very strong hunch about Don Gehman. Unfortunately, Hootie & the Blowfish had a different hunch. In 1992, the band had chosen Don Dixon to produce the album they were going to make for JRS, and they very much wanted him to produce their Atlantic debut. I have to be honest: I never seriously considered Dixon, despite a great deal of personal admiration for him. In the entire half decade I worked with Hootie & the Blowfish, this is the only time I really went against the band's wishes, and I remain glad that I did so. I had a few big reasons for considering Gehman and no one else. First of all, there's that R.E.M./Mellencamp thing. I mean, that's *huge.* Second, I had heard something on *Kootchypop* (and noticed it in the handful of live Hootie shows I had seen up to that point) that concerned me: Darius Rucker has a big, beautiful voice, and the *sound* of it is so rich, so engaging, that you can miss the fact that he *sometimes* sings a little flat. I had thought to myself, to take this album to the next level, we are going to need someone who is going to *push* Darius Rucker, and not just sit behind the board and go, "*Wow, what a beautiful voice.*" I decided that this person was Don Gehman. (This was before there was effective and undetectable voice-tuning apparatus available to music producers and recording engineers; today, these are used by *all* singers, even those who claim they don't use them.)

Don Gehman had an interesting background. He was born in the ludicrously named Blue Ball, Pennsylvania, a tiny town not far from Lancaster. From a very early age, Gehman was fascinated by the way sound emerged out of the nexus of air and machine.

"I remember having a Magnavox stereo in the house," Gehman recalls, "and I was just so thrilled with bass and treble controls and how it worked. I slowly got more and more interested in speakers and how they worked, the physics of it. I was a very scientific person, I had a lab in the basement, and a dark room, and I went through all kinds of things, chemistry and physics and biology, and then electronics, and I started building my own amplifiers."

Before long, Gehman was building not only amplifiers but also entire PA systems for local musicians and events. In late 1964, at a local electronics store, he met Gene Clair, who was also building PA systems in his garage. Clair asked Gehman to join him in his nascent business.

Clair Brothers Sound, the new company that teenage Gehman joined, was the Apple of live performance sound equipment. Clair Brothers, with Don onboard, virtually invented the modern rock band PA system and were the first people to create functional PA systems that bands could bring on the road with them (before that, bands would use whatever speaker the auditorium or stadium had or would run a vocal microphone through a guitar amplifier). They also invented the stage monitor system, a concept that didn't exist until Don and the Clair Brothers decided to solve the problem of how to enable musicians to hear themselves on stage. This is Thomas Edison–level shit we are talking about.

Before long, Don Gehman was going on the road with these PA systems and running live sound for the bands that rented them. He worked with virtually every touring rock band in America until 1973, when one of his clients, Stephen Stills, asked him to come off the road and go into record production. That turned out to be a good fit for Don. In the early 1980s, Gehman began a long run producing very successful albums for John Mellencamp. Chances are every Mellencamp song you've ever heard (including the one you are humming in your head right now) was produced by Don Gehman.

By 1994, Don Gehman was out of the spotlight and doing most of his work with relatively low-profile artists outside the United States. But I got in touch with him and offered him the gig of producing a largely unknown band from South Carolina called Hootie & the Blowfish.

Don Gehman: "I don't know if I was in a panic mode, but since I hadn't had a hit in a while, I was aware that every opportunity offered to me was not to be taken lightly. So I felt I pretty much had to take the job, but I was backed into a corner: You only gave me thirty grand to actually make the record. I was used to having at least a hundred fifty or two hundred. And so, I had to work with less money and, therefore, a very short recording schedule. I think I had eighteen days to record and mix, and it was like, oh my God, how am I gonna pull this off? I can remember making checklists, and being much more organized than I was on other projects, and it forced me into very gut-level kind of decision making that I really cherished after that. Thankfully, I knew that what I had in front of me was the talent to make something great and that I just needed to make sure I got everybody to do what they do best and nothing more."

Darius, Dean, Mark, and Soni arrived in Los Angeles on Friday, March 11, 1994. The band set up house in three rooms at the Academy Village Apartments, an utterly unlovely stack of stucco and concrete buildings in North Hollywood. Built to temporarily house recently relocated employees, rock bands, and/or movie people working in Burbank and the San Fernando Valley (where most of Los Angeles's television, movie, and recording studios are), the Academy Village existed somewhere in the foggy netherworld between hotel and apartment. "We had a two-bedroom apartment, and we were sharing rooms, with one big living room," Darius Rucker remembers.

We began pre-production the very next day, at a carpet-walled hole of a room in the San Fernando Valley. It was a step up from the storage container in back of the soccer field but not too far a step up. Pre-production is not an exotic process, but it is one of the most important parts of making a record. With an experienced four-piece band such as Hootie & the Blowfish, pre-production just entails sitting in a room with the group and listening to them play their songs over and over and over, and making suggestions and tweaking parts. For two very long days, from noon to eight in the evening, Don Gehman and I sat in this carpeted ashtray of a room and listened to Mark, Dean, Darius, and Soni play every original song they had, plus a pile of covers.

The general idea—and this is especially important when working with a very tight recording schedule—is to make it so that you *don't* have to discuss things such as song arrangements, guitar solos, key modulations, lyric changes, or how a song ends in the studio when you're on the clock and the tape is rolling. I recall there being relatively little to tweak with Hootie during pre-production, other than to dial in the melodic aspects of some of the guitar solos and, most important, shorten some of those soon-to-be famous choruses. Hootie and their audiences loved those big sing-alongs on songs like "Hold My Hand" and "Let Her Cry," so we needed to eliminate a couple of the extra chorus repeats that the band had gotten used to playing live.

On Wednesday, March 16, 1994, Hootie & the Blowfish and producer Don Gehman arrived at NRG Studios to begin recording their debut album.

For the next two weeks, Darius Rucker, Dean Felber, Mark Bryan, Jim Sonefeld, Don Gehman, and I worked from roughly ten o'clock in the morning to eight or nine at night at NRG, a squat blockhouse of a building tucked into a low and unattractive corner of North Hollywood. The Northridge earthquake had rattled Los Angeles—especially this part of the city—just seven weeks earlier. All around us, the shattered San Fernando Valley spread from horizon to horizon, but NRG Studios had weathered the tremors almost completely undamaged. Like many recording studios, NRG was half golden-lit magical cave and half survival bunker. Underneath its flat roof, you found a strange contrast of noise and silence. That's what recording sessions are: the quiet and the storm.

Before a single note was played, Don Gehman made it clear that he wanted Darius to play rhythm guitar, just as he did live. This pleasantly surprised the band. They had always assumed that a "real" producer would prefer that Mark, the "better" guitarist, handle all the guitar chores. This was an early affirmation that Don wasn't going to try to make Hootie into anything they weren't but, instead, was going to underline their identity as a compact but expansive sounding four-piece rock band.

Most rock band recording sessions proceed along the same framework, and Hootie & the Blowfish were no different. First, you record basic tracks, which are, essentially a live recording of the band. You do anywhere from one to five takes of each song. You then sit down in the control room and listen back and try to find the takes where the drums and bass gave their steadiest and most inspired performances. This becomes the foundation for the rest of the tracking. Very occasionally, you will grab a "keeper" guitar part or even vocal from the basic track sessions, but that is rare. Next (after some bass fixes), we recorded the guitars. Because these parts were mostly set in stone (and what tweaks needed to be made had been done in pre-production), this was mostly just about finding the right amp and instrument combinations for both Mark and Darius and making sure that Mark had gotten performances on the solos that satisfied all of us.

The process of recording the lead vocals is generally the same for most rock and pop projects (especially in the era before auto-tune technology was common). The singer will do a few takes of a song (commonly, three to five complete takes, although it's not uncommon to do far more). Then the producer and the vocalist (often assisted by the rest of the band) will sit down with a lyric sheet and pencils and, listening to each take, assemble a "comp" take of the best lines from each performance. Once he was inspired or warmed up, Darius often gave very solid full-song performances; so, often our "comps" came mostly from one full take, with just a few words grabbed from other takes.

Then, you do all the important extra stuff, such as keyboards, hand claps, tambourines, and backing vocals. Finally, you assemble some rough mixes and take a little break until the real mixing begins. It makes a lot of sense to take an extended break between recording and mixing. That way you can approach the tracks with fresh ears.

We did most of this stuff—all of the tracking, overdubbing, singing, piano banging, hand clapping, and foot stomping—between Wednesday, March 16, and Tuesday, March 22. This was a time period so compact that, while researching this book, I actually had to double-check, then triple-check, the dates. It was, without any doubt, the easiest recording process I have ever been involved with, *period*. I have worked on sessions in which a folk singer cut three songs that were infinitely more complicated and anxiety filled than the sessions for the entire *cracked rear view* album.

Darius has a similar memory of the sessions. "I remember thinking while making that record, 'If this is what it's going to be like, this is going to be *amazing.*' It was *easy.* We went in every day, and Don was so laid back, and he instantly and instinctively knew how to handle each of us in our own way. Making that record will always go down as one of the greatest times of my life."

"What stands out is how easy the guys were to work with," Don Gehman notes. "And how incredibly unprecious they were. Everybody was always right there when asked to be there and rarely would they argue with me. They were very trusting of me, they really gave me a lot of positive support to do my job. It was all *right there.* At that time, with that collection of songs, we had the combination of the four people working together to create something really honest, so the bones were really there. And it just needed production that made it fit where the world needed to hear something new. Who would have ever thought from where we started that we would be the fresh, new sound?"

"The thing that stands out the most about the recording of *cracked rear view* is how close we were," remembers Darius. "I'll never forget that. That was really our moment. The moment we were closest and the moment we were best, as a band."

I was fortunate enough to be at NRG for almost every moment of the amazing recording session (and the mixing that followed). It's unusual for an A&R person to be such an active part of a recording session, but I felt very attached to this project, and I believed that it was, ultimately, my responsibility to make sure that this thing came out as good as it possibly could.

I had also grown extremely fond of all four band members, and during their time in Los Angeles, I spent nearly every evening with them. Dean, Darius, Soni, and Mark were instantly familiar to me. They felt like the kind of people you meet in your dorm or at your college radio station, and you become friends for life. I *knew* these guys, I recognized them. All of this made the recording of Hootie & the Blowfish's first album *personal* to me, and I think it shows.

The impressions I formed in March of 1994 as we bonded over recording tape, takeout menus, beer, Crown Royal, guitar strings, loud amps and quiet moments in the parking lot, sports, our favorite obscure and not-so-obscure bands, San Fernando Valley jukeboxes, Ventura Boulevard bookstores, and my bad driving, remain very much with me.

Soni was very quick with a joke, a pun, or a raised glass, although occasionally a piercing intelligence and deep, almost mournful sensitivity would poke through. Although he was likely the member of the band quickest to party, you could tell that he was also a searcher; sometimes you would look at him and he would appear to be far away, and then just as suddenly, he would gaze at you with a deep, silent intensity that spoke volumes.

Mark wore his college-radio geekiness as a very visible badge of honor. He could quickly be drawn into any conversation about The dB's, The Replacements, The Smiths, or The Jam, and he was very quick to proselytize for his favorite indie artists from the Mid-South, such as Dillon Fence, Don Dixon, and Cowboy Mouth. Mark was polite—almost to a fault—and even after the band had achieved great success, he would engage in long conversations with strangers without mentioning he was a member of a well-known musical group. He idolized the brash, arrogant intelligence of Pete Townshend and the everyman "grin 'n' grace" of Springsteen, and I got the sense that he wanted to be an exact cross between the two.

Dean was quiet but clearly heard everything that was being discussed around him; when he did offer a suggestion, a comment, or a joke, it would be so on point that it made you realize that not only was he taking every single thing in, but also in any given situation he could probably be trusted to make the wisest decision. At the time, he was rarely seen without a sizable plug of tobacco between his cheeks, a habit that seemed hugely exotic to a lifelong northerner such as myself.

Darius had a way of making you feel that you were the most important person in the room. He was very intelligent and extremely quick to laugh and was one of those people who could make you feel that you were his best friend; yet you soon recognized he was telling you very, very little about himself. Darius reminded me a lot of Michael Stipe (with whom I had been close friends in the 1980s), especially in their strange blend of intensity and privacy; like Stipe, Darius never, ever talked about singing, or being in a band, or dreaming rock 'n' roll dreams. I know he had those ideas, but he just chose not to disclose them. I got the sense that he thought of the positive things that happened to him—both during those amazing weeks in March of 1994 and beyond—as a gift, not a right. During those first weeks, Darius and I also discovered something slightly peculiar about each other: We were precisely the same size. We would regularly borrow clothes from each other when necessary.

Another constant presence during those weeks in March was that of Gena Rankin and Tina Snow. Virtually every evening after the sessions, we piled into a couple of cars and went out to eat or drink— usually drink—with Gena and Tina. Although relatively young, both were music industry veterans. Gena was Danny Goldberg's long-time assistant, and she had great additional insight into the industry because her father, Kenny Rankin, was a much-loved singer/ songwriter, especially in the Laurel Canyon circuit. When I came to Atlantic in March of 1992, Gena had taken it upon herself to show me around the city and make me comfortable with my new working and living environment. In March of 1994, exactly two years later, she took on the same role with Dean, Darius, Soni, and Mark. And Gena was a helluva singer: You can hear her, prominently and beautifully, on two of the *cracked rear view* B-sides, "Fine Line" and "Almost Home." Tina, one of Gena's best friends, also had strong family links to the industry and was involved in music publishing. During Hootie's time in Los Angeles, the seven of us were more or less inseparable. Mark's friends Emma and Stu sometimes joined us, too. Most evenings, we ended up at a super-friendly and completely untrendy faux-British pub on Burbank Boulevard called The Robin Hood. A couple of years later, Hootie did a big tour they called Summer Camp with Trucks; March and April 1994 felt like Spring Fling with Recording Tape.

We once said that if the band ever sold half a million copies, we would have to give a gold record to the Robin Hood. That may have been the only time during the recording process we even *joked* about the record being that successful. We existed in the moment, to a wonderful and rare degree. I do recall our discussing that if we could sell as much as The Jayhawks (who, we imagined, occupied a similar space in the marketplace), that would be *amazing*. If we sold that many records, wow, Atlantic would probably let us do a second album! The efficiency and joy of the *cracked rear view* session means that a lot of it just exists as a happy yet vague blur to me (and I did not keep a diary). It may come as a disappointment—or as a relief—that I am not going to give you dry, Beatle-esque accounts of what was cut on what day and how many takes we did of such-and-such. Nonetheless, certain things do stand out.

After listening to Darius run a couple of takes of "Let Her Cry," I stepped into the vocal booth with him, because I wanted to get in his face and give him someone to sing to. In my entire career as an A&R person, this is the one and only time I ever went into the sanctum of a vocal booth with a singer while they were actually doing a take, and if this is the only time that happens, well, dammit, I sure picked a good time to do it.

I also have two funny memories from the part of the session reserved for cutting keyboards. The group did not yet have a dedicated keyboardist, but there were a handful of songs that we all agreed would benefit from some piano or organ, so we set aside an afternoon to knock this stuff out.

John Nau is a warm and kind gentleman who played piano, with great delicacy and skill, in a local jam band called The Zoo People. We recruited him to come in for the afternoon and add piano to a few songs.

A couple of days before John was due in the studio, I sent him a cassette of rough mixes of the basic tracks of the half-dozen songs for which we were considering adding piano. Late in the afternoon of our second-to-last day at NRG, John showed up, as scheduled. With our time at NRG running out, we ran things very quickly. Rapid introductions were made. John was handed a Styrofoam container of coffee and led into the studio. He settled on a piano bench behind a highly polished grand piano. John brushed his long hair out of his eyes and sat with his fingers poised above the ivory keys. Don Gehman signaled to the engineer, and we ran five songs consecutively, without any break or second takes. It went better than we possibly could have hoped.

Don then smiled with that half-childlike, half-sinister smile of his and said, "That's terrific, John. C'mon in, we're done, and you can fill out your paperwork."

John got a panicked look on his face. *Really* panicked. He bolted up from the piano bench and dashed into the control room, where I was sitting on the studio couch. He caught my eye and urgently indicated he needed to speak to me, and *only* me. We moved into the hallway, out of Don's hearing range.

John: "We've got to take them again."

"But John, that was perfect. Absolutely gorgeous."

"But Tim, I . . . I never listened to the cassette you sent me." John looked like he was about to cry. "That was the *first time* I heard *any* of those songs. Please let me give it another shot. I assumed we were just practicing and getting levels. Now I know how they go. Please, let's do them again."

I conferred with Don. Don thought that the takes were fantastic and saw absolutely no reason to waste our limited time doing any of them again.

Don Gehman, laughing: "He was winging it. And because of his skill and his jazz background, and his ability to find something that was actually in the correct key at every moment, he created some of the most unexpectedly beautiful things. Especially On 'Let Her Cry,' there are things going on that are such a big part of what you experience emotionally."

So here's a great bit of trivia: All the piano parts on *cracked rear view* were not only done in one take but also they were played by someone who had never even heard the songs before.

A little later that same afternoon (very close to the time in the session when everyone is getting a little itchy to get out of the studio and hit the Robin Hood for a beer), we realized we still needed a keyboard part on "I Go Blind," a simple and affecting pop song that had been a college radio hit back in 1986 for a band from Vancouver called 54-40. In fact, it was one of the oldest songs in the band's set, and it had been performed regularly back in the Brantley days.

"I Go Blind" had not been in the pile of songs that we had presented to John Nau, but we all agreed it needed *something*, and that something was probably an organ part. Two different band members, the producer, and an assistant engineer each went behind the glass and tried something, but nothing was quite right.

I announced that I had an idea. I asked Mark and Don Gehman if I could go in and give it a shot. They consented.

The Hammond B3 organ is a beautiful and mysterious instrument. With pedals, a sleek hardwood chassis, and rows of levers to be pressed, flicked at, decoded, and revealed, it is not unlike a classic car. It speaks in subtle, almost human whispers, and it can also roar like the end of the world. It invites infinite possibilities, and for me, the infinite begins and ends with nothing—and just west of nothing is a single note.

I adjusted my headphones. The tape rolled.

I sat out the first verse and chorus. When the song reached its second verse, I reached out one eager, slightly trembling index finger and placed it on a D, one octave above middle C.

And left it there.

For the next two minutes and eight seconds, I did not move my finger. For the duration of "I Go Blind," my index finger remained on the D, one octave above middle C. It would remain there until the song ended. In fact, just to be certain, I kept it there until after the engineer stopped the tape. I proudly took my headphones off and returned to the control room to find the producer, the guitarist, and the drummer smiling and assuring me that the part was "just right" (the singer and the bassist were playing Madden NFL, as usual).

That one note ended up being pretty high in the final mix.

The amazingly efficient tracking session at NRG was over. We took four days off and moved on to a different studio to mix all of our tracks into a coherent, finished recording.

-17-

GREEN JUICE AND POST-IT NOTES

MIXING HOOTIE & THE BLOWFISH

Scream Studios was a small, compact facility dedicated almost exclusively to mixing records. Like NRG, it was an A-level room, and probably half of the records you heard in the 1990s—from Nirvana to Sugar Ray, from Faith No More to Jewel, from U2 to Sublime—were mixed at Scream. From the outside, it was totally unremarkable: a gray, purple, and pink storefront on Ventura Boulevard at the northern base of the Hollywood Hills. If you want to visit, the site is now a Mexican restaurant called Jalapeño Pete's. On Tuesday, all tacos are two dollars, and after nine P.M., if you buy one drink, you get one free.

"I fasted for the mixing," Don Gehman says.

See, Don Gehman is a particularly intense guy. He projects calm, authority, and wisdom, and he has a demeanor that is somewhere between holy man and cult leader. These qualities make him an outstanding producer, and the band—especially Darius—will tell you that there are times when they are fairly certain he hypnotized them into doing their best.

"I decided to go on a cleanse for the mix," Gehman says. "And I drank green juice for eight days, and mixed Hootie & the Blowfish. I think it's some of my best work. I look back at it now and go, 'how the fuck did I make that happen?' I have no idea. It was just the moment. I remember thinking while I was doing it that it was so easy to do, and I think that there was a certain kind of a turning over of a subconscious energy that came forward because of that. I didn't agonize over choices that I was making."

We were becoming aware that there might be some genuine magic in the air.

Don Gehman: "As much as I was in control of every moment every day, I wasn't in control of anything. The sessions for *cracked rear view* had its own consciousness. That's the magic part. They were hard working, they'd made a business, they knew how to stay on the road and make money and pay for food and lodging, and do something they loved. They'd gotten that far well enough that Atlantic research made them noticeable. And then to all go into the studio with that kind of energy, discipline, and the excitement of 'wow we've got our shot,' and that made everybody focus. It really was a special moment, and to be honest, we never really got that back again."

When we were very close to the end of mixing, we assembled in the small studio lounge. Darius and Dean sat on the couch, Mark and I sat cross-legged on the gray carpet, and Soni remained standing, close to the wall. Don hovered, arms crossed, behind us. We had come to a very crucial part of the record-making process: choosing the songs that would go on Hootie & the Blowfish's debut album and what sequence they would go in. Soni wrote the title of every finished song on a Post-it Note. He then put all of the Post-it Notes up on the robin's-egg-colored wall.

First, a very important decision was made: The album sequence would *only* contain original songs. I remember being disappointed, because I thought both "I Go Blind" and "Fine Line" were strong enough to go on the released Atlantic album and had potential radio appeal. However, the group felt very strongly that their debut should only contain songs the band had written.

With that out of the way, determining the shape of side one was pretty straightforward. "Don Gehman was very adamant about putting your best foot forward," Mark Bryan remembers, "that *these* tracks have to be the songs that lead off the album. Once you established the shape of side one based on that line of thinking, side two just became what it was."

Everyone agreed with Don, and we decided we would frontload the album with the songs that were already fan favorites and would clearly grab a listener and tie them up in a Hefty bag of happiness: "Hannah

Jane," "Hold My Hand," "Let Her Cry," and "Only Wanna Be With You." At that time, there was a very common idea—half superstition/ half music industry inside joke—that you *always* put a more laidback song in the fifth slot. So "Running From an Angel" went in there.

Once you had those five stuck up on the wall, the rest of the sequence pretty much wrote itself. The last four songs on the album sequence— "Time," "Look Away," "Not Even the Trees," and "Goodbye"—tell a very different story from the deeply familiar, juicy hits on side one. These tracks display an elegiac, stately grace that compares favorably to any of the big U2 or R.E.M. ballads. I have often thought that if you were to *start* listening to *cracked rear view* where side two (technically) begins ("Drowning"), you hear what is virtually a concept album about race and loss, and you get a completely different impression of the band. Interestingly, when I asked each band member if the relatively clear "concept" of side two was intentional, each says it was accidental. (I shall also note that the band broke down in hysterics the first time I used the word "elegiac" to describe anything they did, and to this day, just saying the word gets them giggling.)

Hootie has a somewhat unusual method of assigning songwriting credits. Every member of Hootie & the Blowfish contributes significantly to the songwriting. Sometimes two or three members will write a song together; other times, a complete song will be composed by just one musician. Fairly often, one member will come up with the bulk of the music and Darius will come up with most of the lyrics (although there are examples where the lyrics were partially or wholly written by someone else). Occasionally, there's a song like "Drowning," which is written by all four band members together.

In other words, there is no one rule about who writes Hootie & the Blowfish songs. Every member writes; sometimes together, sometimes on their own. However, all the songs on *cracked rear view* (and all of Hootie & the Blowfish's original songs through 2003's self-titled album) are credited to "Hootie & the Blowfish." An individual writer is never credited. There are a few reasons for this. First, and mainly, Hootie did this because it's the way R.E.M. did it. Hootie modeled many aspects of their business after R.E.M. Second, by splitting the songwriting credit four ways on each and every song, the band also split their publishing money four equal ways. Think about it: If the money is split four ways on every song no matter *who* wrote the song, there will be far fewer fights about who gets their song on a record. After all, you all make the same amount of money no matter who wrote what. On the other hand, in bands where each member has separate credits and split their publishing on an unequal song-by-song basis, there are frequent fights along the lines of, "But why do *you* have five songs on the album, and I only have two?!" These are exactly the kind of disputes that can lead to long-lasting animosity and breakups. Hootie were adamant about wanting to avoid these kinds of conflicts, so a four-way split, regardless of who actually wrote the song, made sense.

Now, a few words about the twelve songs that made it to the final sequence of Hootie & the Blowfish's debut album (which still, at this point, lacked a title).

---

cracked rear view
Track by Track

Written in 1992, "**Hannah Jane**," the happy buh-BANG that kicks off the record, is named after Hannah Jane Carney, the daughter of one of the band's best friends, Chris Carney.

Mark Bryan: "Soni started showing us those chords, and the first time he played them, they were exactly as they ended up on the album, though we added the big stop on the E-minor. Darius took it from there and wrote the melody and the lyrics. Carney was the first one from our group of college friends to have a kid, so that was a very heavy subject matter. I think Darius did a really nice job of putting that feeling into words."

"If you listen to it," notes Carney (who remains a valued member of the Hootie organization), "it's more about the relationship between Darius and [me] than about my daughter—she hadn't been born at the time it was written, or maybe she had *just* been born. I remember him saying to me, right after it was written, 'Any and every time Hootie & the Blowfish play live, we are going to play this song.' I remember him making this declaration."

What about the real Hannah Jane? What does she think of having the first song on one of the most successful albums of all time named after her?

"I have always loved hearing the song, especially live, and reflecting on my life," Hannah Jane says. "Now I'm married, so I've taken all the 'steps' in the song, though I'm not 'gone.' It's funny to hear what people think the song is about. I've read online that some people consider it a breakup song. That image just makes me laugh, because I just picture little baby me with my dad and Uncle D—that's what I have always called Darius—watching me crawl around, and talking about me growing up. I love the song, but even without it, I would still be so grateful for the extended family the band has always been for me."

We have already talked a little bit about "**Hold My Hand**," the song that cemented Soni's membership in Hootie & the Blowfish and was included on both *Kootchypop* in 1993 and their first cassette in 1990. But here's a remarkable thought from Darius, which puts the song in a different light.

"'Hold My Hand' is the biggest protest song Hootie & the Blowfish ever wrote or recorded," Darius says. "And no one sees it. That song is not like a love an' togetherness song, that song is about why *hate* is wrong. People just missed it, because they wanted to feel good, they didn't want to smell like teen spirit for a moment, they wanted to feel good."

It's a little-recognized fact that David Crosby sings backup on "Hold My Hand." Crosby was an old family friend of Gena Rankin (Gena's vocals are probably in the "Hold My Hand" vocal mix somewhere, too), and Gena and Don hatched the plan to get Crosby down to the studio.

"**Let Her Cry**" was making its second appearance on a Hootie release, having been debuted on the *Time* cassette in 1991. It was also a longtime fan favorite and a popular sing-along in the live show. (Although seven of *cracked rear view*'s twelve compositions had been released before, all of the songs were re-recorded for the debut Atlantic album.) Mark remembers, "Darius wrote 'Let Her Cry' late one night, after he had come home from the bars. The first time he showed it to us was at soundcheck at the Brewery in Raleigh. He didn't even say anything to us, he just started playing it, over and over. I got the sense he was just trying to work it out in his head. He was like mumbling through it. So I joined in and came up with that riff you hear in the chorus, and then the rest of the band joined in, right there on stage at the Brewery. We may have actually played the song in the set that night."

"People responded to it right away, because we didn't have any other ballads," Mark continues. "Everyone can relate to that song. Everyone can relate to the heartbreak. I didn't figure this out until much later, but Darius, *he's* the girl in the song. He didn't even realize it at the time he wrote it, but it's about all the shit *he* was going through, but he made it about a girl. It's almost a cry for help. It's Darius's pain coming out through a song."

When we discussed the *Kootchypop* EP, we covered where Mark's head was at when he wrote the music for **"Only Wanna Be With You"** (he applied the strumming pattern of Pete Townshend on "Pinball Wizard" to the capo chording style of Dillon Fence). But what about the lyrics? "Darius ended up writing lyrics about a conversation he was having with his girlfriend about [the Bob Dylan song] 'Idiot Wind,'" Mark explains. "On the first verse, what he's saying is pretty much straight from that conversation. It's almost literally a transcription. When Darius heard my music, he picked up on the Dillon Fence thing I was going for, so that's why he added the line 'Put on a little Dillon, sitting on the Fence.'"

The fact that "Only Wanna Be With You" lifts a few lines from Dylan's "Idiot Wind" was to cause a significant legal kerfuffle, but we'll get to that later. So let's move on to **"Running From an Angel,"** also making its second appearance on a Hootie release (it had been the lead-off track from the *Time* cassette).

Mark Bryan: "I went out to Vallejo, California—my first trip to California —to hang out with my friend Steve Lipton and his family, for a week. Had a blast. Sitting around their house, Lipton had this old Bradley Stratocaster ripoff, a cheap little guitar, and I was noodling around on that guitar all week. Somewhere in there I came up with the riff for 'Running From an Angel.' I came up with the riff, the chords, the structure, the whole thing, and it was something I was very excited about. So I came home and taught Darius how to play the chords so I could play the riff over it—of course, I hadn't heard the two together yet up until that point—and we locked in immediately. Darius wrote the lyric about his older brother, Ricky, and the fact that their mom was so good to him, but that his older brother wasn't honoring that—how he was literally running from an angel."

The gorgeous violin on "Running From an Angel" is played by Lili Haydn, one of Los Angeles' most sensitive, skilled, and unique violinists. She has also performed with Roger Waters, Jimmy Page and Robert Plant, George Clinton, Nusrat Fateh Ali Khan, and many others, in addition to releasing her own records. Lili also plays on (the *cracked rear view* version of) "Look Away" and occasionally guested with Hootie & the Blowfish when they played live in 1995 and '96.

"'**I'm Going Home**' was written right after Darius's mother died," Mark recalls. "Darius wrote both the music and lyrics. There are times when I have started crying on stage while we played that song. It is *so* heavy. It is the sound of someone capturing the emotion of the moment of loss. It is rare that you can feel that in a song. I think when I first heard it, I felt, 'Okay, be strong for D, don't overreact.' I don't even know how to talk about it, it's so emotional. It makes me cry just talking about it."

"**Drowning**" was another song that had been previously released in a different recording, having ended the A-side of the *Time* cassette. "Dean, Soni, and Darius were messing around with the chords that became 'Drowning,' then I came up with the riff," says Mark. "That is one of those songs that was really written by the four of us, emerging from a jam. We had gotten together for a true writing session. The lyric is all Darius. He is saying, without very much margin for misunderstanding, 'I live in the South, and racism is still a gigantic issue here; we are drowning in it.' I like how he points out Public Enemy and Nanci Griffith, who had gone out of their way to say the same thing."

The reference to Public Enemy is at the beginning of the second verse. It is often overlooked, since it might sound like Darius sings "Peace is coming," when he actually is singing "P.E. is coming." To paraphrase Emily Litella (a character from the 1970s' *Saturday Night Live*), that means something else entirely.

A key line in "Drowning" is "Why is there a rebel flag hanging from the State House walls." Since "Drowning" is one of the more overtly political songs in the band's catalog (although there are many where race and politics is implicitly discussed, or dealt with from a personal perspective), it's worth opening up this subject a little further. At the time "Drowning" was written, the Confederate battle flag was still flying at the top of the state capitol dome in Columbia, South Carolina. It wasn't removed from the dome until 2000, and it was still displayed in the State House grounds until July 10, 2015.

The flag was originally raised above the statehouse in 1962 as a deliberate effort by the all-White state legislature of South Carolina to show resistance to the burgeoning Civil Rights movement. But Professor Jon Hale of the University of South Carolina notes that "there isn't really any resistance to confederate relics in the culture, until the late 1980s and early 1990s. Until then, you are still trying to achieve desegregation, you are still trying to gain the citizenship rights of every citizen in the United States. After we get that on *paper,* and elect some Black politicians, then we can start to expand what's left of the movement to these cultural flashpoints like the Confederate flag. We see lynching of people of color and denying people the right to vote but are slow to grasp why the Confederate flag is such a hateful symbol and why it's a symbol of hate speech. In the 1970s and '80s, we were all complicit: White Americans were listening to Lynyrd Skynyrd, we were watching Dukes of Hazzard, we were cheering on Evel Knievel. We are bombarded by the image of the Confederate flag in apparently apolitical spaces and to a degree, become immune to it."

That's a pretty good summation of the history and rage behind "Drowning." Not only that, but "Drowning" is, almost without a doubt, ironically the most "southern rock" sounding of Hootie's recordings. In fact, during the NRG sessions, Mark was very resistant to my suggestion to add the harmony guitar over the main guitar riff, because he felt (correctly) that it made the song sound even more like a southern rock song. He only acquiesced when I pointed out to him that Thin Lizzy, a band we both admired, also used the harmony lead technique.

Moving on: "**Time**" (the title song from the band's second, Dick Hodgin–produced cassette, released three years earlier) is a song with both music and lyrics written primarily by Soni, although Darius altered the verse lyrics a bit. In its echoing of the rolling, gentle arpeggios of The Byrds or early R.E.M. and its splendid, precise harmonies, it's a terrific example of a Hootie song that could have worked on radio in the 1960s, the '90s, or any time in between. As noted earlier, it's also the song that convinced Rusty Harmon to manage the band.

"**Look Away**" is probably the oldest original song on *cracked rear view* and was actually rehearsed while Brantley Smith was still in the band. It is also one of two compositions on *cracked rear view* that originally appeared on the band's debut cassette in 1990 (the other being "Hold My Hand"). Despite the gentle, R.E.M.-ish lope of the song, it deals with a very serious issue: the fact that the father of Darius's girlfriend at the time did not approve of her dating an African American man.

"**Not Even the Trees**," with music primarily written by Dean and lyrics by Darius, was the newest song on *cracked rear view*. Like (at least) three other songs on the album, it deals with the loss of Darius's mother.

"You can really hear Darius's pain on the album," Mark notes. "It's fascinating to consider how Darius channeled his pain and handled his loss through the songs on that album. Sometimes I ask him about everything he went through, but other times I just think, you know what, he has already said what he wants to say in these lyrics, it's all right there in the lyrics, I don 't need to ask him. I think he got better at hiding the pain as the years went on, in future albums he hides it more, but it really sticks out on *cracked rear view*."

Like "Hold My Hand," "**Goodbye**" is entirely written—words and music —by Soni. "It is so vintage Soni," Mark enthuses. "Soni is the master of the piano ballad; he's certainly got some Elton John in him."

And I suppose I lied when I said the band only wanted original compositions on the record.

Mark Bryan: "'**Motherless Child**' is the only cover on the album! But it was public domain. Yet the significance is huge, because it picks up on the theme of 'I'm Going Home' and 'Not Even the Trees,' that theme of loss. It wraps it up nicely, it makes a lot of sense for sense of closure to the album."

-18-

UNRELEASABLE

In the ten weeks between mid-April 1994, when we got a finished master of *cracked rear view*, and the release date on July 5, a *lot* happened. These were the make-or-break days for Hootie & the Blowfish and their debut Atlantic album.

Sometimes, you are in the exact place you ought to be. Sometimes, something happens that may not have happened if you were anywhere else or anyone else.

I did not "discover" Hootie & the Blowfish. Tens of thousands of people knew about them and loved their music long before I had even heard their name. Nor did I tell Atlantic Records about the band. Our friend in the storage closet, Scott Schiff, did. True, I signed the band and, more important, was so swept away by what they were doing and what wonderful fellows they were that I watched their recording session like a hawk, making sure they met every freaking atom of their potential. Any good A&R person would have done that.

But there is a moment when I was exactly the person the band needed, in exactly the place I was meant to be. This was my greatest gift to Hootie & the Blowfish.

Jason Flom, the head of Atlantic A&R, was based in New York. But in mid-April, 1994, he happened to be in the Los Angeles office. I did not know Jason well and only infrequently interacted with him. There was an unspoken understanding that I was one of Danny Goldberg's people, so there was a bit of a gray area regarding the person to whom I actually reported.

This is an important point: Jason Flom is a very good man. In recent years, he has done extraordinary and selfless work for the Innocence Project, and if I lived eighteen lives, I would likely not benefit humankind as much as he has. I truly mean that. I mean this, too: Jason is not a villain in this story. He was just a man caught up in the same record company politics we all were, only the stakes were much, much higher for him. At that time, every major executive at Atlantic was battling to get Doug Morris's attention and become the president of the label (Jason Flom could not be reached for comment for this book).

Back to mid-April 1994.

Jason stuck his head in my door. He said he wanted to hear the just-completed Hootie & the Blowfish album, in its entirety. This request made sense, since he was, after all, the head of A&R. Earlier that week, I had received a CD master of the album and all the potential B-sides (I still have that somewhere; it's literally the *first* copy of *cracked rear view*, and I am proud to own it).

Jason sat down across from me. I put the disc into the CD player, and the cannon shot of "Hannah Jane" filled the room. Neither Jason nor I said a single word for the next forty-seven minutes. I probably doodled a little bit, and I certainly played with my hair. It is likely I sipped a Diet Coke. Since this was before the era when you could constantly check messages, social media, sports scores, and news on your phone, Jason just sat quietly with his legs crossed and listened attentively to the whole album.

At the end of "Motherless Child," Jason shuffled slightly in his chair and looked at me. With no sense of gravity whatsoever, and with a firm, quiet, and perfectly kind voice, Jason said this: "There's no single on this record. Not one. I had heard good things about this band and we expected more here, but it just didn't make it to tape, or maybe we made the wrong record with the wrong producer. This is unreleasable. We're not releasing this record." Jason was the head of A&R, so for all intents and purposes, what he was saying right now would be the final verdict on whether Atlantic put the album out or shelved it.

I remember feeling a little hot inside. I also remember being completely in denial of his judgment. I didn't defend the record we made but, instead, quickly said, "There's a few other tracks—covers—which could totally be singles." I played "I Go Blind" and "Fine Line."

For some reason—I guess this is what is called "grasping at straws"—I thought if Jason heard those two, it would change everything! I really did think that.

"No. Nope. It's just not there," Jason said. There wasn't any anger or urgency in his voice, his tone was perfectly matter of fact. "We're not putting this out. We might consider getting them back in the studio to try again, maybe we'll do that, but I won't commit to that. Let's talk about this some more at some point."

Jason then walked out of my office.

I remember sitting still for a while. That hot bee-swarm of indistinct feelings continued to buzz in my head, growing more persistent. It wasn't anger, it really wasn't. And it wasn't disappointment. Soon, it coalesced into a warm but hazy sense of denial. "That didn't really happen, did it?" I thought. "Of course, it didn't. That's not going to be the end of this thing, it just can't be."

A few more minutes passed. My thoughts proceeded along that same line, one foot in "That simply didn't happen" and the other foot in "I'm not going to let it happen." Looking back on it, I realize that, even at this relatively early stage, I felt so personally close to Darius, Dean, Mark, and Soni and so personally invested in this project, that I was feeling the way you might feel if a family member's dream was in danger.

What happened next happened quickly, almost instinctually. For a moment that kinda changed the course of music history, it was remarkably efficient. I got up from my chair and stepped out the door. My head was still full of bees, and I distinctly recall feeling out of my body. I walked forty-five feet to my right, to Danny Goldberg's office. The door was open. I placed myself directly in front of his desk. He did not look up, and he did not acknowledge me. Since Danny was not on the phone—which was somewhat rare—I took that as a sign that I could begin speaking. This is what I said to him: "Danny, Jason just told me that he doesn't hear any singles on the Hootie & the Blowfish record, and he doesn't want to release the album. His exact words were that it is 'unreleasable.' Danny, I respectfully disagree. I want us to put out this record."

And this is exactly what Danny said: "Timmy, if it means that much to you, we'll put it out." And that's all he said. When he stopped talking, I understood the conversation was over, and I returned to my desk.

So, friends, this is what I did: I didn't discover the band, I didn't tell Atlantic about the band, and I didn't produce the record. But if I hadn't walked into Danny's office that day and gone over Jason's head, I am fairly damn certain Hootie & the Blowfish's debut album would not have been released on Atlantic.

This raises the question: What would have happened if I had acquiesced to Jason? I'm actually pretty certain of that scenario, based on my observations of other Atlantic acts around that time that had records shelved. I don't think Hootie would have been dropped outright. My guess is, we would have *talked* for the next year about putting the band back into the studio. During that time, Atlantic would have coughed up a couple of grand here and there for demos; and probably, about sixteen or eighteen months later, the band would have been dropped, without any music released. I saw this series of events happen to at least half a dozen acts during my time at the label.

It was a long time before I told the band, Rusty, or Gus anything about what Jason Flom said that day. I didn't want them to feel discouraged, or to feel that they might be better off on their own. It wasn't until well after the album went gold (that is, sold half a million copies), that I revealed what had happened in my office in the middle of April 1994.

-19-

WE VIEWED OURSELVES AS LOWERCASE

Now that we knew Hootie & the Blowfish's Atlantic debut album was actually going to be released (and a release date was set for July 5, 1994), the band needed to come up with a title.

Mark Bryan: "We were down to the wire, like 'You need to go ahead and name this, because the art department is about to hit a deadline.' It was clear that it was time to name this thing, no more fucking around. We hadn't even made any lists or anything, and suddenly had this deadline looming. Names had been shouted out every now and then, but nothing had stuck. And so this moment had come, and all four of us thought, 'We have got to name this thing *tonight!*' And we just happened to be listening to John Hiatt's *Bring the Family* album while this discussion was taking place, while we were throwing out potential titles. When 'Learning How to Love You' came on, Soni heard the lyric [Mark sings], 'There was a life that I was living in some cracked rearview/Where no future was given to a heart untrue.' And Soni just announced, 'How about *cracked rear view*?' And we all looked at each other and it made *so much sense*. It's a beautiful lyric about looking at your past, and no one's past is perfect, and man, there you go, there's your title. So many of the songs on our album were three or four years old at that point, and *it just made sense*, our life in a van for so many years up to that point, it fell into place with those three words."

It didn't occur to anyone at the time to ask John Hiatt, a highly respected performer and songwriter and a founding father of the

Americana movement, what he thought about this, so I asked him, 26 years later. "I was tickled," says Hiatt. "I was flattered. For a lot of years, people would come up to me and say, 'Hey, do you know that. . . .' And I would just go, *well, as a matter of fact I do*, I do know that. It's like somebody complimenting one of your children. That's what it feels like. So I thought, 'Boy, they must have liked that song a lot to take that line and make it into an album title.'"

Of course, with a manufacturing date fast approaching, Dean, Darius, Mark, and Soni needed to come up with an album cover, too. So, let's talk about Wade Hampton III. Hampton was a much-decorated lieutenant general in the Cavalry of the Confederate States of America. He was also was one of the largest slaveholders in the state of South Carolina. After the Civil War, Hampton led a large and powerful paramilitary group who terrorized local Black men and women. His organization, the Redeemers, actively sought, through violence and intimidation, to suppress Black citizens from voting or holding office. In fact, he was so good at this that the grateful White male voters of South Carolina elected him governor, and later, senator. Oh, and his statue is on the front cover of *cracked rear view*, the debut album by Hootie & the Blowfish.

This wasn't any sinister plot, by any means. The band, art director Jean Cawley, and photographer Micheal (not a typo) McLaughlin were seeking iconography that echoed the mystery, character, and social dichotomies of Columbia, South Carolina. Each of the six images on the front sleeve is blurred, colorized, slanted, and meant to be part of a larger design, an asymmetric portrait that provides a new way of looking at an old and familiar city that, like many southern cities, had staggered through the twentieth century with both grace and horror.

Coincidentally, Jean Cawley (back in 1994 she was Jean Cronin) had also attended the University of South Carolina and had been friends with the group while she was there, but this isn't why she got the gig. Hootie landed on her desk only because she was the newest person in the department, and Hootie were not considered a priority.

"My role as the art director was to tell their story," she says. "Their story as friends and their story as a band. I interviewed several photographers for the band to pick from. Once they made their decision, we decided that we would do the pictures in Columbia. Even if it wasn't where the band members were born, it was the birthplace of the band. Micheal McLaughlin was a Quaker, for real, and believed in total equality, that no one should appear more important than the other, and all the band members agreed with this. It was pretty serendipitous: the guys agreed about anonymity in these cover photos. No one wanted to be front and center at that time, they truly were a band that fed off one another, they were equal."

"The style is atmospheric, and lent itself well to a Southern locale," remembers McLaughlin. "That was my style at the time. It was all very deliberate. It was a very small shoot. Just the band, Jean, myself, and my assistant Orlando. The band showed us their town and helped us choose locations. We had a very small crew. No wardrobe or hair/makeup, no higher-ups. It all went very quickly once we had a plan in place."

"The band were funny, gracious, and professional," continues McLaughlin. "I was impressed by how they approached the photo shoot as a serious undertaking but still had a fun time doing it."

Over the years, it has been speculated that the cover images of the band were deliberately blurred to mask the fact that there was an African American in the group. Sara Rodman, a prominent African American journalist who later wrote extensively about the band and Darius Rucker, says that's how she interpreted it at the time. "One hundred percent," she states. "I just remember looking at the album and smirking a little bit like, 'Oh, I see what you did there.'"

Jean Cawley: "I know, especially in retrospect, there was a lot of controversy about their faces not being on the cover, but it truly was a collective decision. When I received the prints, I sent the band three different cover options. They selected which ones they preferred. Once we went through several changes, we arrived at the end result. They were all delighted, as far as I recall. Nothing, absolutely nothing, would have gone through without their total approval."

As for the Hampton statue, both Cawley and McLaughlin distinctly remember that the band chose all the locations, so there was no agenda there, other than to show the different realities that existed in Columbia.

There is one other peculiar aspect to the design of *cracked rear view*: The title is written entirely in lowercase letters. As you know by now, I have chosen throughout this book to honor that choice and always write *cracked rear view* without any uppercase letters. Jean Cawley confirms that the use of the lowercase font was discussed at some length with the band and fully agreed to by Darius, Dean, Mark, Soni, and Rusty.

"The fact that it is in lowercase is kind of cool," says Mark. "It also kind of makes sense because, of course, the title comes from the middle of a sentence."

Soni also thinks that there is something very appropriate about the title of Hootie's debut being in lowercase letters. "If there's a theory about how we viewed ourselves in 1993 and '94, we certainly viewed ourselves, at least within the great big rock 'n' roll industry, as lower case. We were not a big capital letters–type band. We were a band from South Carolina with everything to prove. I think we felt that maybe we had something to prove for South Carolina, and artists from South Carolina."

-20-

MISSION CONTROL

Visualize a classic space launch, like you've seen dozens of times in films and documentaries. They always have that classic mission control shot in these films, right? See all those rows and rows of white-shirted men and women with pocket protectors and headsets? I have no bloody idea what each of those people do, but I am pretty certain of this: If any one of them fucked up, that big ol' rocket is going to end up in the Atlantic, or not taking off at all.

Hootie & the Blowfish had a mission control, too. It wasn't dozens and dozens of people in neat rows, like you see at Cape Canaveral. The key people in the Hootie mission control probably could have been counted on one hand. But the result is the same: Without these people, *cracked rear view* might have fizzled out on the launchpad.

In the nine months between the time Hootie & the Blowfish signed their Atlantic deal and the release of *cracked rear view*, two new friends and essential members of mission control entered the picture.

Evan Lamberg, who worked at EMI Publishing, came into the band's life at the very beginning of 1994. Like me, he resisted both industry trends and the initial opinion of his boss so he could sign Hootie & the Blowfish to a publishing deal.

A publishing deal is very, very important. In many ways, it may be even more important than a record deal, even if it's a little harder to understand. Record deals are relatively easy to grasp: Sign here! I will give you money to make a record and buy a shiny new car and/or guitar! And I will make sure your music gets pressed up/sent to streaming services (unless I change my mind). That's a grotesque simplification, but really not far off the mark.

In the simplest terms, record labels exploit the physical sale of a master recording; publishers help maximize the use of the song that was composed and recorded on that master recording. A publishing deal is about intellectual property; a record deal is about the physical recording of the intellectual property. A good publisher not only assists with ensuring that an artist gets paid when one of their songs gets played in any context or gets covered; they also help find new and unique usages and placements for those songs and make sure the artist gets paid (and paid well) for it. When you hear a familiar song in the background of a scene in a TV show or film you're watching, chances are that it's there because someone like Evan hustled to get it in there. It's called publishing, by the way, because it goes back to a time when people would buy *published* sheet music of their favorite song, so they could play it on the upright piano in their front parlor. Think of it that way: Publishing is the exploitation (in a positive sense) of the words and music, whereas record labels control the artists' *recording* of the song.

Evan Lamberg is currently the president of Universal Publishing, but in early 1994, when he was just starting out at EMI Publishing, he explained that end of the business, in depth, to Mark, Dean, Darius, Soni, and Rusty. "I spent an excruciating amount of time educating them," Evan says, "explaining what a proper publishing deal could do for them. Do you know how valuable it would be when 'Hold My Hand' and all these beautiful songs become hits? And what happens ten years from now when somebody wants to do a cover version of that song? We went through all these real-world scenarios and usages, from airplay to physical record sales, to synchronization licenses— that's when someone uses your music on film or TV—to what happens if potentially somebody wants to turn your album into a play. They're kind of looking at me and they go, wow, yeah, that's a lot. And I said yeah, and that's *all* from the songwriting. It's got nothing to do with you getting up on stage performing, or getting a record royalty for a sale of a CD. This is all about the intellectual property of your melodies and your lyrics. This is a big business. If this goes the way I think it could go, your publishing will be worth millions and millions and millions of dollars. And after the records eventually stop selling, you know what doesn't stop happening? The songs keep getting played on radio."

Evan sold Hootie & the Blowfish on EMI, but the next step was selling EMI on a relatively unknown band from South Carolina. He returned from Columbia after having seen the band play an over-packed show at The Elbow Room, and he sat down with his boss, Marty Bandier.

"I had never really signed anything that had broken in the eighteen months that I had been at EMI," Evan remembers. "I'm kind of new, still in my early mid-twenties, and I'm telling Marty, 'Look I've seen this band we *have* to sign.' I play him the music, and he's not especially impressed. Marty says, 'I know you're really passionate about this, but it doesn't really sound like what's on the radio right now, and it's a *Southern* band.' And he gives me a few more excuses like that."

Here's what Evan and I share: We each chose not to take no for an answer.

Evan told Bandier, "Look, I will put my career on the line that if we sign this band and it doesn't work out, you can fire me. You have to let me do this. Marty, please."

Bandier was impressed that Evan was willing to put his future at EMI on the line for the band, so he said yes. Hootie & the Blowfish signed with Evan, Marty Bandier, and EMI Publishing for an advance of $350,000 (since they couldn't get "dropped" from EMI the way they could get booted off Atlantic, the size of the advance wasn't a negative factor).

If that advance sounds like a lot—I mean, it *is* a lot—there is an enormous amount of money to make from publishing. Most artists and songwriters will tell you that's where the *big* money is in the music business. Without giving specific numbers on Hootie, Evan notes that what he calls a "cultural hit"—that is, just *one* song that you hear all around you, even if you are not familiar with the band—can earn three to six million dollars. A "massive" hit can make seven to ten million. Now, consider that Hootie probably had (and continues to have, through radio, satellite, streaming, film and TV placement, singing teddy bears, and all those damn times you hear them in CVS) multiple "cultural" and "massive" hits, and you can see why a good publishing deal and a supportive publisher are very, very important.

But Evan, like me, was more than a business partner. He was someone who became integrally involved in the social, emotional, psychological, and business sides of the phenomenon we were all about to go through. We became a family.

Another key person in this family was Kim Kaiman. Kim was Hootie & the Blowfish's product manager at Atlantic. During the crucial period between the completion of the album in early April 1994 and its release in early July, Kim (with some help from Rusty and me) was in charge of formulating the strategy that would unveil *cracked rear view* to America.

I have always said that Kim was the godmother of this project. Those words do not even begin to honor the importance of her role on *cracked rear view*. Even after the album was recorded, the odds were stacked against Hootie & the Blowfish. Regardless of my personal enthusiasm, I didn't have the ability to solve most of the problems the project faced. But Kim did.

A native of the northern suburbs of New York City, in the early/mid-1980s, Kim became the program director at the Ithaca College radio station. There, like Rusty Harmon at WKNC and Mark Bryan at WUSC, she actively promoted the interests of alternative and independent artists. After graduating Ithaca in 1986, Kim went into radio and from there started doing public relations for various (largely hip) bands and labels. While she was working with a big indie punk act, Bad Religion, Danny Goldberg reached out to Kim for her help bringing Bad Religion to Atlantic. He also asked her to consider coming to Atlantic and working as a product manager. She ended up both joining Atlantic and successfully wooing Bad Religion to the label.

What's a product manager, and why was it so important to Hootie & the Blowfish?

After an album is completed, the product manager, together with the A&R person and the artist manager, attempt to assess the audience for that artist and develop a strategy to reach those people. The product manager then does his or her best to make sure everyone within the label is doing their job in ticking the boxes of that strategic plan.

"A product manager keeps everyone focused on the goal and the mission and the strategy of how to market that artist," Kim says. "I'm not necessarily calling the warehouses and telling them where to send the records, but I might be calling the person who's in charge of calling the warehouses and showing them evidence of why such-and-such might be a good idea. I help create the tools that are needed so everyone can do their job."

"I was aware that this was definitely not a priority act," Kim states. "But I never really gave a shit about priorities. I'm gonna find out where they fit into the grand scheme of things whether they're a priority or not. So the first thing I had to do was get people as excited about this band as I was."

Kim and I had a plan, and Kim knew how to put plans into action.

In the mid-1990s, record labels were based almost entirely in New York or Los Angeles. Therefore, most A&R people and product manager types thought primarily about impressing people in New York and Los Angeles. In addition, most media were in these two big cities. As a result, new-release campaigns were often geared towards making waves in New York and Los Angeles. You wanted to *see* evidence of your work—hear the band on *your* local radio station, read a review in some big magazine or newspaper published in New York City or Los Angeles, see them stocked in *your* local big city record store. That way, you could say to your boss, "See, the record is in the front window in the store down the street, and written about in the local paper you read every day! I did my job!"

We did something wildly different. Kim called the Atlantic sales department and said (very nearly using these exact words), "We don't give a good goddamn if there's not one single copy of *cracked rear view* in New York, Los Angeles, Chicago, Seattle, or any of those big media-friendly cities. *But in the Carolinas and the Mid-South, stock the fucking thing like it's Pearl Jam.*" Kim then faxed the sales department pages upon pages of retail reports, showing how extremely well *Kootchypop* had done at record stores throughout the Mid-South. She explained to them that, in many stores throughout the Mid-South, *Kootchypop* had been a Top 10 seller, and we could expect *cracked rear view* to perform just as well or better. The reams of paper Scott Schiff had assembled were coming in very handy.

Kim Kaiman: "We were gonna sell this record to their fans first and foremost, and then we were gonna have the fans fan it out and tell the story and infiltrate other regions. Always, always, always the plan was, break this band regionally first."

That was the strategy, in a nutshell. It could not be more different than the usual "We'll get it on MTV! We'll get it on the radio! We'll get it into *Rolling Stone!*" tactic that labels at the time usually used. There was an ancillary part of that plan, too. It was based on the fact that Kim and I knew that no one at the label cared very much about the band. How could we get their attention?

There was (and is) a chart in *Billboard* magazine called The Heatseekers Album Chart. This chart had (only) twenty-five positions, and it tracked the sales of new and developing artists (during the 1990s, CD, vinyl, and cassette sales were tracked through a system known as SoundScan, which literally scanned the barcode of the album or single at the point of purchase). An appearance on the Heatseekers chart—especially high up on it—generally indicated an artist on the rise, someone who could be making big noise in the future. The chart was reserved for developing artists: If you had ever climbed higher than no. 100 on the *Billboard* album charts, you were no longer eligible to be on the Heatseekers chart.

Back in 1994, the Heatseekers chart was very closely watched. And Kim and I knew this: If we could make sure that stores in the Mid-South were heavily stocked with Hootie product, maybe *cracked rear view* could make a Top 10 Heatseekers entry. And if that happened, the rest of the company would very likely sit up and go, "Whoa! They *entered* the Heatseekers chart in the Top 10? We need to pay attention to that band!" Atlantic Records was a label that required some sort of quick reaction from the marketplace, or a project was likely to get abandoned. We knew radio outside of the Carolinas wasn't going to come in for Hootie & the Blowfish any time soon, so the entire future of *cracked rear view* was balanced on that Heatseekers entry.

-21-

THE GA-BILLION PEOPLE
IN THE MIDDLE

cracked rear view, the debut album by a nine-year-old band from Columbia, South Carolina, called Hootie & the Blowfish, was released on July 5, 1994. It entered *Billboard*'s Heatseekers chart at no. 1.

The strategy developed by Kim Kaiman, Rusty Harmon, and myself (and executed, masterfully, by Kim) had worked beyond our wildest hopes. In the Mid-South region where Hootie had already proved their sales potential, the new album was stocked as heavily as any mainstream hit record of the day. On July 5th and the days to follow, it flew out the door, easily making the record a Top 10 seller in the region. Certainly, the sales figures were helped in no small part by a mega-release event at Sounds Familiar in Columbia—Darius Rucker's old employer—where fans lined up hours before the store's opening, and a block party atmosphere was in effect all day.

The album's entry at the *top* of the Heatseekers chart was huge. A no. 1 entry on Heatseekers was very, very unusual because, by definition, the artists on that chart are "developing," and therefore they tend to "sneak up" the chart. The album also entered the Top 200 (*Billboard*'s chart tracking the sales of all albums in the United States) at no. 127. This was also a very impressive number. It would have been the highest chart debut that week if the *Forrest Gump* soundtrack hadn't come in at no. 34. Damn you and all your whimsical wisdom, Forrest.

The week *cracked rear view* was released, I flew to Milwaukee to spend some time with Atlantic's newest (potential) hitmakers. They were playing a sparsely (but enthusiastically) attended show in a park setting. There are a number of reasons this visit stands out for me. First, although we were all mega-excited about the release, I remember absolutely *zero* sense of "Now, we're gonna be stars!" Hootie, as always, were excited to be Hootie. If anyone else wanted to come to the party, well, that's totally fabulous, but Hootie & the Blowfish were going to have a good time with whoever showed up. Honestly, I think that sums up the Hootie philosophy—and attitude toward fame— pretty goddamn well.

Second, when I look back at the Milwaukee trip at the end of the first week of July of 1994, I now realize this was my very last exposure to the compact, highly functioning, drinking, partying, driving, and playing unit that had been working efficiently since 1990. On the road that July, it was just Darius, Mark, Dean, Soni, road manager Paul Graham, and soundman Billy Huelin. That was it. Six guys in a van and a U-Haul. It was the last time I got to really spend time with the "local" Hootie & the Blowfish. It would never, ever be like that again.

On that visit, I also learned a peculiar Hootie superstition: You always keep the TV on when you leave your hotel room. I learned this the hard way: We were stepping out of the room Darius and Dean shared, and I instinctively clicked off the television. Darius turned quickly and said, coldly and deliberately, "You . . . don't . . . ever . . . do . . . that. TV *always* on when you leave the room." Years later, Darius and Mark both confirmed this peculiar habit, although neither could recall how it originated.

With the no. 1 Heatseekers entry, we had the attention of Atlantic Records. We were no longer a small band of mobile guerillas operating under the radar. But it wasn't a straight shot to the top. Some, uh, interesting things happened. August, you see, was a cruel month. The album sales went down, not up, and some problems emerged that proved nearly fatal to the newborn album.

By August 6, 1994, *cracked rear view* had dropped out of the *Billboard* album charts entirely (and on the Heatseekers chart, it had fallen to no. 13). The band's Mid-South fan base had been milked dry, and without radio coming in to support the album, there was relatively little new consumer awareness of the group. The "Hold My Hand" single was out there, but it wouldn't make any impact on radio and the charts for another eight weeks.

This is pretty incredible to consider, but true: For the second time in just a few months, Hootie & the Blowfish came precariously close to being dropped from the label, barely five weeks after the release of *cracked rear view*. Atlantic remained an extremely radio-driven label, and in August of 1994, Hootie were not blowing up—or even puffing mildly—on the radio.

Rusty Harmon's dire prediction of what might happen to Hootie if they had sought a bigger-money record deal came perilously close to coming true. According to someone high up in Atlantic's sales department, in August of 1994, a powerful figure in the New York office strongly suggested that Hootie & the Blowfish should be dropped. Gus Gusler and Rusty are both thoroughly convinced that the *only* reason Hootie were kept on the label during those dark days in August was because they had cost Atlantic so little money.

Scott Schiff, still toiling in his closet and tracking sales data, once again stepped in to help. "Our sales data and information was *still* supporting the idea that *cracked rear view* would sell, it was just taking longer," Scott notes. "So, we started pulling in favors from everyone we knew, and everyone who had asked favors of us. I was personally giving out copies of the album to friends and people I knew who had influence. Because people genuinely liked the band, people wanted to help us and so they continued to work the album. However, this was made very, very clear: If this thing failed it was going to be our head— specifically, *my* head—on the block, not theirs."

The work of Scott and other dyed-in-the-wool Hootie supporters began to pay off. Radio began to dribble in, and the shaky sales picture began to steady. On August 13, 1994, *cracked rear view* re-entered the *Billboard* album charts at no. 161. It would remain one of the Top 200 best-selling albums in the country for the next two-and-a-half years. Still, for the rest of August, *cracked rear view* bumped around in the mid-100s, until a very significant and unlikely event occurred.

In the 1990s, one of the most sought-after television bookings was *The Late Show With David Letterman* (in 1994, it was in its second season at CBS, in the coveted 11:30 P.M. slot). Not only was there an enormous amount of competition among artists and labels to land a Letterman spot, but within Atlantic itself, this high-profile booking was also considered a rare prize. I'll be very frank: In August of 1994, with their album swimming around the bottom quarter of the Top 200, no one at Atlantic Records was calling Letterman or any of the other late-night shows going, "Hey, you just *have to* book this Hootie & the Blowfish band!" This is why everyone was gobsmacked when we got a call that *The Late Show With David Letterman* wanted Hootie & the Blowfish to appear on the program on September 2, 1994.

"It was the moment our career changed," Darius later told an interviewer. "We had been a band for eight years, played a lot. We had put out a record, and it was doing okay in the South, but grunge was king, and nobody wanted to hear 'Hold My Hand,' it seemed like. And then Letterman . . . for some reason, one of the stations in New York played our record, and David heard it on the way home. He pulled the car over and called his talent booker and said, 'I want you to get me this band Hootie & the Blowfish.' That was a Tuesday. And Friday, we were on the show. And honestly, on Thursday we were just another band trying to make it. And Saturday morning, everybody was trying to find a Hootie & the Blowfish record. It was really one of those things, Letterman made our career, and we can never thank him enough."

The effect was immediate. *cracked rear view* began a relatively rapid climb up the album charts, and the "Hold My Hand" single entered *Billboard*'s Top 100 single charts (it eventually peaked at no. 7). The week before Halloween, the album entered the Top 50. (Hootie & the Blowfish were to make their first appearance on *The Tonight Show with Jay Leno* on December 27, 1994; they would appear on the Leno show eight more times.)

The group also started to enlarge their touring profile. That autumn they went on their first "proper" national tour, opening for Big Head Todd and the Monsters. They also continued to pick up smaller venue headlining dates along the way, and whenever they could, they played a run of shows at their old favorite venues in the Mid-South.

Meanwhile, the band was beginning to explode in radio, and music video had begun to influence the picture. VH-1 (as it was then called, now it is known as VH1) was historically geared at playing and promoting "older" artists who already had a reputation, so it was highly unusual that the network would take the "lead" in breaking an artist. David Weir, an executive in the music and talent relations department at VH-1, remembers that VH-1 took a great sense of pride in Hootie & the Blowfish.

"Hootie was the first full-blown success story at VH1 in terms of artist development," Weir says, "and we felt ownership of them. MTV didn't really get on until much later that year, until 'Hold My Hand' had proven itself. They were late to the party. But in the meanwhile, we started booking them on everything. Every interview show, every game show, every event. We would book them because they were articulate, they were music fans, they seemed to have opinions on a lot of things, and most of their opinions were really positive. So they were great to interview, and it wasn't just Darius, it was Dean, and Mark, and Soni, all of them had their own minds, it wasn't just lead singer syndrome."

Of course, the legendary Hootie charm and utter lack of snob-bishness helped. "It was impossible not to like them," Weir remembers. "Their warmth, their humor. We were laughing and joking and having fun the very first meeting in the conference room, and things got only better from there."

Linda Ferrando, the Atlantic executive who was the primary inter-face between the artists and MTV and VH-1, also remembers what a pleasure it was to work with Hootie and how that made her job that much easier. "I was always looking for people with personality, artists that somebody would give a damn about," Ferrando says. "And at that time, there was a huge gap in the video world: It was either urban pop or grunge alternative. Well, what about the ga-billion people in the middle there? The Hootie guys were sweet, they hung out until the end of the road, so to speak. And this quality came across both on TV and in person, you couldn't really help but smile. And what's wrong with that?"

"I've worked with so many acts in so many different situations," Ferrando continues, "and I've said it then, and I'll say it today: The Hootie guys never changed, they were always kind and respectful and smart and worked hard, and I was really appreciative of that because we worked just as hard. Now, 99.9 percent of the people you work with, they *change* and I understand why they change. You get money or you get no money, you get fame, people are talking about you, they're looking at you, they're pointing, they're pushing, you're tired, you change mentally and physically because of everything that's happening to you. And the Hootie guys, I'm sure they had their issues, but outwardly they were just the same guys. They never changed and were the most lovely people."

So, it's the autumn of 1994: The record is moving up the charts; radio and video have come to the table; and a lot of the Atlantic office, from assistants and people in the mailroom to the highest executives, are becoming Hootie & the Blowfish fans. Smooth sailing, right? Not quite. Even at this stage, a major speed bump threatened to derail the momentum in a potentially catastrophic way.

-22-

HOW A MAN NAMED GRAY ALMOST SHOT AND KILLED *CRACKED REAR VIEW*

Early in the autumn of 1994, we got word that we had a problem. A *big* problem. Bob Dylan's publishers were *not* happy that Hootie & the Blowfish had used five lines from Dylan's song "Idiot Wind" in "Only Wanna Be With You" (everything from "I shot a man named Gray" through "I can't help it if I'm lucky" is quoted from the Dylan song).

This was really effing scary on multiple levels. If Dylan's people wanted to, they could demand that we take the track off the record. This happens in about half of these sort of copyright disputes. It's important to remember that at the time this problem surfaced, *cracked rear view* hadn't *really* taken off yet. I was fairly certain that if we had to pull the track from the album, Atlantic would not go to the expense or trouble of re-pressing the CD, cassette, or album. Kim Kaiman, Gus Gusler, and Evan Lamberg (who was the real expert with this publishing stuff) were also panicking in a *major* way and agreed that it was unlikely Atlantic would re-press the album if the track had to be removed.

Considering how hugely successful *cracked rear view* became, it's odd to consider this incident almost derailed the whole project (and how close Atlantic came to throwing tens of thousands of already made product into the dumpster, the ocean, and/or a landfill on Staten Island). But you've got to remember that, to many Atlantic execs, the costs of re-pressing a new *cracked rear view* (without "Only Wanna Be With You") would probably have outweighed any potential money they thought the band could make. I recall sitting in my office in Los Angeles, staring at the bubbles rising in a glass of diet ginger ale and thinking, *well, that's that.* After all, it was totally a crapshoot whether a settlement could be reached with Dylan's people.

How did this potential catastrophe happen in the first place? Well, it turns out Rusty Harmon, and the band thought they already had a deal with Dylan. Remember, "Only Wanna Be With You" had earlier appeared on the *Kootchypop* EP, released a little over a year before *cracked rear view.* Band manager Rusty Harmon says that back in early 1993 he had some casual contact with Dylan's publishers. Rusty goes on to explain that after sending Dylan's people the lyrics to "Only Wanna Be With You," they said there wouldn't be any problem. He says that after that brief amenable conversation, Dylan's people sent Rusty some paperwork.

Apparently, the original *Kootchypop*-era paperwork said that the band could use the quoted Dylan lines for no charge, with no copyright share, and with no credit, *but if the band ever used the song on a major label release, Dylan and his publishers had to be notified in advance.* Rusty, apparently, had forgotten about that clause; and Gus never knew about it in the first place.

Gus Gusler: "The first I heard of *any of* this is when I happened to notice Dylan was suing us. And I called Rusty and the band and said, 'Y'know, it would've been nice if someone had told me about this.'"

No one does slightly sarcastic outrage better than Gus Gusler. "So," Gus continues, "I got on the phone with the Dylan people, and they said, 'Nobody told us you were putting out the song on Atlantic. If you'd just called us and given us some notice, we would've honored the gratis thing, *but you just did it.* Now it's on the radio, and Bob's not willing to do the gratis deal now.' So we had to pay."

(A few years after all this happened, the general drift of this conversation was confirmed for me by Jesse Dylan, Bob's filmmaker son, who had some involvement in his father's publishing at the time of these events.)

Hootie & the Blowfish likely paid $350,000 for the usage of the five lines from "Idiot Wind" (neither the bandmates nor their management will confirm an actual figure). Although this seems like a fortune—it is, after all, roughly ten times what it cost to record the entire *cracked rear view* album—it was a pretty good deal for the band. Here's why: In many similar cases, the songwriter whose work was appropriated demands a significant piece of the copyright of the contested song. For example, it would have been "standard" for Dylan to request 50 percent—or even 100 percent—of the copyright. But Dylan didn't. His people merely asked for a flat buyout. If Dylan had gotten half the copyright, he likely would have netted between five and ten million dollars from "Only Wanna Be With You."

Fascinating side note: Bob Dylan has played over two thousand concerts since 1994, but he has not played "Idiot Wind" once since the release of *cracked rear view*. It seems reasonable to presume that this is because of the appropriation in "Only Wanna Be With You."

On New Year's Eve, 1994, the band appeared on *Dick Clark's New Year's Rockin' Eve* (on tape) and played (live and in person) a celebratory show at the Benton Convention Center in Winston-Salem, North Carolina. It had been a helluva year. In the spring, Hootie & the Blowfish had recorded their debut album and almost had it canned before it came out. In the summer, they had put out the record and almost been dropped five weeks after release. In the early autumn, they had hit the rocky shoals of a copyright suit and almost had the album turned into landfill. And they triumphed over all these challenges, finishing the remarkable year at no. 56 in the charts (and rising), having sold about four hundred thousand albums so far. But the next year was going to be even bigger. *Much* bigger.

-23-

THE YEAR OF HOOTIE

Did you live in the United States in 1995? Then you already know what I'm going to tell you. 1995 was the year of Hootie.

1995 began with Hootie & the Blowfish's first single, "Hold My Hand," having just entered the Top 40. The band's debut album, *cracked rear view*, was at no. 53, and it was closing in on five hundred thousand in sales. At this point, the group and all of us on Team Hootie could be fairly certain of one important thing: We would probably make it to album two. More significantly, everyone was having a good time. Sure, the band had sold a couple of hundred thousand records, but it was all just business as usual for Hootie & the Blowfish.

"I want to make this point," says Paul Graham, the band's tour manager since the very early 1990s. "The thing that made Hootie successful is that they just *embraced* the fact that they were normal dudes. They never tried to be brooding rock stars. Brooding rock stars typically sit at their apartment and brood. These guys, we would all go to a bar and soon there would be twenty people all hanging out and then we'd be, like, let's go see a band play, what band do y'all think we should see? They *embraced friendship*. They embraced the fact that they were social people, they embraced the fact that they easily made friends."

Rusty Harmon: "Every person in that band was good people. They were fair, they were honest, they were polite, they were ethical, they were just good people. We didn't take shortcuts, we didn't screw people over, and we treated people the way we wanted to be treated."

On January 11, 1995, *cracked rear view* went gold. All of us had been hearing about "gold records" since we were children. For as long as any of us had been following music, a gold record was *the* standard by which commercial success in the music industry had been measured. And bands like Hootie didn't necessarily go gold particularly quickly: Hootie's heroes, R.E.M., didn't hit gold until album four (coincidentally, the Don Gehman–produced *Life's Rich Pageant*). Yet five months after the release of *cracked rear view*, it had gone gold.

Hootie & the Blowfish left for their first European tour on January 18, performing in Amsterdam, Hamburg, Munich, Stockholm, Madrid, Barcelona, Milan, and Bologna. After they returned to Columbia on February 5th, I asked them how the tour had gone. I anticipated hearing stories about the historic sights they had seen, the legendary venues they had played, and important updates about how the European label representatives had treated them. Instead, they told me a long story about how one of their road crew had gotten so high in Amsterdam that he had fallen asleep in an elevator at their hotel and rode the elevator up and down, up and down, up and down all night long, undisturbed by patrons and hotel employees who were used to this sort of thing. They laughed so hard and had such a good time telling me this story that they then told it to me again, from a different perspective. And that's all I heard about Hootie & the Blowfish's first trip to Europe.

Shortly after the European tour, WDVE, a radio station in Pittsburgh that had been very early supporters of the band, did a live broadcast of their set at a club in the city called Nick's Fat City (this was later released in its entirety on the twenty-fifth anniversary edition of *cracked rear view*). The Pittsburgh show reveals what were truly the band's final days as a "club" band. It's a fascinating document of the four-piece Hootie & the Blowfish that had been wowing audiences steadily for the past five years and would soon vanish forever. By summer, the group would have a fifth member on stage (and if you saw the group in 2019, there were seven musicians up there). Every time I listen to the Pittsburgh set, I consciously think, "*That's* the band I saw at Myskyns in September of '93."

When they returned from Europe, "Hold My Hand" was in the Top 10 and Soni, Mark, Darius, and Dean embarked on their first coast-to-coast tour as a nationally well-known act. They would be going out as the support band for one of the groups they had idolized back in their cover band days, Toad the Wet Sprocket. Toad was coming off of their most successful album, the Platinum-selling *Dulcinea*. Since the venues were generally medium-sized theatres and ballrooms, sellouts were virtually guaranteed.

On the first week of the tour (the last week of February, 1995), *cracked rear view* pierced the *Billboard* Top 10 Album charts, landing at no. 7. (By contrast, that same week *Dulcinea* was at no. 195 on the charts, having peaked at no. 34.) After just a few days on the road, it was clear to everyone on stage and off that the opening band was the "big" draw on the show, and there was a considerable amount of pressure (from Atlantic, from the booking agent, and from the venues) to change the billing.

But Hootie & the Blowfish, who idolized Toad the Wet Sprocket, would hear nothing of it. "Everyone realized that people were coming primarily to see us," Dean remembers. "But we wouldn't allow them to flip the bill. We were like, *no*, man, it's *their* tour."

Hootie and Toad had an interesting solution for the situation that had developed. Members of Toad would join Hootie on stage at multiple times during their set, and Darius, Dean, Soni, and Mark would be on stage for a lot of Toad's headlining set. By midway through the tour, it was essentially a seamless evening of music, with both bands intermingling and contributing to each other's songs (and a couple of choice covers). It made for a wonderful event, with the stage full of musicians who seemed to truly enjoy each other's company.

When I spoke to Toad the Wet Sprocket guitarist Todd Nichols about the spring 1995 tour, his primary memories were not musical. "When I think of Hootie," Nichols says, "I don't think much about the music. I think of golf. They almost were a band that played golf more than a band that played music. Everything revolved around golf."

I pushed Todd a little. After all, he was on tour with one of the hottest bands in the country. Isn't there *anything* else that stands out?

"It really was the golfing," Todd affirms. "I would spend the night on their bus so we could wake up at six in the morning, and keep in mind we had usually just gone to sleep an hour or two earlier. They had so much energy, it was unbelievable how they could do that. Our band is much more mellow, but Hootie would stay up all night and wake up early to play golf. They knew everyone at the golf courses too, they would get hooked up with tee times and golf clubs, and they would give *me* golf clubs 'cause they were just *overflowing* in swag. They would give you shoes, they would give you balls, and man, it really seemed like it all revolved around golf. And after that, drinking. The music came third, it seemed like, after golf and drinking. I'm not digging on them, it's just that was their personality: Have as much fun as you can."

In addition to the booming sales figures and the vast increase in the band's profile on radio and VH-1, in the first few months of 1995, there was another sign of the rapidly changing industry perception of Hootie & the Blowfish. The same executives who had been extremely wary of Hootie just a few months before (if they were aware of the band at all) began to seek out the band to contribute to high-profile soundtracks and compilation albums. One of the most remarkable of these is the track they recorded for *Encomium: A Tribute to Led Zeppelin.*

Encomium was released on Atlantic (a company long associated with Led Zeppelin) in mid-March, 1995. The album also features Sheryl Crow, Big Head Todd, Blind Melon, Cracker, and Tori Amos, among others. There's something very interesting about this lineup: Barely a year after the music business was all grunge all the time, the artists chosen to contribute to *Encomium* reflect the industry's awareness that the landscape had quickly shifted away from the Seattle sound. Hootie's contribution, "Hey, Hey What Can I Do" (recorded at Reflections Studios in Charlotte with Don Gehman behind the board) speeds up Zeppelin's arrangement and brings out the bluegrass element that was only hinted at in the original. It's the first time (on record) the band dabbled in bluegrass, a genre that was to surface frequently on every subsequent album the band recorded. There's also a nuanced Darius vocal that entirely avoids the squealing, squelchy histrionics of Robert Plant.

But something else important happened at the sessions in Charlotte. For the first time, Hootie & the Blowfish worked with Peter Holsapple, who would become an integral part of the group's life and a vital member of their touring band. Peter was eight years older than the youngest member of the band, and throughout his long tenure in the group he added a powerfully wise, playful, avuncular presence to Hootie & the Blowfish. In the 1970s, Peter had been part of the groundbreaking independent music scene centered on Winston-Salem, North Carolina, and was a co-leader (along with Chris Stamey and Will Rigby) of The dB's. The dB's not only had an acute impact on the shape of American jangle pop/power pop but also profoundly influenced R.E.M. In 1988, in a harbinger of his role with Hootie & the Blowfish, Holsapple joined R.E.M. as their fifth touring member, a position he held until 1991.

I had long hoped that Peter would join up with Darius, Mark, Soni, and Dean. In the spring of 1994, shortly after we had finished mastering *cracked rear view*, I sent a pre-release cassette of the album to Peter. I enclosed a note that said, "If this band can ever afford a fifth touring member, this gig would be *perfect* for you." I will confess that even I, a true believer, wasn't entirely sure the band would be able to afford a fifth member, but I wanted to give Peter the heads-up nonetheless. About a year later, Holsapple finally came to meet Mark, Dean, Darius, and Soni in Charlotte to add mandolin and organ to "Hey, Hey What Can I Do." They got along famously, and not long after that, Peter packed up his accordion, his guitars, and his mandolin and joined Hootie & the Blowfish on the road.

Mark Bryan: "He really embraces the role of, 'What can I do for this song?' He would *find* the part. It might be an organ, it might be a mandolin, it might be a slide guitar, whatever the right part, he'd find it. And he might end up playing piano in the verse and big power chords on guitar in the chorus, and then organ on the bridge. It's so amazing to have that *instant* complement on stage, that voice, as it were, from that side of the stage adding what you *know* will always be the right thing. He is the perfect utility man, and a *wonderful* soul, full of life and light, and as passionate about music as anyone I've ever met. In his own words, he is the possessor of a vast amount of useless information. I am the same way. We are both people who spent too much of our adolescence reading liner notes."

-24-

TOP OF THE CHARTS

On May 27, 1995, *cracked rear view* reached no. 1 on the American charts, edging out the *Friday* soundtrack, which had been in the top spot for two weeks. In our wildest dreams—*and I do mean our wildest dreams*—I don't think any of us could have imagined that this band would reach this height. The utter down-to-earth quality of Hootie & the Blowfish and all the people around them made it impossible to think of all this as some big rock star adventure. Hootie were just doing business as usual. Only now they were doing it at the top of the charts.

Paul Graham: "They were most decidedly *not* the kind of guys who were like, I'm not going to sit and have a drink with you because I'm in the band. That's fine, if that's what you want to be—but that's not who the Hootie guys were. You know what kind of guys Hootie were? After the show, we would grab some college kid and say, 'Hey, where's the party? Where do we go next?' *And we would go with them to the party.* And that was not something we did to get fans, or create some everyman image of the band, it's actually that we wanted to go party and to meet girls and do the same exact thing we did when we were in college. Every night—drink beer and meet girls. Every night. And it was awesome."

"Listen," Paul concludes, "I do think there's validity to the loneliness and despair that causes you to write great songs. But to have fans, and cultivate those fans, it takes some kind of social gift, and that can be a huge part of success."

In the post-grunge mid-1990s, artists such as Hootie, Dave Matthews Band, Phish, Tori Amos, and Alanis Morissette spoke directly to their audiences' needs, fears, hopes, and lifestyles. They approached their audiences on equal terms.

Populist political legend Huey Long once said that, when addressing an audience, you have to stand high enough on a soapbox so people can see you but not so high that you are looking down on them. Hootie & the Blowfish wasn't "music for the rest of us," as an Atlantic marketing campaign trumpeted. They were us, making music.

cracked rear view by Hootie & the Blowfish stayed at no. 1 from May 27, 1995, until June 17, 1995, when Pink Floyd's *Pulse* replaced it for just one week. It then returned to the top spot on July 1, in time to celebrate the first anniversary of its release. Hootie's second single, "Let Her Cry," was also heading up the charts, on its way to peaking at no. 9 in the Hot 100.

In the second week of June 1995, Hootie entered a dramatic new phase of their career—headlining the enormous sheds, amusement parks, and beachside venues that the very biggest acts played during the summer. Amphitheaters, pavilions, Summerfests, multiple nights at legendary venues like the Greek in Los Angeles and Jones Beach on Long Island . . . many lighters were lighted, many hands were shaken, many long miles rolled under many wide tires. Much Jägermeister was spilled, much golf was played, all around the land. It was business as usual for Hootie & the Blowfish.

I recall one moment that really typified the spirit of that summer and the grace and goodwill of Darius, Dean, Mark, and Soni. It was a hot, dark, thick day in August, and the band was playing one of those giant outdoor amphitheaters—I think it was the World Amphitheater in Tinley Park, Illinois, about forty-five minutes from Chicago. I was watching from backstage, the stage-right side—Dean's side. Through the first third of the show, from our elevated vantage point, we could see that a giant storm was rolling in. The wind kicked up in a pretty scary way, and although the worst part of the storm didn't hit the venue head on, it got close enough that the power cut out.

When the electricity went out, the band did not leave the stage.

Instead, they had a brief meeting in front of the drum kit, and then they did something that seemed like such an incredibly beautiful yet natural thing for them to do. They separated (so they could cover more ground), and each member walked to the front of the stage and stepped into the pit. Then, for the entire duration of the power outage—about forty minutes—they shook hands, signed autographs, and talked with fans.

In mid-1995, the nicest band I had ever met became the biggest band I had ever known. And we all still felt like family. It felt like we were in the back of the biggest station wagon ever, surrounded by the nicest brothers and sisters, with the best ever parents behind the wheel. And no one was ever shouting, "Are we there yet?" Because we were already there; the destination had been the journey, as they say.

If it was the end of an era in the music business, it was ending with Hootie & the Blowfish sitting on top. For the entire summer of 1995, *cracked rear view* remained at either no. 1 or no. 2 in the charts, except for two weeks when it was bumped to no. 3 by the entry of Michael Jackson's *HIStory: Past, Present and Future Book 1.*

The success was certainly helped along by the fact that the band, three singles into their album, finally had a signature video: "Only Wanna Be With You." Of course, Hootie had already made two videos, both of which had gotten a lot of exposure on both MTV and VH-1 (Hootie were one of the rare bands that were simultaneously in high rotation on both channels). But the clips for both "Hold My Hand" and "Let Her Cry" had been, well, functional. They weren't "must-see TV" in the way that, say, Weezer's "Buddy Holly," Nirvana's "Smells Like Teen Spirit," or Blind Melon's "No Rain" had been.

It all began with a little chat backstage. On December 31, 1994, Hootie & the Blowfish ended the year with a packed New Year's Eve show in Winston-Salem, North Carolina. I had flown in from Los Angeles to spend the holiday with the band. The band was about a minute away from taking the stage. I was standing in the wings, next to Darius. He already had his guitar strapped on.

I turned to Darius and said, "Y'know what would be a *great* video?

Imagine if you are sitting at home watching TV and flipping channels, and SportsCenter comes on . . . only it's *not* SportsCenter, it's a video for 'Only Wanna Be With You.' Like, it looks exactly like SportsCenter, same set, same anchors, but in every highlight, it's *you guys*, doin' shit and playing the song."

Darius's eyes widened. He jumped in and elaborated on my idea, explaining what the band could do, and what the SportsCenter anchors could say. He only stopped when it was time to walk on stage.

Seriously, that's really how it happened.

The next day, Darius and I told Mark, Dean, Soni, and Rusty about our idea, and everyone got a big kick out of it. They immediately brainstormed on the possibilities, throwing in different gimmicks, ideas for cameos, that sort of thing. Quickly, it emerged that the band wanted to feature manufactured "highlights" that made them look silly or incompetent.

The video Darius and I conceived on the side of the stage at the Benton Convention Center on New Years Eve got made, almost exactly as we imagined it, and it became *the* element that pushed Hootie & the Blowfish into the stratosphere.

ESPN was excited to be a part of it, and network anchors Keith Olbermann, Dan Patrick, Mike Tirico, Charley Steiner, and Chris Berman readily signed on. In 1995, ESPN was just one network (this seems unimaginable, doesn't it?), and the brand still wasn't exceptionally well known outside of the world of (mostly male) sports fans.

"We were cult heroes in the beginning," remembers Chris Berman, who has the last word(s) in the clip. "I was doing a lot on the network— all the football, four times a week, the Swami, and the Sunday and the Monday and the blah blah blah—but we were still somewhat cult heroes. But because of that video, I started getting stopped by younger people who probably weren't huge sports fans, and in Europe sometimes, someone will be, like, 'Wait a minute I know you. You were in a rock video!'"

"I think it helped us get out of being 'just' sportscasters," remembers Dan Patrick. "We were becoming a brand, whether we knew it or not. I didn't look at it as, oh, they're going to take away our journalism degrees for being in a video. We knew we could have some fun. And back then on SportsCenter in the mid-1990s, we were having a lot of fun."

"On the day of filming," continues Patrick, who was to become a close friend of the group, "the band were in the area, so they could have come to SportsCenter in Bristol, Connecticut, or they could have gone to the Adidas golf plant in Massachusetts. They made the decision to go up there and get gear instead of going to SportsCenter. I gave them grief about that for a *long* time . . . 'You guys passed up coming to SportsCenter so you could get golf equipment?!?' And they were like, 'Yeh . . . of course.'"

With the ESPN personalities in place, the band and their management lined up the sports cameos. Eventually, golfer Fred Couples and basketball stars Alonzo Mourning, Muggsy Bogues, Alex English, Walt Williams, and Charles Smith joined Hootie for clips that were half slapstick and half something that could just *maybe* be a real ESPN highlight. But most exciting to Darius was the participation of Dan Marino, the star quarterback of his favorite sports franchise, the Miami Dolphins.

The cameos and the ESPN gimmick aren't the only reason the "Only Wanna Be With You" video really worked for the band. For the first time, they had made a video that showed them being silly, joyful, grinning, jumping up and down, laughing at each other, and having a ball. Everything you see in that video—the shooting hoops, the relentless self-ridicule, the embarrassing dancing—is just Hootie being Hootie. I'm not sure they ever made another video that captured this nearly as well.

Initially, the clip confused the hell out of Atlantic. "I just knew they were on the trajectory of *enormous*, and then here comes this video," recalls Linda Ferrando, who was responsible for bringing the clip to MTV, VH-1, and any other potential television suitors. "I distinctly remember going, 'I just don't understand this. Who are these people? Is this a joke?' And someone goes, 'No, these are actually people on an actual cable network.' I'm like, 'What network?' I was not really a sports person. And at that time, SportsCenter wasn't known like it is today. So, I'm just watching, thinking '*What is this*? What are we going to do with this?' And at this point, of course, we're rolling, the band is doing amazing, and this video comes in and I don't understand it at all."

"But then," Ferrando continues, "so many people that I'd never heard from before called me. People from other labels, other music people, other friends in the business, and even my family, and they all said, 'That's the greatest thing I've ever seen, that is the coolest clip I've ever seen.' And I'm, like, '*Really?*' Even then, we still had this significant problem: We thought networks like MTV or VH-1 might be reluctant to play something that contained branding of another network. But of course, there's no way to really edit the ESPN angle out of the clip."

David Weir, who was at VH-1: "When Linda brought me the clip, we had that conversation prior to watching it. And I said, 'Listen, you know what? ESPN isn't VH-1, but there's a considerable overlap in the audience. I think it might be something that is validating in certain respects to the audience that also watches VH-1.' The ESPN aspect, it worked, it made sense. It was *perfect* for us. We thought it was not only very representative of who the band were as people, but also very reflective of the audience that we were serving at that time. 'Cause VH-1's audience, the target was a little older. We were 30–45, 25–45. It was post-collegiate, it was we have a family, we've got one kid and a second on the way, we have jobs, we like to still have fun, we still love music, we play golf, we go to the kids' soccer games. That video spoke to not only who the band was, it also reflected the audience that we were catering to."

It's a long-time cliché that athletes want to be rock stars, and rock stars want to be athletes. Not too long after we shot the "Only Wanna Be With You" video, I asked Darius an important question.

"Darius, would you give this *all* up"—and with a wave of my arms, I indicated the dressing room we were sitting in, the arena full of adoring fans waiting above us, and everything amazing that had happened in the last year or so—"to throw one pass in the NFL?"

Darius took my query very seriously, and he was quiet for about forty-five seconds. Finally, he looked me in the eye and said, "Would I give all this up for one pass? No. But for one season in the NFL . . . yes. Yes, I would."

On October 21, 1995, "Only Wanna Be With You" peaked at no. 6 in the *Billboard* Hot 100. It was Hootie's third hit single in a year, and the *cracked rear view* album was still sitting very firmly in the *Billboard* Top 10.

For a young African American music fan (and later journalist), the ubiquity of Hootie & the Blowfish in 1995 had an even deeper meaning. "It was amazing that you could flip on MTV and you could see yourself in a way that wasn't Michael Jackson, that wasn't Jody Watley, that wasn't dance, pop, or soul," Sarah Rodman says. "Those are all wonderful things, things that as African Americans are important to our heritage and that we have dominated to an extent. But to see somebody doing rock music that was infused with this bar band stuff, that was infused with this country stuff, that was infused with the Southern sensibility in a way that wasn't scary at all . . . From the perspective of a Black person that was very exciting. It's the kind of thing that you can't name necessarily or articulate when you see it, but you're just glad to see it."

Hootie & the Blowfish had ended their summer tour on September 13 with a gigantic homecoming show at Capital City Stadium in Columbia. They turned it into a festival atmosphere, adding three of their favorite local(ish) bands to the bill: Cravin' Melon (who were to rival Clemson what Hootie were to the University of South Carolina), Edwin McCain (who had just released his major label debut on Atlantic), and one of their biggest inspirations, Dillon Fence from Chapel Hill, North Carolina. The bill also included Cowboy Mouth from New Orleans, old friends who had been on the road with Hootie for most of the summer.

In the autumn of 1995, Hootie & the Blowfish took part in three highly visible mainstream music industry events, the kind of things you only get invited to if you're one of the biggest bands in the country.

On October 1 at Cardinal Stadium in Louisville, Kentucky, Hootie & the Blowfish joined John Mellencamp, Neil Young, Willie Nelson, Steve Earle, The Supersuckers, John Conlee, and the Dave Matthews Band for the tenth annual Farm Aid concert. Hootie played a rousing and electric nine-song set that was one of their loosest and most engaging concerts of the year. They also welcomed Radney Foster onstage to sing "Fine Line" with them, Willie Nelson joined in on "Let Her Cry," and Foster and Earle helped out on "Mustang Sally" (which had become a staple of Hootie's live sets).

It also felt as if the band was saying goodbye to something. That evening, for the last time, the group played a set centered almost exclusively on songs from *cracked rear view*. Even as they sat at the top of the world, they were moving ahead, because that's all that Hootie & the Blowfish had ever known: Playing, moving, playing, driving, playing, writing, staying in motion. Why should success change that?

The pros and cons of moving forward a little too fast would become a major factor in the year to come. There was a hint of this at the next big event Hootie & the Blowfish played, Neil Young's ninth annual Bridge School Benefit at the Shoreline Amphitheatre in Mountain View, California, on October 28, 1995. The yearly event raised money to support The Bridge School, a unique facility that assists children with severe physical and speech impairments. It was a *loaded* lineup, including Bruce Springsteen, Beck, Emmylou Harris, Daniel Lanois, The Pretenders, and, of course, Neil Young.

While Darius, Mark, Soni, and Dean were off signing posters and guitars to be sold and auctioned off, and meeting some of the children who would benefit from that evening's concert, one of my all-time favorite Hootie-related moments took place. Paul Graham and I were alone in the band's dressing room/trailer, sitting on a ratty couch. Like most dressing room couches, it had been so significantly abused that the only place we could sensibly sit without falling either off or into the thing was dead in the center.

Suddenly, Neil Young bounds into the trailer.

He had a lot to do that day, and he was clearly in a hurry. He grabbed an acoustic guitar off a stand and then he wedged himself into the ten inches of space between Paul Graham and myself. I've got to underline how very little room there was between Paul and me, but somehow Neil found just enough space to fit in.

He began talking, breathlessly. "So, you know we end each one of these things with everyone up on stage doing '[Rockin' in the] Free World,' right, so let me show you the chords, I mean, it couldn't be simpler—you with me?"

Paul and I looked each other. Wordlessly, we mutually agreed to not disabuse Mr. Neil Young of the idea that he was talking to guys who were actually *in* Hootie & the Blowfish.

"—Okay, so, this is dead simple"—and Neil begins to play and sing "Rockin' in the Free World," his guitar neck literally two inches from my chin—"E minor, *colors on the street*, then D to C, *red white and blue*, an' keep going with the E minor to D to C, until y'get to the chorus, then it's G to D to C and back to E minor, *keep on rockin' in the free world, keep on rockin' in the free world*, and there's an instrumental bridge in A, but that's the basic idea, *got it?*"

Paul and I nodded. Neil Young had just performed a (very short) private concert just for us, so we were, understandably, speechless.

Neil said, "Great! See ya up there!" He ran out of the trailer as quickly as he had arrived.

Later, as Mark Bryan and I were strolling in the artists' area, I witnessed another great Hootie moment. Mark stepped up to Bruce Springsteen, introduced himself, and they shook hands. While still holding on to Springsteen's hand, Mark explained how very, very much Springsteen had meant to him; how he had studied his records and absorbed the way he loved rock 'n' roll and interacted with his audience; finally, Mark said, "Mr. Springsteen, you are the reason I am here today." Springsteen, silent the entire time, embraced Mark in a bear hug, and held it for a long time.

Hootie's set that night was the first public sign of the impatience and (slightly out-of-character) creative adventurism that was to affect their decision making in the next half year. After opening their seven-song set with "Hannah Jane" and "Running From an Angel," The band (performing acoustically) elected to play four brand new, unrecorded songs (all of which were to appear on *Fairweather Johnson*—"Fool," "Let It Breathe," "When I'm Lonely," and "Be the One").

Personally, I thought this was a very peculiar decision, especially since three of those four were slow-tempo numbers. It was rare that I strongly disagreed with a choice of the band, and even rarer that I confronted them about it. But before their performance, as we sat in the trailer going over their setlist, I told them I thought they were making a mistake. I explained that they had been invited because of their status as hitmakers, and, well, they weren't playing any of their hits. But I didn't push it. Hootie, to my mind, played the most underwhelming set of the entire evening.

However, it was largely forgotten a few minutes later, when everyone piled on stage to do "Rockin' in the Free World." At one point, I looked up at the big video screen, and I saw a shot of Darius Rucker and Bruce Springsteen sharing a microphone. And I thought, man, *that* displays the dreamlike aspect of 1995 better than any words.

There was one more high-profile event left, and this one was the strangest of the lot.

On November 19, 1995, a literal galaxy of stars gathered at the Shrine Auditorium in Los Angeles to pay tribute to Frank Sinatra on his eightieth birthday. The event was going to be broadcast as a primetime special on CBS, produced by one of the legendary names in television production, George Schlatter. Among the artists honoring Sinatra that evening (either in speech or by performing one of the songs he made famous) were Tony Bennett, Bono, Ray Charles, Natalie Cole, Johnny Depp, Bob Dylan, Steve Lawrence and Eydie Gormé, Little Richard, Gregory Peck, Salt-N-Pepa, Arnold Schwarzenegger, Seal, Tom Selleck, Bruce Springsteen, Don Rickles . . . and Hootie & the Blowfish.

For the evening, Hootie had worked up a fairly straightforward arrangement of one of Sinatra's trademark songs, "The Lady Is a Tramp." They would be accompanied by a full big band.

Darius (dressed in full suit and fedora, as the whole band was) took "The Lady Is a Tramp" by the teeth and made it a monument to his personal love for Sinatra, and to his own ability to play ball in the biggest of big leagues. Performing with complete confidence and composure (and singing with a near-exact enunciation rarely heard on any Hootie & the Blowfish track), Darius not only owned the moment, but likely, the evening. Of all the times I have seen Darius perform in extraordinary public settings—special guest shots with other artists, national anthems, historic nights at the Opry—I have never seen a moment where Darius so totally slam-dunked an opportunity.

The producers had situated the aging Sinatra and his wife, somewhat awkwardly, at a stage-side table. During almost all of the evening's acts, the great man had sat stone-faced, looking disinterested at best, feeble at worst. But while Darius and Hootie were doing "The Lady Is a Tramp," the cutaways of Sinatra show him beaming, clapping his hands, snapping his fingers, and grinning with joy and approval. It was virtually the only moment of the long evening when Sinatra came alive. When they finished, the audience roared with happiness and surprise, and the band, especially Darius, were almost limp with relief that they had gotten through the number. I honestly believe Darius could have walked off stage that night and gotten himself a variety show on CBS.

But we all had something else on our mind. The band was already recording their next album. By deciding to go into the recording studio in the fall of 1995, Hootie were, well, just being Hootie. Even though they were at the top of the charts, the band still followed the models set by their college rock heroes. And what these bands had done—The Replacements, early R.E.M., The Connells, The Reivers, Cowboy Mouth—was live in an endless cycle of stage, van, studio, stage, van, studio, stage, van, studio. That's what Hootie & the Blowfish thought being in a band was all about, and why should being the biggest band in America change that? In addition, Hootie & the Blowfish were tired of *cracked rear view*, tired of playing the same songs they had played for Dick Hodgin and Rusty back in 1990.

But even if Soni, Mark, Darius, and Dean might have been growing tired of *cracked rear view*, America wasn't. During the 1995 holiday season, *cracked rear view* was selling a quarter of a million copies a week. This was not something *any* of us could have predicted eighteen months earlier. It had not been within the realm of our imagination. It was like we had entered an alternate universe where the good guys won.

-25-

TO BE *THRILLER*, OR NOT TO BE *THRILLER*?

1996 was a very strange year for Hootie & the Blowfish. They released a new album that went straight to no. 1. It became one of the biggest selling albums of the year. Yet it was also a year that revealed cracks in the foundation that had built the band, and even larger fractures in their relationship with Atlantic Records.

What happens when you lose control of your dreams, not to failure but to success? When a group achieves enormous popularity, there comes a moment when your band no longer belongs to you but belongs to the people who have made your music the soundtrack to their memories. Audiences can become very possessive of a gigantic record. If you have done your job very well, listeners won't just hear your song; they will remember exactly when they heard it at a very special moment in their life. They will remember one perfect moment, or that one incredible summer, when *your* music was always in the air.

All songs are about place and time. They start out being about the composer and performer's place and time. But when these same songs start being about someone else's place and time, when they become a place keeper, a mnemonic for a place and time in the listener's life, then they stop belonging to the artist. By the end of 1995—and far, far beyond—*cracked rear view* had become a mnemonic for the memories of millions of people. It was forever wedded to a million first kisses, last goodbyes, moments of tequila-fueled madness, car rides to the beach the week before school ended, the first friend made in a new place the week school began.

Usually, when an album becomes a part of the culture—that is, something that is wedded to our memories and our experiences—that release comes fairly deep in an artist's career. *Rumours* was Fleetwood Mac's eleventh album. AC/DC's *Back in Black* was their seventh LP. Even *Born to Run* is Springsteen's third album. Oh, and the R.E.M. album with "The One I Love" is their fifth album ("Losing My Religion" doesn't appear until album seven, *Out of Time*). But Hootie & the Blowfish arrived at that place very quickly. They were just one album into their career, and they already had made a record that was a *part of the culture*. And as 1995 ended and 1996 began, there were many who felt that *cracked rear view* still had plenty of history to make.

Every major record label is known for doing one thing better than another. This was especially true in the 1990s, the last years before the big mergers and the streaming revolution entirely changed the function and character of the major labels. Atlantic was known for a few things; most notably, being very radio driven and very political. It was also known for this peculiar trait: It didn't do "blockbusters." A blockbuster is a record that sells a lot and keeps on selling. Then it sells some more. It's a record that you bought twice because you lost your copy when you moved back home after sophomore year. And then you bought it again, because you wanted it on CD. Think of those albums *everyone* had growing up, regardless of musical taste. Think of those albums you kept on getting for Christmas or Hanukkah, because it was the one album your aunt or your grandmother knew about. Michael Jackson's *Thriller*. Fleetwood Mac's *Rumours*. The first Boston album. Pink Floyd's *The Dark Side of the Moon*. The Eagles' *Greatest Hits*. *Frampton Comes Alive*. Remember those albums that *everyone* had, even those kids who didn't really pay attention to music? That's what a blockbuster is. *Bat Out of Hell*. *Nevermind*. The *Titanic* soundtrack.

Because Atlantic was a radio-driven label and generally halted promotion of an album once the single started winding down, building blockbusters wasn't necessarily in its DNA. Certainly, Atlantic in the 1990s had records that hit and hit big—Stone Temple Pilots, Brandy, Collective Soul, Jewel—but a *blockbuster*, the kind of record that sells five, eight, ten million? Atlantic hadn't had one of those since Phil Collins's *No Jacket Required* in 1985 and, before that, AC/DC's *Back in Black* in 1980.

"When *cracked rear view* had sold a million copies, everyone wanted to pull the plug," remembers Val Azzoli, who had been promoted from within the company to replace Danny Goldberg as Atlantic's president in mid-1995. "In those days Atlantic was all hit-song driven. And I kept saying, 'There's more songs on this record.' Then we were at *two* million records and I remember everybody wanted to pull the plug *again* and move onto something else and I said, 'No, let's work on this. Why can't we sell five million records?' And then we started doing television advertising, and every time we did a television advertisement, we'd sell a hundred thousand records. Then, we were like, oh my God, we're at five fucking million records. [laughs] And then I started to realize, not to get too technical here, but the incremental cost of selling a record once you're at five million is considerably smaller than selling it when you're at five hundred thousand. So we're up to four, five million records, and [head of radio promotion] Andrea Ganis started putting out more singles and then *they* started happening, and *then* I thought, why can't we sell it in bookstores? Why can't we sell it in Starbucks? Why can't we sell it in supermarkets? This aspect of retail was just beginning to open up in the early and mid-1990s. So we started doing *that*, and then it became clear that *cracked rear view* might be able to go to *really* historic places."

So Atlantic was thinking: *cracked rear view* might be a true blockbuster.

In the second week of January 1996, "Time," the fourth single from *cracked rear view*, peaked at a very respectable no. 14 and pushed the album back up to no. 4 in the charts. Executives at Atlantic Records in New York were beginning to have some remarkable thoughts about *cracked rear view*. Eighty weeks after the album's release, the album was at no. 4, and there was literally no sign that this thing was slowing down. They started thinking, What if they released a fifth single, a sixth single, maybe even a seventh single, and made this thing into *Thriller*? After all, there were seven singles released from *Thriller*. Meatloaf released five singles from *Bat out of Hell*. There were seven singles from Springsteen's *Born to Run*, and nine from *Purple Rain* by Prince. You only had to *listen* to *cracked rear view* to know that you could keep on going after "Time": "Drowning," "Hannah Jane," "Goodbye," any one of these (and more) could have been issued as singles, and goddamn good ones.

Atlantic's confidence in the potential for *cracked rear view* was underlined by a night of triumph in February of 1996.

The Shrine Auditorium is a squat, enormous, dusty old pile of Moorish domes and arches situated in South Central Los Angeles, a stone's throw from the campus of the "other USC," the University of Southern California. Erected in 1926, the Shrine looks like an armory built by someone who wanted to impress a cousin of an Ottoman emperor. The Shrine seats sixty-five hundred people, and until relatively recently, it was the home to a many of the major Los Angeles-based awards shows, including the thirty-eighth annual Grammy Awards, which took place on February 28, 1996.

In 1996, the Grammy presentation and telecast was very different than what it would become. Today, the Grammys are a giant performance-based show, with a small handful of awards handed out somewhere amid the pyrotechnics, lasers, and elaborately staged performances. But back then, in the moldy old Shrine days, the show centered on the hopes, dreams, and disappointments of award nominees. Major and minor celebrities read names. Awards were handed out. Between the awards, some artists performed.

Hootie & the Blowfish were nominated for Grammys in two categories: Best New Artist and Best Pop Performance by a Duo or Group with Vocals. In the Best New Artist category, Hootie's competition was Shania Twain, Brandy, Alanis Morissette, and Joan Osbourne. In Best Pop Performance by a Duo or Group with Vocals, "Let Her Cry" would be up against "Waterfalls" by TLC, "I'll Be There for You" by The Rembrandts, "I Can Love You Like That" by All-4-One, and "Love Will Keep Us Alive" by the Eagles. I was not extremely optimistic about Hootie winning either of their categories, but we were determined to have a good time.

Hootie & the Blowfish won both of their categories.

Yet even at this high point of their career, there were many who still saw Hootie as the dullest form of mainstream entertainment.

This misplaced, formless resentment against Hootie was made painfully and visibly evident that night. During the band's live performance (which immediately preceded the announcement of the Best New Artist award), the sinister, glowing red mark of a laser pointer appeared on Darius's forehead. I knew enough from police procedural TV shows to guess that this could be the harbinger of something very bad indeed. This is a bangeroo of a story, and I'm going to let Rusty tell it.

Rusty Harmon: "I grew up idolizing KROQ [a major Los Angeles radio station, and a significant force in breaking alternative music in America]. So when we get to town to do the Grammys, I land and I'm in the limo, and I tell the guy to turn on KROQ. And the *first thing* I hear when the guy turns on KROQ is [morning show hosts] Kevin and Bean talking about a promotion they had been running about what would *you* do to screw up Hootie's performance at the Grammys if you had the chance."

"So," Rusty drawls, "they are getting all these people calling in and suggesting all these horrible ideas to screw up Hootie's performance. So I called Andrea Ganis immediately. I'm like, what *the hell* is this. Andrea, *This has got to stop*. I understand Andrea has to be very conscious of her relationship with the station—she has other records she's trying to get on KROQ. So she was being fairly casual about this and she says 'I'll tell them to stop,' but I said 'NO. NO. No. You don't tell them to stop. This HAS got to stop, and I want a public apology.'"

"At that point I don't even want to speak to the head of KROQ, I want to speak to whoever runs the company that owns them. And Andrea pulls that off—yes, she does—so I speak to them, and they agree with everything I say, and they promise me a public apology, and I'm like, 'Okay, tell me when it's going to be on, I want to listen.' So they did it, I listened, and I figured it was over."

"So we rehearsed for the Grammy show all week, I'm hanging out, I get to be friends with everyone at the venue, I make buddies with the head of security. So it's show time, and during the band's performance, and I look up and there's that red dot, that red laser dot, on Darius's forehead."

"And the first thing I thought of," Rusty continues, "was, 'Oh my God, someone is getting ready to shoot Darius.' So I bolted around in my seat and started looking for it, and then the laser beam hits me dead smack in my eyes. In the middle of the band performing—and they are about to be given an award for Best New Artist, from Kiss and Tupac, I mean what a *moment*—while all this is going on, I follow the laser beam, and there is a dude standing in the back. And when I am about ten feet away, he realizes I am walking right at him. And he slips whatever he's got—at this point, I still have to consider it might be a gun—into his pocket. So I told my friend Bob the security guard to have him arrested. They informed me they couldn't have him arrested, but they could escort him off the premises."

"So we win our two Grammys, and we party all night back at the Four Seasons and we're having a blast, and I am so fired up and happy I can't go to sleep, so I happen to turn on KROQ. The Kevin and Bean morning show is on. And Kevin starts telling this story. 'I'm at the Grammys last night, and I wanted to have a little fun, so I got my laser pointer out, and I got it pointed at Darius during their performance, you might have seen that on TV! When all of a sudden, the manager of Hootie & the Blowfish shows up, and he has me escorted out!'"

"*I went ballistic.* I got Andrea on the phone, she was pissed that I woke her up, and I said 'I don't care. Whatever this takes. Whatever has to happen. This ends right now.' So for about two hours, I'm on the phone with KROQ's owner, and the GM. They apologized again and may have suspended him for two weeks. The thing that bothered me the most is, at that moment when I could have been enjoying a long-earned triumphant moment for the band, I am in the lobby dicking around with Kevin of the Kevin and Bean Show."

Now back to our regularly scheduled 1996.

Shortly after the Grammys, in the first week of March 1996, I was in New York City, visiting the main Atlantic offices in the heart of Rockefeller Center. Atlantic President Val Azzoli had asked if he could meet with me. I walked into his large, extraordinarily well-paneled office and sat down across from him. He had an impressive row of baseballs in front of him. Some were signed and in neat Lucite cases. Others were free-range baseballs and sat guard at the front of his desk.

Val said he had something serious to talk to me about.

cracked rear view was still doing huge business, Val explained, tossing a baseball from hand to hand. We were "only" four singles in, and even if we shut down all promotion today, it was clear that we were going to do at least ten million sales with Hootie & the Blowfish's debut album. True, he continued, the band was already well into recording album number two, *but* . . . but what if we delayed its release until 1997? If we delayed album number two, he said, we could easily go to singles five and six on *cracked rear view*, then around Christmastime '96 maybe even put out a seventh or an eighth and push this thing to twenty-five million.

That's right, Tim, Val asserted: twenty-five million.

I'll admit, it was a fascinating idea. The walls of Val's office seemed to glow with gold, even though it was just the wood paneling (oh, so very much of it). And it certainly appealed to my ego. So, I thought, why not? Why not just keep going with *cracked rear view*?

I explained to Val that I was under the distinct impression that the band was chomping at the bit to record and release new material and that they had made Atlantic so much money—I believe I said they had "kept the lights on," which wasn't much of an exaggeration—that we owed it to the band to let them do what they wanted. It wasn't as much of an "artist knows best" argument as it was a "this artist has earned the right to do whatever the hell they want" argument.

Nevertheless, Val deputized me to go up to the studio in northern California where they were recording album number two and speak to them about delaying the release.

The band was recording at a sprawling residential studio in Marin County called The Site Recording. I flew up to San Francisco. I did not know that the Oakland airport was closer. I rented a car. I fumbled with the directions my assistant had printed out for me. I pointed the car up US-101 North. I then fumbled with the instructions once more. I found the all-news radio station. I put it on and started driving. All-news radio is my spirit animal. I continued to fumble with the directions my assistant had printed out for me, and took a PayDay bar out of the inside pocket of my jean jacket, and I fumbled with that. I drove pretty deep into the hills of Marin County and then took a left up an imposingly long, narrow, and steep road. I thought about how I was not the kind of guy who was going to be comfortable telling the members of a band that they shouldn't be making the record they apparently very much wanted to make, and how my presentation was going to be half-hearted at best. I thought about how I didn't want to make the drive back down the hill to my room at the Embassy Suites in the dark. At the top of a great pile of green and stone, I found The Site.

I walked in. Dean was playing, so help me God, a bass fishing video game. Without looking up he said to me, "This is no more interesting than actual bass fishing. That is what's so interesting about it." This was an extremely Dean Felber-ish thing to say.

Mark was listening to R.E.M.'s debut album, "*Murmur.*"

Soni was studying the board in the recording studio, intently watching the relationship between the knobs, levers, lights, and the sound they conjured.

Don Gehman smiled at me in that way Don Gehman has of smiling that is not a smile at all. Don could look at you, smile, and you would know, without him saying anything, "We ought to be worried. Really, really worried."

Darius was nowhere to be found, but was summoned relatively quickly, from some unused vocal booth that he had turned into a combination chillout spot and hookah cafe.

Hootie & the Blowfish were now sitting in front of me, on the plush, buttery, leathery studio couches that announce, "You, my friend, are in a high-end recording studio." I explained to the band that history was knocking. That Atlantic felt they could make *cracked rear view* the biggest selling rock album at time of release in history. That if they didn't have to worry about another album coming down the pipe, Atlantic could work a fifth, sixth, maybe even a seventh or eighth single, all (more or less) while the boys were sitting at home playing Madden or smoking weed and drinking on the beach in Bermuda.

That is what I said.

Hootie & the Blowfish said no.

It wasn't a very long conversation, and Mark did most of the talking. The whole thing lasted less than five minutes. Mark then showed me some new guitars, and after that, Dean and I rummaged for something to eat.

Because they spoke with one voice on that late afternoon in March 1996, I had always assumed that this crucial decision to go ahead with recording and releasing the second Hootie & the Blowfish album was a unified, relatively easy decision. It turns out that wasn't the case.

"There was most certainly an inner battle within the band about that," says Dean Felber, twenty-four years later. "We had already played our chips with Mark to get him to wait even *that* long. He wanted to go into the studio before we had even finished the big 1995 summer tour. Rusty kept him at bay, but we still had big—*really big*—arguments about it. I certainly felt it was a good idea to give it a little more time, but look, we *lived* on the road, so we didn't know anything but touring, going in the studio, and touring."

Although Dean disagreed with Mark, he hints that if Hootie had hit pause on album two and worked *cracked rear view* even deeper into the history books, it might have had a negative effect on the band. "Part of me thought, hey, I'd love to go to the South of France for a year and figure life out, but the other side of that was, *would we be any good at that?* None of us had stopped moving, not for ten years, so would taking a break have been a good thing or a bad thing? In the abstract, I know it would have been a good thing for us to have taken some time off and delayed the second album, I just don't know what waiting would have caused. *There would have been a price.* Part of me thinks it would have been a *good* price to pay, and part of me thinks it would have been tumultuous, since you have to understand there were people who were vastly against us taking a break. A true break from the band at that point could have broken the band up. If we had stuck to our guns, it could have gotten very ugly. Let's put it this way: No one felt *that* strongly about taking a break, but Mark in particular felt *very* strongly about not taking a break."

Had Val or I "stepped in a bit more aggressively," Dean said, "it might have swayed things. Who knows?"

I told Darius that, after all these years, I was extremely surprised to hear that the band was having the same second thoughts about the timing of the second album as we were. Why didn't I have any clue about this?

"Because Rusty wouldn't give you that information," states Darius, firmly. "Rusty wouldn't tell you guys that. Rusty didn't want to see it, Rusty didn't want to hear about it, Rusty didn't want to talk about it. At that time, our lives were not about 'What's best for these guys.' It wasn't about, 'Let's look at these four guys and see what's best for them and their future, as artists and human beings.' It was about how can we sell more records and put more asses in the seats, and that's *all* it was about. That's *all* that mattered. 'I don't want to hear that you're fucking tired—get in the bus.'"

"We should have taken a year off," Darius continues, "not toured, let Atlantic work two more singles like they wanted to, *then* sit around for another six months or a year and *then* say, 'Hey, we are putting out a new record.' I look back on that and I say, without any doubt, that we put the second record out too early."

Dean Felber: "There were some times where I wish someone had intervened, or that someone like you [Tim] or Rusty had sat us down and been more straight with us. A lot of times we had good advice and made good decisions; other times, we had good advice but still made bad decisions. I think this is one of the prices we paid for being a counterintuitive success: There is no script for it as it becomes big, because there was no script for it to begin with. The industry and the label were so wrong about everything having to do with Hootie & the Blowfish and *cracked rear view*. So how were we to be sure what was the right advice?"

Soni, also, has spent a great deal of time considering the crucial timing of the second album. "I have looked back and imagined rearranging the order we did things, imagined inserting a year's vacation in that spot and delaying the second album for a year, I have tried this many different ways with many different outcomes. But the truth is we had to release an album *then*. For our hearts, for our sanity, for our souls, we had to do it then, and I don't regret one bit about how we did it. Period. End of sentence. *But* [laughs], the fact is, if someone at the label we trusted—whether it was you or Kim or anybody—would have said, I am in charge of your careers, we will not be putting out a Hootie record until 1997 or '98—I think we would have said okay. It would have made more sense as a business plan, but as you know, Hootie & the Blowfish were not formed for business reasons, and we did not write songs for business reasons, *ever.*"

Finally, let's hear from Rusty. Rusty—did we put out the second album too soon?

Rusty Harmon takes a deep breath and waits nearly thirty seconds before responding. "I have asked myself this question a lot, and I have never found quite the right answer. I feel in the organization, to a man, we all felt that *cracked rear view* had run its course. *But it wouldn't go away.* I tend to feel that America, at that time, was sick of Hootie & the Blowfish. Hell, we were sick of Hootie & the Blowfish. We had four singles out, we had been on the cover of everything, we had done every conceivable TV show, we had toured the world, we had done everything we had ever wanted to do or imagined we could do. And frankly, to a man, I don't think any of us had any idea what to do next. Nobody in our organization, and no one we were working with at the record label, had ever been through something like this before. But we *knew* we had a lot more music in us. We *knew* we had more records to make. I think we felt that the best way to *end cracked rear view* was to put something else out."

My perspective was simple. At a time when Atlantic Records needed an infusion of cash and commercial prestige, Hootie & the Blowfish and *cracked rear view* had supplied both. In addition, the band had been a label's dream: They had shaken every hand and done it with a smile—again, and again, and again. The label would have had a hard time inventing a more cooperative or more successful act. In return for all this, I believed Atlantic should allow Hootie to record what they wanted, when they wanted. The mistake I made—and Don Gehman, Kim Kaiman, and Evan Lamberg made the same error, too—was in thinking that the band was approaching the decision to record the second album so "soon" in a unified, certain way. In fact, there were many holes in their unity, and in reflection, we should have investigated further.

26

NOT ALLOWED TO BE DONE

Hootie & the Blowfish's debut album, *cracked rear view*, was recorded and mixed in eighteen days by a band who rarely left each other's side and who acted, at every moment, like lifelong best friends.

The process of recording the second album could not have been more different. I visited the Site Recording studio frequently throughout the long slog of the making of *Fairweather Johnson*, and it was constantly evident how different things were. The band members did not seem to be communicating on any regular or functional basis. Instead, they appeared to be focusing on their own parts, their own songs, their own video games, their own brand new, high-priced instruments. Most significantly, they—at least Dean, Mark, and Soni—were writing material in the studio, something that could not be further away from the tight collection of finished songs the group brought into *cracked rear view*. No one seemed to be having a particularly good time, and *a lot* of weed was being consumed (even by Hootie & the Blowfish standards). Perhaps, most noticeably, Darius's interaction with the rest of the band seemed to be minimal, at best. I distinctly recall that he would surface in earnest—as opposed to merely making cameo appearances—just one day a week, when he would attack the role of recording vocals with a diligent, mostly joyless, business-like approach. Attempts to get him in front of the microphone any more frequently would usually result in slurred, incomplete, lifeless performances.

Darius Rucker: "We were as close to breaking up as we ever, ever have been. The other guys act like they don't remember it. But I was miserable. I did not want to be in Hootie & the Blowfish. When we first went to the Site to start making that record, and of course it's a residential studio with a lot of beautiful little houses and luxurious bedrooms, I rented a hotel room in San Francisco. My plan was to stay in the hotel in San Francisco, with the intention that I would just drive to the studio when they needed me. So the first day I drove in, and I just didn't want to be there. And we have a meeting on that first day, and Don is talking to me, and he pulls me aside. Don says, 'Man, we cannot make this record if it's going to be like this.' And I said, 'What are you talking about?' and he says, 'It is so obvious you don't want to be here.' And I said, 'You're right, I don't want to be here.' So Don said to me, 'Man, you need to go get stoned or something, because we have *got* to make this record' [laughs]."

"So we made the record," Darius continues. "But I did *not* want to be there. I was *tired*. We were *never* stopping. I had just had a kid. Cary was six months old. We were working all the friggin' time, and we were all worn out, and I was just *done*, but I wasn't allowed to be done. It's like, 'I'm saying I'm done, people!' and no one is hearing me, they're going, *no, we've got to work*."

Don Gehman adds his perspective. "It was obvious to me then that we were in trouble and that there was just no real interest in all four of them doing things together. Also, Darius was smoking a *lot* of pot at that time, since he had gone from drinking to smoking pot, because he was having trouble with his stomach, I believe. And so he was stoned out of his mind a great deal of the time. And the stuff he was writing . . . it was just nonsensical. It didn't connect. Darius was becoming more and more disconnected from the band. And everybody had lost the craft of what they had done so well before, of melody and lyric. The previous material really made sense. And now all of a sudden they were going to this place that was . . . these were not good songs."

"There's a lot to say about *Fairweather Johnson*," Soni says. "It's . . . uh . . . *different*. Going into the album, we faced a relatively big problem. We all wanted to start a new record, but we were aware that we already had a considerable handful of songs that had been tested in front of audiences and hadn't made *cracked rear view*. We were aware that we had this existing quality material that might get passed over because we were so hungry to write and record brand new music. We had a lot of deep discussions and arguments about this. We had songs like 'If You're Going My Way,' which had been very popular with audiences in 1992 and '93, we had 'Sorry's Not Enough' from *Kootchypop*, which audiences really liked. These songs had all passed the audience test, if you will. 'Old Man & Me (When I Get to Heaven) [as titled on *Fairweather Johnson*],' of course, was in the same category."

Darius weighed in on the fact that the band used only one of their older, audience-tested songs, "Old Man & Me (When I Get to Heaven)," on *Fairweather Johnson*. "That's something, I think, we all look back on and think was an error. We should have really looked at the older songs we left off *cracked rear view*. We should have at least *tried* to record them for *Fairweather*. But we were kids, we were stubborn, we thought we were artsy, and those songs were *old* . . . but we absolutely should have."

In many ways, *Fairweather Johnson* doesn't necessarily *feel* like a second album (or the follow-up to a mega-successful debut). With its eclectic mix of styles, odd little asides and experiments, handful of numbers that 100 percent hit the target, and instrumental and vocal performances that range from intense and adventurous to obligatory and detached, in many ways *Fairweather Johnson* feels like a fourth or fifth album from an established (and perhaps fractured) band. *Fairweather Johnson* takes you on quite a little voyage: From the almost Zep-ish "Honeyscrew" to the bouncing, neo-ska/beach music of "She Crawls Away"; from the early R.E.M. meets Cheap Trick hyperpop of "Sad Caper" and "Silly Little Pop Song" to the impassioned, melancholy sobs of the album's four deep, stoned, late-night ballads.

I think this sums up my personal assessment of *Fairweather Johnson:* Because of how diverse and inconsistent it is, it feels so much like a double album that, to this day, I sometimes mistakenly refer to it is as such. Now, that is not to say that *Fairweather Johnson* isn't full of muscle, heart, joy, and meaning.

"Tucker's Town," gentle yet firm, like a bittersweet dream on a beach with a college-rock arpeggio guitar leading us in and out of the dunes, is one of the handful of Hootie & the Blowfish songs that deal explicitly with race and the struggles of being an African American in the United States. Specifically, it addresses how no one in Tucker's

Town, Bermuda, assumes that Darius is going to "hurt the population" just because of the color of his skin. In some ways, it echoes a theme expressed on "I Don't Understand," released on the band's first cassette in 1990. Likewise, "Old Man & Me (When I Get to Heaven)" also explicitly addresses prejudice, touching on the deeply divisive fact that African Americans who fought in two world wars, Korea, and Vietnam were still prevented by Jim Crow from voting in their native South.

The album is filled with odd little in-jokes, deliberately ambiguous titles, and songs that make stylistic left and right turns from Hootie's wheelhouse—all the things artists do when they are struggling with their own high visibility—but it is also filled with some gems. "Silly Little Pop Song" (based on a very early Hootie original called "Kiss Me") is one of the most R.E.M.-ish pieces the band has ever recorded. It's a terrific reminder that if Hootie had never achieved great pinnacles of success, they would have been a *very* credible college rock band in Bongos/Toad the Wet Sprocket/Neats mode. "Earth Stopped Cold at Dawn," a powerful song about a death in Mark's family, has an insanely catchy chorus and guitar hook, and would have fit in perfectly on *cracked rear view*. Although the album is plagued by songs that were not fully fleshed out and vetted in pre-production, the album closer "When I'm Lonely" proves that this technique could sometimes lead to great results. Written entirely in the studio and with the lazy yet deep feel of a track by the Grateful Dead or The Band, "When I'm Lonely" is rich, warm, loose, and heartfelt, and a wonderful showcase for organist John Nau.

I should also note that one of my favorite songs from the *Fairweather* sessions was left off the album, and in many ways, this omission reveals the fault lines that ran through the whole project. During the basic tracking part of the session, the band cut a big, cinematic, weepy, mid-tempo Mark Bryan song called "City by a River." I was bloody certain it was a flat-out big, fat Hootie & the Blowfish light-yer-lighters and wave-yer-hands-in-the-air hit. As the *Fairweather* sessions evolved into a series of fascinating digressions and passionately felt neo-soul ballads punctuated by some brilliant light pop, it became more and more clear to me that "City by a River" was exactly what the album needed. I personally thought it could be the difference between a big seller and a really big seller.

But Darius had no affection for "City by a River." He never even completed a vocal take on it, mumbling his way through about two thirds of a couple of takes before giving up. The inability to finish "City by a River" reflects a number of the sessions' consistent problems, notably Darius's reaction to and rejection of the more blatantly pop side of Hootie & the Blowfish and the inability of the band to communicate well enough to act in their own best commercial interest. Eventually, the band would come to terms with these issues and come together to create a truly smashing, diverse and fully rounded third album; but a lot would happen between 1996 and 1998. (By the way, "City by a River" did eventually see the light of day. Mark cut a fine version on his 2000 solo album, *30 on the Rail*. And in 2002, Hootie, accompanied by a big ol' gospel choir and the considerable talents of BeBe and CeCe Winans, finally did a full-band version that appeared on a somewhat obscure soundtrack project, *Music From and Inspired by Jesus: the Epic Mini-Series*. Go listen to it, now. Tell me it isn't exactly the kind of song that wouldn't have pushed *Fairweather Johnson* completely over the top.)

Before the second album was even in the can, yet another factor affected Hootie & the Blowfish's relationship with the marketplace and desperately complicated the already contentious discussion about the timing of the release of album two. Remarkably, this element was completely out of the control of the band, Rusty, Gus, and even Atlantic.

In early March of 1996, despite that *cracked rear view* was *still* hanging around at no. 10 in the album charts, we planned on giving the oversaturated marketplace a tiny little break from Hootie in anticipation of the late April release of album number two. Let's at least give them six or eight weeks without a new single, we thought. But these plans were ruined when a competing label—Warner Bros—released "I Go Blind" as a single.

How did such a thing happen?

The author raises his left hand slightly above his desk and waves his coffee-stained fingers. "My bad!" he says, meekly.

And I would do it again.

In early 1995, Danny Goldberg had left Atlantic and become president of Warner Bros. Records. In mid-1995, Danny called me and said that Warner Bros. was assembling a soundtrack to accompany the TV show *Friends*. Danny asked me if there might be a Hootie song lying around that they could have for the *Friends* album. Not only had Danny Goldberg hired me, but he had also been enormously supportive of Hootie & the Blowfish. Because of Danny's faith in me and in Hootie, back in 1994, I had been able to override Jason Flom's verdict and release *cracked rear view*. So I did not hesitate for one second when Danny Goldberg asked me for this favor. Since "I Go Blind" had been left off of *cracked rear view*, it seemed like an obvious—and at the time, completely uncontroversial—choice to give to Danny.

"I Go Blind," released on Warner Bros., was an enormous hit on radio. It was also featured prominently in an episode of *Friends* ("The One with Five Steaks and an Eggplant," season 2, episode 5, originally aired October 19, 1995). To complicate things, the last single from *cracked rear view*, "Time," performed far better than expected, so *both* "I Go Blind" and "Time" were still kicking around at radio in April of 1996, when "Old Man & Me (When I Get to Heaven)," the first single from *Fairweather Johnson*, was released. Hootie & the Blowfish were not only overexposed. They were competing with themselves.

27

THOU SHALL NOT DISTURB
THE FLOW OF COMMERCE

Fairweather Johnson was released on April 23, 1996. It entered the *Billboard* charts at no. 1, replacing another mega-seller of the mid-1990s, Alanis Morissette's *Jagged Little Pill*. *Fairweather* also sold four hundred thousand copies in its first week, an extremely impressive number. That very same week, *cracked rear view* was at no. 21 in *Billboard*. There was probably no time when Hootie & the Blowfish were more visible in America's consciousness than these weeks in late April and early May 1996. The band had two hit albums, three visible and active singles, a full slate of talk show appearances, and a pile of other tracks still bopping around on radio and MTV/VH-1 almost constantly. The band was everywhere, an almost constant grace note in the American experience, in a way that so very, very few pop artists ever achieve.

Fairweather Johnson stayed in *Billboard*'s top spot for weeks, helped, no doubt, by the visibility of a massive concert on the University of South Carolina campus, broadcast frequently on MTV, filmed on April 16, 1996. It was to be a triumphant evening for the band and a celebration of local boys made good. It would also mark the first time in over six years that former drummer Brantley Smith appeared on stage with group, albeit just as a cellist in a string quartet.

Something else came along with being the biggest band in America: a backlash of enormous proportions. This was to be expected. To the vast majority of American music fans, Hootie had come out of virtually nowhere, and within a remarkably short space of time, they were *everywhere*. The reality of who Hootie & the Blowfish were, how long they had toiled, and the credible influences that actually formed them barely mattered to these naysayers. If you didn't know about the band's deep college roots and the pointed lyrics about race tucked within some of their most famous songs, you might believe that Hootie & the Blowfish was some corporate plot to invent the anti-Nirvana.

"Death to Hootie!" Trent Reznor of Nine Inch Nails proclaimed in the pages of *Rolling Stone* magazine. Reznor's big problem with Hootie, according to the same interview, was that they were "safe" and "legitimate." Around this same time, Marilyn Manson said that, "Blaming me for what my fans do is like blaming Hootie and the Blowfish for making your life completely boring."

I *get* it. As someone who grew up treating anything mainstream with aversion and suspicion, I understand why your average, alternative-inclined fan might have a negative reaction to anything as popular and as visible as Hootie & the Blowfish were in 1995, '96, and '97. True, most of America didn't know the band as well as I did. My insider knowledge allowed me to know that Hootie & the Blowfish were more creatively honest and emotionally and politically complicated than 99 percent of the people who criticized them.

Shortly after the release of *Fairweather Johnson*, an event occurred that served as a major focal point for people's resentment at Hootie's mainstream status. This came in the form of a loud and public donnybrook inside—and outside—the pages of *Rolling Stone* magazine.

Today, Jim DeRogatis is one of the most respected music journalists in America. He is largely credited with breaking the story about the profound sex abuse committed by rapper R. Kelly in a series of piece in the *Chicago Sun Times*, in late 2000, and he has a long history of articulate and important support of groundbreaking alternative acts. In 1996, DeRogatis was a well-liked senior editor at *Rolling Stone* magazine. He explained to me that when *Fairweather Johnson* was released, no one at *Rolling Stone* wanted to review it, even before anyone had heard the album. According to DeRogatis, this was because every writer and editor believed that, with *Rolling Stone*, there was no room for genuine subjectivity, actual commentary, or critical nuance when talking about an artist as successful as Hootie & the Blowfish.

"Thou shall not disturb the flow of commerce," DeRogatis says, describing what was perceived as the prevalent philosophy of *Rolling Stone*'s record review section at the time. "Now, you can give a bad review to the Melvins' record or any number of other albums that aren't big sellers, but you could *not* give a bad review to something that's selling. So no one wanted to do the Hootie record."

When every journalist he reached out to turned him down, DeRogatis decided to handle it himself. DeRogatis handed in a fairly deep, witty, negative-leaning (but not *too* negative) review of *Fairweather Johnson*, with a few choice barbs directed at the mainstream appeal of the band. Undeniably, the review had an overall snarky tone. DeRogatis said that Darius Rucker sounded like "Eddie Vedder imitating Otis Redding" and the lyrics "reek of Hallmark-card sentimentality" and asserted that Peter Holsapple only joined the band for the health insurance. True, DeRogatis does get in some funny slams (for instance, insinuating that Hootie fans consider "Bud Lite a psychedelic drug"); but by consistently comparing Hootie to a respected and long-lasting outfit like the Grateful Dead (something DeRogatis does throughout the review), he at least accords them a certain amount of respect.

When he saw the review, Jann Wenner, the legendary founder and editor-in-chief of *Rolling Stone*, completely flipped out. He refused to run DeRogatis's piece and immediately replaced it with a far less interesting review by Elysa Gardner (which, curiously, wasn't that much more positive; I have read both reviews and say, without any doubt, that DeRogatis's initial review would have made me *more* interested in hearing *Fairweather Johnson* than the second, supposedly more positive review). That would have probably been that, except that in the immediate wake of his rejected review of *Fairweather Johnson*, Jann Wenner fired Jim DeRogatis, a journalist who was much admired by the hipster music community. DeRogatis almost certainly wasn't fired because he wrote a negative review of Hootie but because he talked to the media about it. However, at the time, the perception was that he was fired *because* he wrote the negative review. You can imagine how this was fodder for the Hootie haters.

Jim DeRogatis tries to set the story straight: "Wenner blows a gasket and pulls it out of the magazine, and now people are shouting censorship. I get this call at home from this *New York Observer* reporter who says they're doing this story about the Hootie review being killed. And I say, firmly, 'I can't talk to you.' And the *Observer* reporter says, 'Well we have the whole story already, we just want a comment from you.' I say, again, 'I really can't talk to you.' And the *Observer* writer says, on the third attempt, 'Answer me one question. Is Jann Wenner a Hootie fan?' And I say, 'That son of a bitch is a fan of anything that sells eight-and-a-half million copies.' And now *that's* in bold as a pull quote in the *Observer*."

When DeRogatis got to work the next Monday morning, he found that his desk was packed and he had been fired. The media had a field day with all this: A popular and hip journalist is fired (ostensibly) for writing a negative review of Hootie & the Blowfish (even if he actually was fired for slagging Jann Wenner in the press). For much of the world, this cemented the narrative that Hootie somehow represented the pro-establishment, anti-progressive interests of mainstream America. For decades after this, there was still the vague yet persuasive smoke of the idea that Big Brother Hootie had gotten cool Daddy-o Jim DeRogatis fired.

-28-

THE RIDE WAS GOING TO END

On July 8, 1996, two years and three days after the release of *cracked rear view*, Hootie & the Blowfish started the American tour to promote their second album, *Fairweather Johnson*.

When they had left for a European tour back in April, *Fairweather Johnson* had been no. 1 on the *Billboard* charts. When they returned and kicked off the U.S. tour in Noblesville, Indiana (with John Hiatt, who, of course, had provided the name for *cracked rear view*, as a support act), the album had fallen to no. 9 in the charts. Only a week later, on July 13, 1996, for the first time in 17 months (!), there was no Hootie & the Blowfish album in *Billboard*'s Top 10 (*Fairweather Johnson* had dropped to no. 13, and *cracked rear view* was at no. 55).

From there, the new album fell precipitously. Even though Hootie & the Blowfish were barely a few weeks past their absolute peak of exposure and popularity in the United States and they were about to embark on their biggest and longest tour yet, in the summer of 1996, all of the pieces were in place for the band's commercial decline:

- A record label that was rapidly losing interest in the band and that was actively disappointed by some of their choices.
- An almost comically oversaturated radio profile.
- A touring strategy that lacked long-term foresight about audience burn rate.
- A lack of interest (on the artists' part) in staging a more elaborate, engaging, or consistent live show that might inspire audience loyalty and anticipation about upcoming tours.

- An unwillingness by the band members and their organization to dig in and do what might be necessary to build a higher profile outside of the United States, in markets that could help sustain the band if the going got rocky in America.
- Four band members who had lost much of their initial spark of friendship and joy, and who profoundly needed a break.
- And last but certainly not least, a manager who did not have the insight to plan for icebergs that were not yet visible and who naively believed that a label that once loved the band would always love the band.

Although the truly negative effects of some of these factors weren't going to blossom for another two years, in the summer of 1996 they were already falling into place. It was certainly evident in the relatively rapid decline in the charts of *Fairweather Johnson*, which fell roughly five chart points a week for the rest of 1996.

Regardless of the errors made within the Hootie & the Blowfish organization and the inability or unwillingness of those closest to the band (specifically, Evan Lamberg, Don Gehman, Kim Kaiman, and myself) to confront potentially negative decision making, I maintain that the darkest cloud on the Hootie horizon was still the Atlantic factor. In an ideal world, one devoid of record company politics, Atlantic Records should have been taking better care of the act that had made the biggest selling album in the label's history. When I consider *why* that didn't happen, it really comes down to this: With the departure of Danny Goldberg in early 1995, there was no upper-tier executive at Atlantic who could look at Hootie & the Blowfish and say, "That is *my* baby, that happened on *my* watch, when they do good, I do good." Simple as that. Without that kind of protection, Hootie's future was always endangered. Circa 1996, among the executives jostling to take over the company, the fact is that not one of them would have their interests advanced by *Fairweather Johnson* succeeding.

If Hootie had delayed the release of their second album and pushed and pulled and promoted *cracked rear view* to the point of selling fifteen, eighteen, twenty, twenty-five million records, that likely would have been a different story. Val Azzoli, who was both a true fan of the band and a genuinely artist-friendly executive, would have been able to take credit for that burst in sales. He would have been able to say, "That album became a blockbuster on *my* watch." This would have given Val a sense of ownership in Hootie's success and given him a far greater incentive to protect and make a strategic investment in the band.

Product manager Kim Kaiman, who was more aware of the nuts and bolts of the band's changing status within the label than practically anyone: "I was scared because I know that the minute that Atlantic Records stopped feeling passionate about the band that they could bury them. I was worried that for all the success that they had, as soon as the band stopped cooperating with Atlantic and elongating the life of that first album, Atlantic could shut the spigot off and focus on something else, because that was the nature of record companies. And I was really frightened for them. I knew the ride was going to end."

Rusty Harmon acknowledges these issues but still wants to give us a much-appreciated reality check: "Let's not forget, *Fairweather* sold four million records—it sold four hundred thousand the first week. Yet people talk about it being a failure. It was the third or fourth best-selling album of the year. It wasn't a failure."

Hootie & the Blowfish toured extensively in support of *Fairweather Johnson*. The touring was done in three distinct legs: the United States, from early July through late September of 1996 (with Jolene, a sensitive, twanging, alt-country-meets-R.E.M. band, opening the first half, and Bela Fleck, the pioneering avant-bluegrass/fusion banjo player, supporting the second half). October and November were spent in Hawaii, Canada, and the Upper Midwest (They Might Be Giants supported most of these shows, with Speech, the progressive rapper from the group Arrested Development, opening the last two weeks).

Hootie then took the first few months of 1997 off and completed the *Fairweather Johnson* touring cycle in March and April of 1997, with their first-ever visit to Asia and Australia, performing in Hong Kong; Tokyo, Nagoya, and Osaka; Singapore; Bangkok; Kuala Lumpur; Jakarta; Manila; Christchurch and Wellington; and Melbourne,

Brisbane, and Sydney. Generally, in the Far East, the band performed in venues a little smaller than the ones they played in the United States but considerably larger than the places they played in Europe and the United Kingdom.

It was toward the end of the second leg of the *Fairweather* tour when I began to notice significant cracks in the organization. On November 22, 1996, I flew to British Columbia to see the band perform at the hockey arena in Vancouver, General Motors Place. *Fairweather Johnson* was flopping around the U.S. *Billboard* album charts in the 80s. The album's first three singles had performed fairly well, but only the first one, "Old Man & Me (When I Get to Heaven)," had made it into the *Billboard* Top 10 (the second single released from the album, the exquisite "Tucker's Town" peaked at no. 23). Make no mistake: the overall sales numbers for *Fairweather Johnson* were extremely impressive (unless you compared them to the once-in-a-lifetime performance of *cracked rear view*). The album had been a hit, by any reckoning. What worried me was what I saw on stage in Vancouver.

First of all, the arena was barely half full. Since Hootie were, for all intents and purposes, still riding the great, bucking pony that was their 1995 and '96 peak of visibility and success, this was a curious omen. The empty seats indicated one of three things (or a combination of all them): First, there was some essential flaw in the band's touring strategy. They were, likely, overtouring, or routing themselves badly. Second, they were choosing the wrong support acts (for the entire Atlantic era, Hootie picked their opening acts out of love, not with ticket sales in mind). Traditionally, a support act should be someone that is not only artistically and spiritually comparable with the headliner but who also can push some of those maybe-I-will/maybe-I-won't ticket buyers over the finish line. Speech, regardless of his extraordinary abilities and credibility, wasn't that sort of artist (and neither were John Hiatt, Jolene, Nanci Griffith, or Bela Fleck). Third, the band was not putting on a dynamic or consistent show that would encourage repeat ticket buyers.

But what I found most disturbing was Hootie's performance. The band, frankly, seemed to be half-assing it. They looked tired, dispirited, and, worst of all, predictable. At this point, Hootie & the

Blowfish were still not using setlists on stage; whereas this once led to a certain spontaneity, in late 1996 it seemed to give the show a hesitant, start-and-stop feel that greatly affected the show's momentum. Likewise, the band's lighting and video-screen program were lackluster, certainly not the kind of dynamic, engaged presentation you would expect to see in a successful arena act.

I knew that some of these factors could be due to the fact that I was seeing the group on an "off" night. But I also knew that, a year earlier, the band would never have had an "off" night. After the show, I asked Soni, Darius, Mark, and Dean if I could speak with them. We gathered in the back of one of the three buses that were being used to transport band and crew on this tour. Here's what I said:

"You have been doing this for *so* long—over ten years now. I understand that for you guys, and for Rusty, too, being in Hootie & the Blowfish, being *in a band*, is synonymous with playing shows. I think you guys think that's what it means to be in a band: It means climbing up on stage in any city that will have you. I mean, that's good and everything, but things are *different* now. You have to think of a definition of this band for the long term—and the short term—that isn't just about taking the gigs, getting in the bus, getting out of the bus, and staying on the road. Look at you guys. You don't even get hotel rooms most of the time, you just sleep on the bus, and move from town to town. I mean, that's okay, if you're Cowboy Mouth, or an oldies act, or someone who *needs* the gig income to stay afloat. But you're Hootie & the fucking Blowfish. You don't need to do that. Why don't you take a step back, and get off the road? You guys are millionaires living like hobos. Why not live like millionaires for a while?"

Twenty-four years after that conversation in Vancouver, Darius tells me, "You were absolutely right. That's what we thought a band was. A band goes and plays. They play every friggin' weekend. They play on Monday and Tuesday if they have to, but what they do is go out and play. Being in a band, we didn't feel there was any other option *but* to play. So that's what we did."

It was 1996, and Hootie & the Blowfish were still working from the Johnny Quest Playbook.

Another problem for the band was that Rusty Harmon was significantly distracted in the second half of 1996, and this was likely affecting some of the decision making. Some of that distraction came from Breaking Records, the label that the band had started with funding and distribution from Atlantic Records.

It is very common for a big-selling act to ask the parent company to fund and distribute their own label imprint. Frankly, these almost never succeed. But because of the fact that some of the very earliest of these artist–label partnerships—the Beatles' Apple and Led Zeppelin's Swan Song—were very high profile and yielded some successful artists, the idea has been passed down, from generation to generation of artists, that *they* should have their own label, too. Almost without fail, these boutique subsidiaries labels are drains on the band's attention and resources and the patience of the parent label.

Rusty, interestingly, doesn't exactly stand up and cheer for Breaking, even though he was the prime mover and shaker behind the enterprise. "It was a vanity label in every sense of the word," he says. "I sat with Val on a plane flying back from Detroit, and I looked at him and said, 'Val, we've been thinking about starting a label.' And he said, 'I'll do that, how much money do you need?' I said three million dollars. And he said, let's do it. It was a ninety-second conversation. That was that. There was no direction. I thought I knew what I was doing, but I didn't know the first thing about running a record label. I did not know *the first thing*. It was never going to succeed. And if any of the people we hired gave us good advice, we weren't listening. And I should have been paying more attention."

Breaking Records actually released some very good records, notably by Jump, Little Children from Winston-Salem, North Carolina, and Treehouse from Liverpool, England. Jump, Little Children played an artier, shimmering take on North Carolina jangle pop; they really are quite wonderful and sound, at times, like an exact cross between Radiohead and Toad the Wet Sprocket. The record they released on Breaking, *Magazine*, is something more people ought to be aware of. Treehouse took the chiming Hootie/Edwin McCain/Dillon Fence sound and gave it a distinctly northern English hyperpop feel, sort of like a cross between The dB's and Oasis. Both of these terrific artists deserved better, but virtually all boutique labels have the odds stacked against them.

1997 began on a sad but inevitable note: On January 18, 1997, *cracked rear view* finally dropped out of the *Billboard* chart of America's 200 best-selling albums, after a stunning 131 weeks on the chart. On March 8, 1997, *Fairweather Johnson* dropped out of the Top 200, after 44 weeks on the chart. For the first time since August 13, 1994—two years, six months, and 23 days—no Hootie & the Blowfish album was in the Top 200.

PART IV

1998-2003

The People They Lend Money To

MUSICAL CHAIRS

As 1998 dawned, enormous clouds, both personal and professional, loomed on Hootie's horizon. Yet at the beginning of the year, I distinctly recall thinking that their third album presented an opportunity for the band to make a focused piece of work which would recapture the vigor and melodic joy of *cracked rear view* while also incorporating their growth and diversity as humans and musicians.

The new songs that I heard (composed in dedicated writing sessions in Jackson Hole, Wyoming, and Phoenix, Arizona) seemed to indicate that they were on the right track. The group appeared to have moved past the understandable (but still, quite literally, sophomoric) problems that had plagued *Fairweather Johnson*, when the weight of success and expectation triggered the band to deliberately do something "different," lacking the natural bliss that marked *cracked rear view*. Also, unlike the *Fairweather* process, we did a concentrated pre-production period for album three, much like we had for album one. Dean, Soni, Darius, Mark, and I holed up at Rockafellas, one of the band's favorite venues in Columbia.

In a conscious effort to reproduce the efficiency of the *cracked rear view* sessions, Don Gehman and the band elected to record the album in relatively compact fashion at a studio in the San Fernando Valley section of Los Angeles (but we would be working at Royalton, not nearby NRG, where we had made *cracked rear view*). But there was a big difference between the 1998 sessions and the first Los Angeles recording session, almost exactly four years earlier: Back in the spring of 1994, Darius, Dean, Mark, and Soni had all piled into two bedrooms at the Valley Village complex in North Hollywood. This time, the band rented a glamorous, enormous mansion on Sunset Boulevard in Beverly Hills.

Hootie & the Blowfish's third LP ignores the deliberately quirky asides and self-conscious efforts to be "different" that plagued *Fairweather*. It is mature without being pretentious and expands the palette without going too far away from the expectations created by the millions who knew the band from *cracked rear view*. *Musical Chairs* picks up on the veins that built Hootie: college rock, the friendlier edges of classic rock, a love for big-ass melody that would encourage sing-along, and the roadhouse sincerity of Mellencamp/Springsteen, all while integrating the insights of a more mature band. Notably, it also dives repeatedly into bluegrass and southwestern-tinted folk, which the group embraced with simplicity and great happiness.

"When we made *Musical Chairs*, I thought it was amazing, and I still do," says Darius Rucker. "On *Musical Chairs*, we took our time writing, we took our time figuring out how the album was going to feel and sound . . . I love that record. We were listening to so much New Grass Revival and Nanci Griffith back then, so there's a lot of that on the record. *Musical Chairs* really is a precursor to where I am now."

Musical Chairs is straightforward but full of dynamics, dynamite, and depth, made by a band that sound like they love each other and love what they can do together. In many ways, it is the album that underlines Hootie's strengths and their claim to being both a classic American rock band and the forerunners of the commercial end of the Americana movement that erupted into modern country in the twenty-first century.

It also, undeniably, contains some of their strongest material. "I Will Wait," a vigorous, chiming rock song with echoes of both classic rock and '80s college rock, features music by Soni and Darius, with lyrics inspired by Darius's friend Rick Johannes, who had a family member in the military. "Wishing"—with both music and lyrics by Mark—also picks up on the blend between classic rock and college rock (in this sense, the album's first two tracks mine territory similar to what R.E.M. explored on their 1987 commercial breakthrough, *Document*).

"Only Lonely" is a classic, arm-waving Hootie ballad, and it should come as no surprise that it was composed and recorded to be an Oscar contender. It was originally written and cut for the Tom Hanks–Meg Ryan film *You've Got Mail*, and the lyrics were inspired by that movie's narrative. But it ended up being used in another film, the somewhat less successful *Message in a Bottle* (starring Kevin Costner and Robin Wright). David Campbell, a noted string arranger who also happens to be the father of the musician Beck, did the dramatic string arrangements on the track (we really went full-blown orchestra on this one, imagining the way it would look and sound when the band played it at the Academy Awards).

"Desert Mountain Showdown" may be one of Hootie's best bluegrass songs, and the band sounds joyous, loose, and sincere on a track that has aged extremely well and probably could be released as a hit single today. It should come as relatively little surprise that the song was inspired by a fierce game of golf the band had. Likewise, both "Michelle Post" (with words and music by Dean) and "Closet Full of Fear" also occupy that space between classic Americana and modern country. It's likely that "Closet Full of Fear" could be released as a Darius Rucker song today, nearly a quarter of a century after it was recorded, and people would think it was brand new.

I won't hide my affection for *Musical Chairs*. I happily recommend it to people as a sign that Hootie truly had more than one great album in them and must be very seriously considered as a deep and diverse band. While we were making it, I thought it had the ability to be the album that firmly put the band back on top and lay the foundation for their future; but I was, quite naively, not counting on the music industry to step in and get in the way.

-30-

BLIND(ERS)

Even before the release of *Musical Chairs*, Hootie's status at Atlantic was declining rapidly. On the face of it, this is certainly baffling. Less than four years earlier, the band had released the biggest selling album in the label's history. *Fairweather Johnson*, released only two years earlier, had been one of Atlantic's biggest selling records of 1996. And in early 1998, the group still was a steady moneymaker, with many friends at the label. Regardless of all these positive factors, the band's relationship with Atlantic was going nowhere but down. How did this happen?

Throughout the 1990s, Atlantic was riven with internecine politics and executive competition. In 1997 and '98, that competition had reached a furious pace. In 1998, not one of the people competing for executive power at the label (namely, Val Azzoli, Craig Kalman, and Jason Flom) was going to benefit in the slightest from Hootie selling any records. In addition, many of the key people who had plotted and built Hootie's success—Danny Goldberg, Kim Kaiman, publicist Jim Lawrence—were no longer at Atlantic. Their replacements were good, hard-working people but not nearly as invested in Hootie's success. Generally, it is up to the band management to be fully aware of these kinds of corporate shifts, and it is likely that a more experienced (or more cynical) band and manager might have been able to work their way through these troubled waters. This is usually the way things work: The artists make the music, happily unaware of the deeper level industry politics, and the manager (and often the attorney) stands guard, ears and nose close to the ground, sniffing out rumors and testing the corporate winds on virtually a daily basis. But Rusty Harmon and the band had blinders on regarding this reality and seemed unwilling to do anything at all to compensate for it or amend it. Hootie assumed that because they had been good to the label, the label would take care of them.

"I only became aware of the deterioration after we put out *Musical Chairs*," says Soni, over twenty years later. "See, when you've got a mansion rented on Sunset Boulevard and you've got your rented sports cars that you can drive all over L.A., and you are in a nice, posh studio being waited on hand and foot, there's no fucking problem with the record label. You feel like you're the most important artist on the label. And that's all well and good until you put out the record and it crashes, and you go, 'Okay, it seems like we're not the most important artist. We're just the people they like to lend money to.'"

Simultaneously, while the band was in Los Angeles recording *Musical Chairs*, I became aware of a shift in my relationship with my employers and that the end of my relationship with Atlantic Records might be inevitable. Throughout 1997 and into 1998, I had increasingly come to think that I worked for the artists I signed and A&R'd, and not the label (in '97 and '98, these artists included a Canadian progressive rock band called the Tea Party; Stone Temple Pilots' vocalist Scott Weiland; the Canadian comedian Bruce McCulloch; Broadway vocalist and actor Michael Crawford; a quirky Los Angeles band called Rat Bat Blue; and the Seattle punk rock band 7 Year Bitch). Again and again, I positioned myself as a close witness and advisor to the artists' creative process and an adjunct to their management team. This was, after all, the role I had taken with Hootie & the Blowfish and that had worked out pretty well. This might sound good on paper, but it was highly dysfunctional. After all, the label signed my paychecks; the artists did not. Also, since Danny's departure, I had no functional day-to-day relationship with any major executive at the company, and this was a big problem, largely of my own making. I had simply not done enough politically to insinuate myself into the structure of Atlantic.

Toward the very end of the recording of Hootie's third album, Val Azzoli was visiting the Los Angeles office. He called me in for a meeting. Val, whom I considered a friend (and still do), was very straightforward.

"Tim, I get calls from the managers of your artists, and the artists you work for, and people who work for our label. They all tell me the same thing. The artists like you. They *really* like you. And they trust you. The artists often like you and trust you more than they like and trust us, their label. *And that's a problem, Tim, because you work for us.* I'll hear back from a manager, who will tell me, 'Tim says the radio promotion department lied to us today, but it's okay because he told us what we should *really* do.' 'Tim told us that the publicist we met with today is full of shit, but it worked out, because he told us who we should *really* talk to.' Do you see how this is a problem, Tim?"

"I could ask you to correct this, Tim," Val said, evenly, "But there's actually another problem. Jason is insisting that you start reporting to him."

Val paused and changed his tone of voice, from slightly upset schoolteacher to friend.

"Jason wants you to report to him, and there's no conceivable scenario where that works out for you, unless you become a *totally* different person. So why don't you just go home, travel a little, enjoy yourself, and ride out your contract? You have about a year and a half left on your contract. Just go home."

With that, Val directed me out of his office.

I had been expecting this, but it was still shocking to be confronted with the reality. And Val had assessed, correctly, that I had become spoiled by being able to make all my own A&R decisions, without supervision. However, I felt my departure posed a unique opportunity for Hootie & the Blowfish. I envisioned a way for them to pull a possible victory from the jaws of defeat.

I organized a meeting with Darius, Dean, Mark, and Soni the next day at the recording studio, where they were finishing the mixes for their (still-untitled) third album. We met under the gold studio lights of NRG. High-end recording studios exist in a permanent stage of dawn light, a little blue, a little gold, a touch of pink. Recording studio light always reminded me of how sunrise is portrayed in a planetarium.

The band members sat around me, in various rolling chairs and folding chairs, in a half circle. I can still picture the order they were seated in, from my left to my right: Darius, Dean, Soni, and Mark. Don Gehman was sitting just behind them, leaning against the mixing console, between Darius and Soni.

"I am going to be leaving Atlantic," I said. "This is not necessarily my choice, but I am not surprised. I cannot make the following more clear, and I want you to listen very carefully, and take me very seriously. Some of this will come as a surprise to you, but it really shouldn't."

"I am leaving Atlantic," I repeated, "and you should, too. I know this is a lot for you to digest, so let me make it as clear as possible: You are *done* at Atlantic. This label does not give a damn about you. A part of you, deep down, may know this. I will no longer be here to protect you and run interference for you, and by far, the smartest thing for you to do right now is to buy your contract out. Rusty and Gus should walk into Val's office, as soon as possible, and I mean *like today or tomorrow*, and this is what they should say: How much money do you want for our contract? How much money do you want for this record we are making right now, so we can walk out of here with the tapes and bring it to another label? Whatever number Val says . . . say *Yes, thank you*, and give it to him. Then take this album to a new label while there are still labels out there that would jump at the chance to sign Hootie & the Blowfish. You will be *much* better off at another label. I know for a fact that Val would be happy to sell you back this album, and your contract."

This was actually a guess, but a good one. I had a very strong hunch that Val would be perfectly happy to let another company put out Hootie's new album and have Atlantic take an override (that is, a percentage of the profits). Years later, Val confirmed that I was absolutely correct, and if Rusty, Gus, and the band had approached him at that moment and asked to buy back their contract, they could have come to a mutually beneficial agreement.

It was heavy, sobering stuff, and the band listened intently.

I then called Rusty and Gus and gave them the identical speech.

And then . . . nothing happened.

In the spring of 1998, Soni, Dean, Darius, Mark, Rusty, and Gus found it completely impossible to even consider that Atlantic would turn its back on a band that was one of the biggest acts in the history of the label. But I knew it was possible. The band would learn the same thing, in due time.

Musical Chairs was released on September 15, 1998. It entered the charts at a very respectable no. 4 (behind Marilyn Manson's *Mechanical Animals*, *The Miseducation of Lauryn Hill*, and *Hello Nasty* by the Beastie Boys). However, it dropped out of the Top 10 in just one week, and by Thanksgiving, it was no longer in the Top 100.

For the rest of 1998, Hootie & the Blowfish scaled down to (mostly) playing large theatres and radio promotion shows (you know, those things where six or eight bands play at 'KMOM's High Flyin' Julyin' Fourth Fest!'). Hootie then returned to Europe for some shows in England, the Netherlands, and Germany, along with some well-received USO shows in Hungary and in Bosnia and Herzegovina.

One other very significant change had occurred in the Hootie camp in 1998. After three years, Peter Holsapple left the group, and John Nau took his role as onstage fifth member/master of all instruments. Nau had played on every Hootie album and retained a close friendship with the band, so he seemed like a natural choice to join the live band, once Peter decided it was time to move on (Peter Holsapple would rejoin the band in 2003 and remains a treasured part of their live performances through today).

Hootie & the Blowfish ended 1998 with a New Year's Eve show at the Hammerstein Ballroom in New York City, broadcast live on VH-1. On the bass drum, Soni had placed a large sign that said "HI TIM!" He did this because, for the first time in 5 years, I wasn't spending New Year's Eve with Hootie & the Blowfish.

I wasn't there because I was in the midst of a significant health crisis. This is a decidedly odd part of the story but, you know, shit happens.

When I left Atlantic, I decided to do some traveling. In late September of 1998—around the time *Musical Chairs* came out, the first album Hootie released without me riding shotgun—I went to central Europe for two weeks. Not too long after I left, I thought to myself, "Huh, your contact lens is a little dirty. You're going to have to change it as soon as you get back to Los Angeles." Well, it got dirtier and dirtier throughout the rest of the trip, and at some point, I realized it wasn't my contact lens. By the time I returned to Los Angeles, all I could see out of my left eye was a foggy, snowy image, like someone had completely covered your windshield with soap or grease (the right eye was unaffected).

The day before Thanksgiving 1998, I was diagnosed with a craniopharyngioma on the optic nerve. That's a relatively rare form of nonmalignant tumor. Although it usually impacts the pituitary gland, mine was adjacent to the pituitary gland, wrapped around the optic nerve. Although it was benign, it was both fast growing and clinging to my optic nerve like an octopus, which made removal difficult (you couldn't just cut, laser, or burn it away, because you would most likely take a chunk of the optic nerve with it, likely blinding me in both eyes). I had five surgeries between December of 1998 and November of 1999 to chip away at the thing. None of these actually worked, and by the autumn of 1999, I had completely lost sight in my left eye (except for a few dim shadows), and my right eye was beginning to be impacted. At that point, the doctors at UCLA Medical Center switched tactics, and wheeled me in for sixty straight days of focused radiation. That did the trick, and by February of 2000, my eyesight had (almost completely) been restored in my left eye, although I was dealing with significant medical (and psychological) complications from the whole ordeal.

I remained in touch with Hootie during most of this medical crap—they even visited me in the hospital, twice, en masse, as a whole band—but we didn't discuss business.

And business was not especially good. On March 13, 1999 *Musical Chairs*, the third album by Hootie & the Blowfish, dropped out of the Top 200 after twenty-three weeks. By contrast, it had taken *Fairweather Johnson* nearly a year to disappear from the Top 200, and *cracked rear view* had hung around the Top 200 for over two-and-a-half years.

Throughout 1999, the band's live audiences were contracting, too. In the smaller places—that is, venues with four thousand or fewer seats—the band was still selling out, or coming relatively close. But throughout the spring, summer, and autumn of 1999, when the band performed in the arenas, outdoor sheds, and fairgrounds they had easily sold out just a few years earlier, the results were decidedly unimpressive. In many of these larger venues, Hootie were filling only about 50 percent of the seats, and as the year wore on, the results became even graver. In September 1999 at the Universal Amphitheatre in Los Angeles, they sold only a little over two thousand seats in a hall that sat well over six thousand, and a few days later in Denver, they played in front of 703 people in a 3,600-seat venue.

I take no pleasure saying this, but the two separate warnings I had laid out for the band (in November of 1996 and March of 1998) appeared to have become true. Overtouring, low-drawing support acts, and the lack of a "must-see" live show had sapped their touring base; and regardless of the fact Hootie & the Blowfish were coming off of a Top 10 album (and only thirty-six months earlier they had been the biggest band in the country), the label had essentially completely stopped promoting the band.

Soni Sonefeld: "The hard part is that you make friends along the way, which we so easily did, probably to a fault. It's hard to recognize, down the road, that you were just in a *business* relationship with these people. That hurts. Some of these people you considered friends sat across you in meetings and lied to your face, because that's what you do in business. And the fact that this is what you do in business doesn't make it hurt any less. There's that realization—'*Shit*—that meeting we had three months ago was a complete fucking lie.' I did hold a grudge for a number of years, sometimes with a specific person, sometimes with the entity known as Atlantic Records. But over the years, the more I learned about the music industry, the more that resentment lessened."

Darius echoes this. "I think the problem that we had was that we just thought, 'We've done *so much* for you guys.' I mean, when grunge had *killed* so much of the industry and so much of the non-grunge record sales, we brought it back! You *have* to respect us."

"And we were wrong," Darius continues, darkly. "Garth Brooks said it best, and I am glad he said this: In 1995 and '96, people were going into record stores to buy our records, and they would buy somebody else's while they were there. We *carried* the industry for two years. We paid all the bills at Atlantic, and we just thought, you *have to* respect us because of that. Yet they proved to us, multiple times, no, we don't."

Dean, however, thinks the blame possibly could be laid a little closer to home. "I don't think the label was making the mistakes. I think we were. I don't think that we were making the right records. I don't think we were making smart decisions about our touring. I think we were on autopilot in a lot of ways. From 1990 until 1996, the five of us were *one person*. We were one voice, one mind, one opinion. We were cohesive, and we did everything together."

"And when you go from having relatively little money and living, basically, within the same four square walls and traveling together all the time," Dean says, "to running a multimillion-dollar business, to having girlfriends, then wives, then children, then living in different parts of the country, and when you tour you have different buses and sometimes even different hotels and you don't show up for soundcheck and sometimes don't even see each other until showtime, and then you leave and don't see each other again for another two weeks . . . you are no longer one band, one vote, one opinion. You are fragmented. And your wife has an opinion, and your checking account has an opinion, and the car you're driving has an opinion, and the Monday Night Football game you are on the sidelines for has an opinion, and all those things start taking precedence."

"I don't want to sit there and bitch at Atlantic Records," Dean continues, "because Atlantic was working with what they had to work with. And I don't think we were giving them the product to work with that they used to have. And when I say 'product', I do *not* mean the actual records being made—I mean the band, Hootie & the Blowfish."

-31-

A POLITICAL CASUALTY THAT STILL HAD A CONTRACT

Hootie & the Blowfish recognized it was time for some changes. On May 1, 2002, Rusty Harmon, who had been managing the band for ten years, resigned.

Soni Sonefeld: "We were beginning to assess and understand our place in the music business, which was a place of *less* influence than just three years earlier. And we felt we needed a dynamic change. We looked to the only person who didn't write our songs to make that change, and that was Rusty."

"It was emotional," Soni continues. "It was deeply thought out and far from spontaneous, even when we started to talk about the idea amongst ourselves, no one wanted to go forward and undertake what was required to part with someone who is not only one-fifth of your corporate entity, but who was with you since you were playing to two people in Greensboro, North Carolina. We all had a general *fuuuuuuck*, with a long sigh, *dammit* we don't want to do this, but we *need* to do this. We didn't just show up one day and say, 'You're outta here.' We had sent up many flares, and there were many serious and deep talks."

Dean emphasizes that Rusty's inability to stand up to Atlantic when the going got tough contributed significantly to the mutual decison to move forward without Rusty. "There was one key event with Atlantic Records that shaped my perspective," Dean says. "I flew up with Gus and Rusty to meet Val. Before the meeting I told them, look, we are going to walk into Val's office, and we are going to ask him this question, and he has already lied to your faces, but this time when we ask him, he is going to lie to *my* face. So sure enough, we walk in and ask Val this question, and he just lies. Now, he doesn't have a choice but to lie, but my perspective was, dude, he is sitting here lying to your bass player, to a member of your band, right in front of you, and that is a situation where you have to confront him on this. Deal with this. Why are we with a label that's just going to lie to us, and not do anything for us? There were smaller things, too, but that was the big moment for me. Once I saw that and felt that in person, I knew. You have *got* to be able to go toe-to-toe with these guys. Even if you lose, you have got to go toe-to-toe, and get some respect from them."

"You had left," Dean tells me, "so we didn't have anyone at the label. Atlantic wasn't doing anything. They were just taking our money and telling us whatever they thought we wanted to hear. I could tell, even while sitting in Columbia, South Carolina, that they weren't respecting us at all. They were giving Rusty lip service, and then he was coming home and giving us lip service. Nothing was happening. That infuriated me. Of course, labels are going to do things like that, but are you going to let your manager just keep on letting it happen?"

"If Rusty hadn't been there with us since the beginning, I don't think we would have gotten where we got," Dean concludes. "He was an integral part of Hootie & the Blowfish. But it got to the point where, well, it's hard to tell if people just didn't respect him, or if mistakes were being made, but things were starting to fall apart. And it was transactional in that sense. It was clear things needed to change and things needed to happen, but those things weren't changing and weren't happening."

Nonetheless, the band remained on Atlantic, and the Hootie product continued to flow. On October 24, 2000, a fifteen-track collection of all the (mostly) wonderful covers Hootie & the Blowfish had released over the years—on B-sides, soundtracks, tribute albums, and so forth—was released. The title of *Scattered, Smothered and Covered* was yet another in-joke, but this time, much of America could identify with it. As anyone from the Southeast (or who has traveled through the South) can testify, scattered, smothered, and covered is one of the ways you can order your hash browns at the Waffle House quickie-food chain (it specifically means that you want your hash browns smashed up with onions and cheese, and, I mean, who doesn't?).

Scattered, Smothered and Covered is a fine record. Not only does it include "I Go Blind," but it also features Hootie's remarkable version of Tom Waits's "I Hope I Don't Fall in Love With You" (which was a highlight of their 2019 tour). Throughout, *Scattered, Smothered and Covered* shows that Hootie & the Blowfish had damn good taste, and with covers of Don Dixon, The Reivers, The Silos, Vic Chestnutt, early R.E.M., and The Smiths, it underlined that Hootie & the Blowfish had deep roots in the user-friendly edge of hipster 1980s college rock. However, it didn't exactly tear up the charts. *Scattered, Smothered and Covered* entered the *Billboard* Top 200 at no. 71 on November 11, 2000, and vanished from the Top 200 just two weeks later.

I can only imagine how angry and cynical Mark, Darius, Soni, and Dean must have been to find that the label they made so much money for was squeezing product out into the marketplace they had no intention of promoting in any significant way.

"Cynical doesn't describe it," says Dean Felber. "We were angry. Now, we are not the type of people to be, like, 'You owe me something.' But we were a political casualty that still had a contract. The label wasn't going to help us, but they also weren't going to push our head under the water and drown us, just in case something comes out that someone can buy. It was a weird kind of existence: You had to do everything on your own like it was before we got signed, but if something had succeeded, someone else would take all the credit. Labels have always had the attitude that they would eat their young before they would give their young away. They have always been that way, and I have never understood it. If you are so sure that it's not going to be successful, why are you holding on to it?"

Curiously, the album that pissed off the Hootie members the most during this period was one that Atlantic *didn't* release. In 1999, Darius Rucker began recording an R&B-flavored album for Atlantic. There was no doubt that this was a significant departure for Darius, but it was a project he held very closely to his heart. He also thought he had a great deal of support from Atlantic when he began the project. This was because one of the upper-tier Atlantic executives we spoke about earlier—Craig Kalman—had great expertise in the R&B field, and he had initially been very encouraging of Darius moving in this direction. Kalman had indicated to Darius, Gus, and Rusty (who was still manager at this time) that it would be exciting for Atlantic's powerful and much-respected R&B department to sink their teeth into a Darius Rucker solo project. But according to Darius, Gus, Rusty, and then-Atlantic president Val Azzoli, when the Rucker solo album was completed and handed in, Kalman ignored his earlier commitment and refused to allow the R&B promotion/radio department to work the record. They say he insisted on handling it through traditional rock and adult rock channels.

"It was shocking," Darius answers. "I thought I made this great record, and it was critically acclaimed, and people thought it was cool, yet my record label, who paid for the whole thing, didn't want to put it out. They wouldn't even try. I was, like, *Wow,* that is fucking nuts. But this is also around the time where we really started to realize where we stood with Atlantic. We had paid their bills for six or seven years, and now they were ready to fuck us."

"I love that album," Darius continues. "I still think it's great. And I understand why Atlantic didn't want anything to do with it, because it was so different. They wanted me to make a solo record that was *cracked rear view.* And that's not what I wanted to do. So I made this little hippie R&B record, and they didn't have any idea what to do with it, and they said it had no hits, and I'm, like, 'Have you heard "Exodus"? Have you heard "Wild One"?' These songs are hits. Someone at the label said, 'Yes, they're hits, but not for you.'"

Val Azzoli then did something that was relatively generous for a record label president: He gave the record back to Darius ("We fucked it up, and giving it back to him was the mensch thing to do," Val says). Darius tweaked it a little, and in the summer of 2002, he released his first solo album, titled *Back to Then,* on Hidden Beach, the label then best known for having had some success with neo-soul singer and poet Jill Scott. *Back to Then* didn't fare any better than the contemporary

Hootie product: It spent one week in the charts (entering at no. 127) and then vanished.

Throughout 2001 and 2002, Hootie & the Blowfish still played live, but only sporadically. Sometimes these shows went well—smaller venue shows in Philadelphia, DC, Cape Cod, Charleston, St. Louis, and Atlanta that sold out or came damn close—and sometimes, not so well (a show at First Avenue in Minneapolis only filled a third of the fifteen-hundred-seat club, with Hootie barely making more money than they did in the frat days).

At the beginning of 2002, Hootie & the Blowfish began work on their fourth studio album. Regardless of the public perception of the band, and in active defiance of their label's blasé attitude, Hootie & the Blowfish were undergoing a creative renaissance.

The band decided, for the first time since *Kootchypop*, to work with a producer other than Don Gehman. Their choice was Don Was, one of the most well respected and artist-friendly producers in the business. Don Was had produced successful and much-loved albums for Bonnie Raitt, the Rolling Stones, Willie Nelson, the B-52's, Bob Dylan, and many, many others. In addition, he had co-led a pioneering pop/jam/funk band, Was Not Was. After a concentrated and positive song-writing session at Mark Bryan's house in Awendaw, South Carolina, the group traveled to Los Angeles to meet with Don Was.

"We set up our meeting with Don Was at John Nau's home studio in Venice," Mark says. "John was touring with us at that time, and at that moment was very much the fifth Hootie. We had tweaked the space before he got there and spent some time setting up, so when he got there we sounded *fucking good*. Don Was came with Ed Cherney, his amazing engineer. After he was done listening to us, Don said, 'Let's just do it here!' We took a step back and chatted amongst ourselves for a few hours to see if it was actually feasible, and then we made it happen."

In May 2002, the band, Don Was, and Ed Cherney set up inside John Nau's home and began recording.

Soni emphasizes that it really felt like the band was making an independent record. "I cannot honestly remember someone from Atlantic fucking Records showing their face in that studio during that entire session. That's not a good sign for your standing on the label. And no one is taking you out to schmooze the national or local promotion people, not a good sign. It seemed like we were already on our own, without a label."

Whatever the process, it worked from a creative standpoint. The 2003 self-titled album is full of light and grace, and it's an absolute treasure. The last thing it sounds like is the fourth album from a tired, overworked, much-derided band whose label does not give a damn about them. *Hootie & the Blowfish* (the second piece in the Hootie discography to have this name, after their first-ever cassette release in 1990) swings, sways, dances, and skips. It has a lighter, funkier touch than the band had used before. I'm not sure that Hootie have ever sounded so *comfortable* in the studio. It is as if, with any expectation of success lifted, the band members let themselves *go*, and this deep, pleasurable, funky collection emerged.

Gone are the thumping rhythms. Gone are the square and fixed guitar lines; it's as if Mark stopped listening to Cheap Trick and The Smiths and started listening to The Meters and The Band. And there is not a mumbled vocal in sight. These are Darius's cleanest, clearest vocals since the Dick Hodgin days, yet at the same time Darius has never sounded more soulful. *Hootie & the Blowfish* is both Hootie's most mature album and the one they sound the most relaxed on. *Hootie & the Blowfish* is also the final Hootie & the Blowfish album (to date) comprising only songs written by Darius Rucker, Dean Felber, Jim Sonefeld, and Mark Bryan. Along with *Musical Chairs*, *Hootie & the Blowfish* is one of the group's overlooked treasures, and it contains one of the very best ever ballads, "Tears Fall Down."

"I loved working with Don Was," Darius says. "He had a totally different approach to everything that we did, every way we ever worked. And I love talking to him about *why* he did that record, 'cause Don will tell you right now that he had no desire or idea to do a Hootie & the Blowfish record. He took the meeting because we asked him. Simple enough. Out of respect, he came to see us. And when he came to see us, he thought we were going to all sit around and listen to some tapes we had made, that we would play some demos for him. And he said that the reason he decided he was going to work with us was because when he arrived in the studio, we all picked up our instruments and started *playing.* And while we were playing, he thought, 'I'm going to fucking produce this record.' I love that record, I think it's one of our best records, and it's also one of the best times we ever had making a record."

Released on March 4, 2003, *Hootie & the Blowfish,* certainly one of the band's essential albums, was on and off the *Billboard* charts in just four weeks. It is the lowest selling of any of the band's studio albums. The touring cycle that followed the release of *Hootie & the Blowfish* was, well, erratic: Although Hootie had a fair number of sellouts in small to medium venues (i.e., fifteen hundred seats or so), they also had their share of half full and one-third full houses.

"Those were dark times," Soni says, laughing. "The allure of the mid-90s, of being welcomed in each market with a label rep and a radio person to talk to and a radio station to visit, a single that had some hopes attached to it—when that stuff isn't there, you kind of feel like a bar band again, no matter what size venue you're playing. And the tours were being scotch-taped together, because we were out of the big amphitheaters, and we were having to tour without something on the radio, and that is *hard.*"

"We held together as best as we could," Soni says. "We were still brothers in arms, for the most part, but we all had different and unique life challenges. From 1989 to 1996, we all had the exact same challenge. But as years pass, you find that you have differing challenges: Somebody has a baby, somebody has a marriage, somebody has this, somebody has that, it was all being more pulled apart."

But there was some good news on the horizon.

PART V

2003-2008

Paying Dividends

-32-

DOC

2004 may appear to have been a relatively low-key year for Hootie & the Blowfish, but the band members recall this time with a fair degree of fondness. Significantly, they found someone who could help them make the most of their changed status. Thanks to a new manager, for the next half-decade Soni, Mark, Darius, and Dean were able to thrive within a new normal that was comfortable and lucrative, even as it was realistic about the band's contemporary standing in the world.

"We split with Rusty and we were thinking about managers," remembers Darius. "I called Jon Bon Jovi. He had left Doc at this point, but I said, 'Doc McGee wants to be our manager, tell me what you think.' And Jon Bon Jovi said to me, 'If Doc McGee wants to be your manager and you don't let him, you are an idiot.' And he said, 'Doc McGee will take that idea you have that you want to do in a club, and when Doc McGee is done with it, you'll be doing it in a stadium.' He was right. Doc could take the smallest idea you had—any idea you had—and figure out a way for it to make money."

By the time he came into the Hootie & the Blowfish family in 2003, Doc had managed Motley Crüe, Bon Jovi, Skid Row, and Kiss and had done very, very well with all of those acts. Doc came into the Hootie picture at the very tail end of the Atlantic era, before the release of the band's fourth album, *Hootie & the Blowfish*. He elected not to take the band off the label right away. Instead, he wanted to observe, and fully assess the state of the band's relationship with the label before making his next move.

Doc McGhee: "The enthusiasm at Atlantic Records was less than favorable for Hootie. And there was an extreme sword fight at the top regarding who could take Atlantic Records into the new millennium in the wake of this horrible new digital world that nobody knew anything about. And because of Hootie's then-lack of success—which wasn't really a lack of success, just a *declining* success—Atlantic had pretty much discounted them and forgotten about them, even though they were still making money. Atlantic wanted to know about bands selling millions, not hundreds of thousands."

Doc analyzed the situation and realized that, with some tweaking, Hootie's (somewhat) hangdog status in the early 2000s could be turned into a positive, moneymaking situation. After watching the way Atlantic worked—or rather didn't work—the band, he negotiated a release from their record contract in exchange for a greatest hits album.

Dean Felber: "I love Doc. He was organized. He wouldn't promise us stuff he couldn't deliver. He knew everybody, and everybody liked him. He knew how to make money with what he had, with us. As people, primarily, we want to be able to make our music and have fun, and it doesn't have to be for Atlantic, it can be for somewhere that wants us. When Doc came on, we did the tours we wanted, we did the albums we wanted, money wasn't going out the window—we weren't spending money that wasn't paying dividends. Doc had been around bands enough and the business enough to know how to make money with whatever size you are at on that day. He knew how to make it so that you would come back with a smile on your face and a check in your pocket."

The greatest hits LP Doc and the band gave to Atlantic in exchange for their contract release, *The Best of Hootie & the Blowfish (1993 thru 2003)*, was released in March of 2004. It features five songs from *cracked rear view*; eleven tracks spread around the other Atlantic albums; and the well-treaded covers of "I Go Blind," "Hey, Hey What Can I Do," and "Use Me" (the same version that appears on *Scattered, Smothered and Covered*, recorded live at Reflections in Charlotte in June of 2000, in a session that also involved Don Dixon and Edwin McCain, who sings a powerful counterlead on the song). It also contains one new recording, a cover of David Gates's "Goodbye Girl," made for a little-remembered 2004 TV remake of the movie of the same name.

The greatest hits album did a little bit better than the self-titled fourth studio album, released a year earlier. *The Best of Hootie & the Blowfish (1993 thru 2003)* hung around the *Billboard* charts for six weeks, although it never climbed higher than no. 62. It's interesting to contrast this with the sales performances of greatest hits albums by Dave Matthews Band and Matchbox Twenty, both of which made it into *Billboard*'s Top 10. The difference, of course, was a label that readily supported the act (in Matchbox Twenty's case, that label was Atlantic). With the release of *The Best of Hootie & the Blowfish (1993 thru 2003)*, after ten-and-a-half years and (as of that time) roughly fifteen million records sold, Hootie & the Blowfish were finally off of Atlantic.

Once the band was off of Atlantic, Doc's new strategies kicked into gear. "In two years we took them from six hundred thousand dollars a year to fourteen million," he says, with justifiable pride. Doc and the band did this through carefully considered touring strategies, well-paid performances on the private and corporate touring circuit, and expanded licensing of the band's existing music in film and TV. "They were easy," Doc continues. "They did setlists, the production was great, they didn't call out songs anymore, it wasn't that cluster-fuck, and it was a well-oiled, fine-tuned machine. We put together the entertainment segment of Hootie and the Blowfish where they could compete as entertainers out there."

Jeff Smith, who had been working closely with Darius and assumed some managerial duties in the wake of Rusty's firing, also exits around this time. Jeff had worked hard for the Hootie organization for nine years and was well liked. His departure appears to have been precipitated by a very public event that left everyone who loved the group a little baffled.

After the release and relative failure of Darius Rucker's first solo album, it was natural that Jeff Smith would seek out new opportunities to create mainstream, national visibility for Darius. However, it is questionable whether dressing up as a surrealist neon cowboy and singing about wanting a Tender Crispy Chicken Cheddar Bacon Ranch Sandwich from Burger King was the kind of thing that was going to bring Darius Rucker to the next level of his career. Darius says that he really had no idea what he was stepping into, and when he arrived on set, he almost walked (but refused to, because of his sense of professionalism). Even after being stuck inside a rather elaborate production and extensive editing, in the finished commercial, Darius looks uncomfortable, if not downright somnambulant. Everything about his gaze and the way he moves through the set says, "I smoked something I shouldn't have and woke up in Pee Wee's Western Playhouse." His uninspired, talky vocals lack any evidence of intent or effort. On the other hand, in a way, I suppose, it anticipates Darius Rucker's future solo career, although from the wrong side of the looking glass. It was, according to Doc, the last straw for Jeff's involvement with Darius.

Doc also added an aspect of professionalism and organization to the band's already established charity events and especially focused on creating a strong local profile for the band's HomeGrown concerts. Hootie & the Blowfish's HomeGrown concerts have been an (mostly) annual event since the year 2000. This benefit event impacts, in a real and direct way, the needs of local Charleston schools and the children who go to them.

Even before Mark, Darius, Soni, and Dean were signed to Atlantic, they regularly played charity events, both for community and national causes. This sounds terribly corny, but it's true: Giving seems to be something built into the DNA of the band.

"You always sensed that some sort of philanthropy was going to be a part of what they were doing," says Paul Graham, who began working with Hootie & the Blowfish as a road manager and general amanuensis in the very early 1990s, and continued in that role for many years before transitioning to sports management and running Hootie's Monday After the Masters event. "They just had that *in them*. There was never any doubt that they were going to give back."

In 1994—again, a time when the band was barely known outside of their native Mid-South region—they began an association with an existing event called Monday After the Masters. The celebrity professional–amateur (pro-am) charity golf event was soon rebranded under Hootie's name, and it has become one of the central events in Hootie's calendar of charitable giving. Monday After the Masters is now an internationally recognized event on the pro-am golf circuit. The tournament—and the accompanying Hootie-plus-special-guests concert—has run every year since 1994 (with the exception of the pandemic-affected years of 2020 and '21).

Monday After the Masters is the main (but not exclusive) funding source for the Hootie & the Blowfish Foundation, a nonprofit group that was established in 2000 so the bandmates could efficiently, productively, and continuously support charities that were especially important to them, as individuals and as a group. Currently, according to the band's old friend Chris Carney, who left a career in law enforcement to run the foundation, the Hootie & the Blowfish Foundation has a five-million-dollar endowment. With an endowment this large, the band hopes that the Hootie & the Blowfish Foundation can keep helping people not only past the life of the band, but even after Soni, Mark, Dean, and Darius have passed on. They have already set a framework in place to get the band members' children involved, so the Hootie spirit of giving can continue on into the next generation.

"It occurs to me," says Mark, "that a day may come where people don't necessarily remember our music, but they know of the charity."

The Foundation has also committed sixty thousand dollars a year to the South Carolina Junior Golf Foundation. The idea of making golf a sport everybody can enjoy, regardless of race, class, or age, has long been a mission of Darius, Dean, Soni, and Mark. The South Carolina Junior Golf Foundation helps them achieve this goal.

"The guys in the band took it for granted that *everyone* should be playing golf," says Paul. "The stigma around golf was nothing they ever understood. We just never *got* it. There were a lot of people who wanted golf to be a country club environment, end of story. But there was a reason to try to change that. This happened more or less simultaneously with the emergence of Tiger Woods, who is a friend of theirs. Golf is one of those sports you can do for your whole life, and while you are on the course, you can get the attention of somebody for a long time. It's a way to get some ideas across, to underline and solidify a friendship. And I think the band has not only been instrumental in South Carolina golf, they have also had a nationwide influence. They have said, 'Hey, *everybody* can come do this sport—Let's go out and have fun.'"

In addition, both Hootie and Darius Rucker have been continually involved in numerous other charities that raised funds and awareness throughout their home state. More recently, Darius was significantly involved in the One SC Fund, which has greatly assisted in disaster preparation, relief, and recovery throughout the state. "South Carolina is so proud of them," says Ambassador Nikki Haley, a South Carolina native and former governor. "They never forgot where they came from. I think that's at the heart of everything."

-33-

END OF THE NEVER-ENDING PARTY

With the label drama finally behind them and an aggressive and experienced new manager steering the ship, Hootie & the Blowfish began to make plans for their first post-Atlantic album.

For album five, Hootie & the Blowfish would be recording for a large independent label, Vanguard Records. In the 1950s and '60s, Vanguard had been an extremely well-regarded imprint for classical, jazz, blues, and folk. After an extended period of near-dormancy, the label was resurrected in the mid-1980s and released a large number of well-received albums from new and legacy folk and roots rock artists, including Julia Fordham, Peter Case, John Fahey, Victor Wooten, Big Bad Voodoo Daddy, and Camper Van Beethoven. In other words, there were a lot of reasons to think that a newly independent Hootie & the Blowfish might be a good fit with Vanguard.

But Hootie did not end up making a particularly credible-sounding album for their Vanguard debut. In fact, they intentionally did the opposite. The band opted to work, once again, with Don Gehman, the producer who had been behind the board for their first three Atlantic studio albums, including *cracked rear view*.

"There was a very deliberate intention to make a comeback at radio," Mark Bryan says. "There hadn't been a single off of the fourth album that had made any impression, so we thought, let's construct a situation where we can come back and have a radio song, or even two, three, four, or five. Don Gehman was working out of Nashville at that point, which meant that we could drive [from Columbia and Charleston] instead of fly, which was *huge*. Doc had moved to Nashville. And we had all agreed we would start writing and co-writing outside the band, and Nashville presented a good opportunity for that."

Looking for Lucky is not a bad album. It's just not necessarily the first, second, third, or even fourth Hootie & the Blowfish album I would listen to. Most of it sounds simultaneously overthought yet underfelt, as if someone was trying too hard without quite understanding why they were trying so hard in the first place. "Hey Sister Pretty," for instance, sounds like someone trying to write a "big" song without really *feeling* it. That's a fairly consistent problem throughout *Looking for Lucky*. There's one big, fat, gigantic exception to all this: "Autumn Jones" is terrific, a deep and sad country song with a big, wave-hands chorus. It's the album's one indisputably great song, and it belongs on every Hootie mixtape. "Autumn Jones" also gives a fascinating preview of a future that never happened: What would it have been like if Hootie & the Blowfish—and not just Darius—had pursued a country direction at this point in their career?

"We were faced with the big question—" Soni says, "are we supposed to sound like Hootie & the Blowfish, or are we not? What's the goal? It's a very difficult way to approach the making of an album, any album. Country was beginning to influence us more overtly, without anyone saying it out loud. We could have made a big turn towards country at that point, if someone had told us it would be a good idea."

(Note to band: It would have been a good idea.)

Looking for Lucky was released on August 9, 2005. It spent six weeks on *Billboard*'s U.S. album charts, peaking at no. 47, a sales performance that was fairly consistent with Hootie's last few releases. The tour that followed found the band playing mostly smaller venues but selling them out a little more consistently than they had in the days before Doc McGhee took charge.

There was a very significant landmark for the band during the *Looking for Lucky* era. Soni became the first member of this legendary party band to stop partying—the first one since Brantley Smith, anyhow.

"It was an enormous change in dynamic," Soni recalls. "The drummer and the ringleader of the nightly, never-ending party decided he was going to quit his position as ringleader. That was a big challenge to the band dynamic, me stopping drinking. I was trying to make an album without drugs or alcohol for the very first time. When we started the album, I was just two weeks into my sober journey, which was all new ground for me. It was like walking on ice. *Thin ice.* The thing that I had needed to navigate relationships and a dwindling career was *gone.* I was left empty handed and had to learn how to walk again."

It was a voyage that was to have extraordinary positive benefits for Jim Sonefeld, who remains sober.

Hootie & the Blowfish stuck around Vanguard for one more album, *Live In Charleston.* The record (and simultaneously released live DVD) was drawn from an August 12, 2005, concert at Volvo Car Stadium in Daniel's Island, South Carolina. Released on August 8, 2006 (almost exactly a year after *Looking for Lucky*), *Live in Charleston* became the first ever full-length Hootie & the Blowfish album to fail to chart in the United States. Twelve years and two weeks after entering the *Billboard* charts for the very first time, Hootie & the Blowfish's recording career had reached its nadir.

-34-

ANOTHER TOUR WOULD HAVE BEEN A ROLL OF THE DICE

Let's clear up two things.

First: Hootie & the Blowfish never broke up.

I do not think Hootie are any more capable of actually breaking up than, say, your family is capable of breaking up. Maybe your mom's brother, Uncle Sol, won't talk to your dad for a couple of years, or your older brother Benny went two whole months without speaking to your big sister, and great aunt Magda is still angry at your mom about running over her hydrangeas at that Memorial Day picnic in 1986. But *no one is breaking up*. No one is saying, "See ya, I'm gonna have a solo family now, maybe we'll do a reunion in ten years."

In 2008, Hootie & the Blowfish went on a mutually agreed-upon hiatus. This was a decision made among friends who had every intention of staying friends, whether they played one gig a year or one hundred.

Second, Darius Rucker did not gather Dean Felber, Mark Bryan, and newly sober Soni Sonefeld in a room and make a big announcement that he wanted to start making country albums and, therefore, the band needed to take a break. Didn't happen like that. Around the same time Darius began to seriously consider a country career, Dean and (especially) Soni independently decided that it was time for Hootie & the Blowfish to take a break. This was good timing for Darius, but even better timing for the emotional and psychological health of the band unit.

Hootie & the Blowfish toured extensively during the summer of

2008 and did pretty well. Even if the venues were considerably smaller than the places they played in the 1990s, they were selling out (or coming close), and making very decent money. Nonetheless, at the end of the 2008 touring cycle—after a show on August 25th in San Diego—Soni took the major step of saying, hey guys, it's time to stop. The great Hootie & the Blowfish road show had been running hard for eighteen straight years (and more or less continuously for twenty-two years). During that time, the band went from taking requests at wing joints to playing their own hits in stadiums, and then back down to working in theatres and casinos. It had been a fantastically long road, impossible to detail unless you were there, unless you were the winner/victim of this marathon of tires changed, guitar strings changed, incredible amounts of diesel fuel consumed, Crown Royal swallowed, weed inhaled, early morning tee times, late-night blackjack, endless numbers of strangers who knew your name, hands shaken and pictures taken, ballgames watched and ballgames missed, coffinlike tour bus bunks that were as familiar as any home, a couple of hundred showers in hockey team locker rooms, and on and on and on. It was a happy/unhappy grind that could give you a reason to live, and it could kill you.

Soni Sonefeld: "I had a strong desire to get off the road and stop making records, and even if we didn't speak about it out loud, this coincided with Darius's desire to make a solo record. I think these things were happening without either of us necessarily knowing about the other person's needs and journey. Darius got a record deal while I was struggling as a divorced, single dad and learning to prioritize my children."

Dean is a little more straightforward when discussing the decision. He says half the band really needed to take some time away from the business, and half the band did not.

"If we had kept touring beyond 2008, I think Hootie would have broken up," Dean says, firmly. "The fact was, we needed a break. It was just time. People were getting on each other's nerves in ways that haven't happened before or since. And there was only one solution for that—hey, let's all go in different directions for a bit, and then come back and see what's up. Physically, I was certainly ready to take a break, and I know Soni was ready to get off the road for a multitude of reasons."

"But Mark wasn't, and Darius wasn't," Dean continues. "If Hootie had said, we are going to go out for one more tour, would I have said no? I don't think so. But I knew that another tour would have been a *major* roll of the dice, and we might not come back with our band intact. I have no doubt it was the right thing to do and the right time to do it, and Darius was already on the path to the country thing. Taking a break at that time maintained the band, and the relationships, and the friendships."

Yet Hootie never considered themselves broken up.

Mark Bryan: "There was never a 'Hey, fuck you! We're done!' moment or fight with this band. Never happened. There was a cool, calm, collected conversation at Darius's house where Soni said, 'Man, I can't do this anymore, I've got to take a break,' and Darius said, 'Well, I'm getting ready to do my country stuff, anyway,' so we all agreed, let's take an indefinite hiatus. We never discussed it again. We just did our events every year, and had fun playing with each other, and we continued to play golf together and went to each other's kids' birthday parties, and then when it was time to make an album again, *that* felt like the right thing to do at the right time."

There was yet another major change, one that has been the subject of a considerable amount of misinterpretation, especially when the band returned to the spotlight in 2019. A few years before the start of the hiatus—just about the same time that Soni embarked on sobriety and reconnected with his faith—Mark's longtime wife, Laura, began taking the same life voyage, quite independent of Soni. Mark was not at a similar stage in his life, and this was one of the multiple reasons that Mark and Laura decided to amicably split. Two years later, well after Mark and Laura split, Soni and Laura found that they had a great deal in common and decided to get married and move forward together. Today, the Bryans and the Sonefelds have a remarkable shared family, and Soni and Mark remain close friends and highly functional bandmates.

Around the same time, the band relationship with manager Doc McGhee amicably ended, although Doc did stay involved with Darius Rucker until early 2016. This partnership turned out to be vitally important not just to Darius but to the history of music.

-35-

HE JUST NEEDS TO BE

This is the elephant in the room. It is also a wonderful, deep, and powerful vein that runs through the entire Hootie & the Blowfish story.

Darius Rucker is Black, a descendent of enslaved Africans, fronting a band much loved by White America. Since 2008, he has also become an African American superstar in a genre overwhelmingly associated with White America. If you think this doesn't matter, if you think this isn't worthy of discussion, if you think this isn't something Darius Rucker isn't keenly aware of every day of his life, you are wrong.

And we cannot end this story without talking about this.

We must recall this deeply important idea: All rock 'n' roll, all rhythm-based pop music in the United States, is political. It may not seem that way, but this is true.

That's because the architect of rock 'n' roll is suffering. Rock 'n' roll is built on rhythm, rhythm was born out of work song, and work song is, inevitably, the sound of suffering. For eons, rhythm is the noise that the disenfranchised have made to ease their burden. Throughout history, from the days when the world was lit only by fire and moonlight, rhythm had three functions: To ease your babies to sleep; to allow unity of syllable and sound when praising a higher spirit; and to relieve your burden when you hauled stones, harvested crops, planted seeds, picked cotton, and laid rail.

The priests of Stonehenge, the pharaohs who built the great pyramids, and the kings and archbishops who commissioned great cathedrals did not haul the stones upon which civilization and worship was built. The slaveholders in their column'd plantation houses did not bruise and bloody their fingers picking cotton.

The legions of the disenfranchised built every culture, and they did not do so silently. They sang, they stomped, they chanted. The sound those builders made, when plugged in, became rock 'n' roll.

Rock 'n' roll is the sound of America's disenfranchised, made electric. It is that simple. There is nothing, and I mean absolutely nothing, in modern pop and rock that cannot be traced, in some very direct way, to the sounds made in slave shacks, Southern cotton fields, Blue Mountain hollows, Midwestern rail yards, and inner-city tenements by America's willing and unwilling immigrants.

From Stephen Foster's faux-slave songs to the modified Appalachian howls of Jimmie Rodgers and Hank Williams, from the sex calls of Elvis to the rhymes of Run-DMC and *all* the manifold descendants of *all* these pioneers, American music was the creation of those forgotten by the American dream: truck driving sons of Parchman convicts, the urban and rural poor, the immigrant Jews and Italians and Irish. All of the people who had nothing and built America, they built American song, too, American pop, American rock 'n' roll.

No other art form was born of more suffering and brought us more pleasure. Sadly and joyously, we announce that rock 'n' roll is the only good thing to come from the American stain of slavery and the institutionalized race hatred of Jim Crow. Make no mistake: What we hear on our radio, what we make with our own fingers on Amazon-bought guitars, can be traced back to the stinking hulls of slave ships, the blistered and bleeding fingers of bent-backed children in the hell-hot cotton fields, the black-lunged miners in grim Appalachian shacks, and so on.

During the years when Hootie & the Blowfish stood on top of the *Billboard* charts, the idea of race in relation to Hootie & the Blowfish was very rarely mentioned. One great exception was Robert Christgau, for decades one of the most respected and well-known music critics in America. In August 1996, in the Village Voice (in his review of *Fairweather Johnson*), Christgau wrote the following, which is still enormously valid today, a quarter of a century later: "As a black son of the civil rights movement whose 'Tucker's Town' is his second hit about racism, making two more than Tupac or Dre has bothered with, Darius Rucker is all too aware that he's damned if he does and damned if he doesn't, and all too normal not to resent it. He knows he's not a 'sellout.' . . . It's not his fault that in the era of O.J. and gin-and-juice he's come to embody what many Whites hope is the Regular Black Guy . . . holding out a hint of a possibility that somehow this problem that makes them feel bad will fade to gray. It's not his fault that by not only accepting but mastering a white-identified cultural style he revalidates it as the Gin Blossoms, say, never could."

Darius Rucker just being Darius Rucker is an enormous political statement, a profound act of courage.

Journalist Sara Rodman: "He doesn't need to speak, he just needs to sing, *he just needs to be.* That's what the representation is. And going back to whatever institutional racism may be baked into the country format, the minute Darius starts making statements is the minute that people who like him start to shut him down. Which is not to say he isn't deep, thoughtful, or introspective, but he is not somebody I feel walks around being angst-ridden all the time. I think that's part of why he has been able to be successful in many aspects but in that aspect specifically. He knows that just being is enough. And maybe even doing more than that would be detrimental."

"So much is expected from people of color from the South, those in a position of fame or popularity are expected to speak out," says University of South Carolina professor and author Jon Hale. "But when you look on the ground at what's happening, especially in South Carolina, sometimes just *being* is an act of resistance. It's like not walking off the sidewalk to make room for a White person in 1940. To a northerner, it may not look like anything, but to the southerner, it is an act of resistance. Sometimes it takes a while for a northerner to understand what resistance really looks like in the south. It's subtle, but profound. Darius may not fit into our expectations of what an activist is, but within a southern Black context, he *is* an activist."

Hale stresses that even as Darius's success is a landmark in country music, his high visibility as an African American in a traditionally White milieu has many dimensions. "He's a narrative of progress for White people, without seeing the complicated nature of his very being in South Carolina. Darius Rucker provides a way for White people in country music to say, 'We're not racist, look at Darius Rucker.' But that doesn't allow people to know Darius, or his issues with the flag, or his struggles growing up."

Hale underlines that Darius would have encountered implicit and explicit racism, on any number of levels, even as he entered the University of South Carolina in 1984, just twenty years after the school's integration. "For one, you had the Confederate flag flying over the State House, just blocks from the University," Hale notes. "Culturally, the Confederate flag is embedded into the region: You're going to see it displayed in Five Points, you're going to see it on the shirts of students, and when it's not on display, it's *just* below the surface. Darius would have seen all this. Frats and sororities were still doing events that featured people in blackface in the mid-1980s. He would have been exposed to all of that. Though in the late 1980s and early to mid-1990s, there is some racial parity at USC—close to 25 percent of the students are African American. Nevertheless, culturally speaking, racism is just part of the fabric."

In fact, there was a very public display of this, at precisely the apogee of Hootie's success and public visibility. As the band was preparing to take the stage for their massive outdoor homecoming show on the University of South Carolina campus on April 16, 1996, a large and well-lit Confederate battle flag was unfurled from the third-floor window of a building near the stage. The positioning of the flag was very deliberate. It could *only* be seen from the stage-center position of Darius Rucker.

Rusty Harmon had the flag removed before the show began, but it was a reminder that race was never far away from the Hootie story, even when the band was at their peak of success in mainstream America.

Implicit racism, not always evident to even the best intentioned non-African Americans, continues through today.

Darius Rucker: "I talk to my friends, and they react to everything that is going on and they are shocked, and they are awakened, and they say, 'Oh, this is just crazy.' And I'm like, I understand that you feel that, but this is *not* crazy to me. I live this every fucking day. *Every fucking day.* In May of 2020, I was standing in the Apple Store with a mask on, and the guy talked to the White lady in front of me, then went and talked to the White lady behind me, and I was, like, *are you fucking kidding me.* Are you kidding me?! And the thing is, White people will say, oh, that's not racist, I am sure he wasn't thinking about race, and he may not even know he is, but what *we* see is the racism *inside* of him that would make that even happen, that would make him just unconsciously skip over the Black guy. Because he *knows* what's going on—I was standing there thirty fucking minutes. And he probably thinks in his heart, I am not a racist, yet something inside of him made me skip me. What was that?"

"There were times when the whole band would be standing in a first-class ticket line at the airport," Darius continues, "and we all looked like hell, all four of us looked like we had been partying all night *because we had been partying all friggin' night.* And Dean walks through, and Mark walks through, and then they ask me, 'First class?' Are you kidding me? And there was no question that those two looked rougher than me, and they're okay, but you are going to stop *me* and ask me if I'm in first class? *Yeah, I am.*"

-36-

SOMEBODY WHO LOOKS LIKE ME

In the first decade of the twenty-first century, manager Doc McGhee had taken Hootie & the Blowfish from commercial irrelevance and disorganization into profitability and efficiency. However, the greatest gift Doc McGhee was to give Hootie & the Blowfish—and the world—was yet to come.

Darius Rucker imagined that he might become a country singer. Doc helped make that dream come true, on a scale virtually no one, not even Darius, could have dared to imagine.

This is a fact that cannot be sugarcoated: In 2008, country music was White. Now, that doesn't mean that its fans were exclusively White (this was far from true) or that its origins were White (this was not remotely the case). But for eighty-five years, the artists who visibly and commercially made mainstream country music, who were showcased to the world as representatives of the genre, and who were played on country radio and distributed by country record labels were overwhelmingly White.

Darius Rucker became the first African American in a generation to make a mark in country music and one of only a handful (and I literally mean handful, as you can count them on the fingers on one hand, *omitting the thumb*) to become a big star in the industry.

This monumental story begins with a Hootie & the Blowfish band meeting.

Actually . . . it begins long before that. On Saturday, December 10, 1927.

DeFord Bailey looked nervously at the studio clock. It was a handful of seconds before nine o'clock P.M. in the Central Time Zone. In 90 seconds—no, 88—no, 86—he would go live on the radio as the first act of the night on a popular radio show, the WSM Barn Dance. On a clear, cold late autumn night like this, WSM could be heard as far north as Chicago and as far south as New Orleans, from Raleigh in the East to Little Rock in the West.

The WSM Barn Dance was the second most popular hillbilly radio show on the airwaves (and moving up quickly to no. 1). The type of music the program showcased wouldn't be called country for another twenty years. Most people referred to it as hillbilly, although sometimes they called it mountain music or just old-time music.

Bailey, a fierce and inventive harmonica player, would be opening tonight's Barn Dance with one of his audience favorites, "Pan-American Blues." It was a noisy, churning, almost avant-garde sound painting that succeeded in evoking the new era of gleaming silver cross-country trains lancing valley and mountain, desert and city. It is still resonant and affecting today.

Nine o'clock approached, and the clock counted down to zero. The lead-in to the local Nashville show would be a program fed from the national NBC Red Network, a classical music show called "The Music Appreciation Hour." The founder and host of the Barn Dance, George Dewey Hay, whose wide politician smile and full head of Brylcreemed hair earned him the nickname "Judge," stepped to the microphone to welcome listeners to the Barn Dance and to introduce Bailey.

Hay ad-libbed, which was not uncommon for him. "For the past hour," he said, "we have been listening to music taken largely from Grand Opera. From now on, we will present the Grand Ole Opry." He then smiled and cued Bailey with his index finger.

DeFord Bailey, an African American grandson of slaves, was the first artist ever heard on the newly renamed Grand Ole Opry radio show.

Not long afterward, Bailey was formally inducted into the Grand Ole Opry, a powerful and utile honor that allowed him to use the Opry name to promote his performances, put him in good stead with the Opry's leviathan booking service, and ensured that he would regularly appear on the radio program that would very shortly become the gold standard in hillbilly music.

It would be a full forty years before another African American was inducted into the Grand Ole Opry—Charlie Rich, in 1967. Forty-five years after that, country superstar Brad Paisley stepped to the microphone at the conclusion of Darius Rucker's Opry performance on Tuesday, October 16, 2012, and invited him to be the third African American (out of a total of one hundred ninety-three members) to be formally inducted into the Grand Ole Opry.

Country music wasn't always considered an exclusively White medium. Before 1933, "country" featured many integrated recording sessions, including those by the legendary industry leaders like the Carter Family and Jimmy Rodgers. At the time, both the common and commercial repertoire for country was full of songs learned from African American performers and composers. In the mid- and late 1920s, hillbilly music was, in many ways, as thoroughly cross-cultural as rock music would be in the mid-1960s.

The racial division of country music was more the process of record industry economics coming from up North than the product of Jim Crow coming from the South. As the modern record industry developed, companies found that it streamlined their marketing if they could divide the marketplace into "race" and "hillbilly," and sell to record stores and retail outlets serving these color-divided markets, more or less without crossover. As detailed in Diana Pecknold's fascinating book, *Hidden in the Mix: The African American Presence in Country Music*, this in turn created the myth that "hillbilly" was a genre largely of Celtic origin and "an authentic folk expression of southern mountaineers," as opposed to the truth: Extensive racial, cultural and geographical mixing was essential to the foundations of country. Likewise, these marketing decisions underlined the myth that "race" music was a product of the plantation and the narrow and noisy tenements of New Orleans, Chicago, and New York.

The marketing terms "race" and "hillbilly" were industry standard until well after World War II, when they were replaced by "rhythm and blues" and "country and western" by record company offices, industry trade magazines, and record stores. These terms denied the common roots and cross-cultural and interracial collaborations that had contributed to both styles. But what had begun as a ploy to simplify marketing soon became a myth that was ingrained into the public and corporate fabric of country music. By the mid-twentieth century, most of America considered country an aspect of White heritage, and both the media and the industry rarely referenced its multicultural roots or the reality that country had many African American fans.

It is important to note that the nearly unbelievable gap between Charley Pride's success in the late 1960s and the emergence of Darius Rucker in 2008 was not a completely empty space for people of color. Cleve Francis scratched the lower ranges of the country charts in the early 1990s before returning to his career as an esteemed cardiologist. Trini Triggs appeared in the middle of the country charts in the late 1990s and early 2000s; and a handful of Hispanic performers, like Freddy Fender, Johnny Rodriguez, and Rick Trevino, made some impression on the country landscape. In addition, Aaron Neville, Tina Turner, and the Pointer Sisters occasionally popped up in the country charts with faith-based, seasonal, and gospel crossovers, and Ray Charles famously scored some country hits in the pre-Charley Pride era, parallel to his pop and R&B career.

But this is a fact: Not one African American artist sustained a hit-based career in country music between Pride and Rucker, and the number of artists making country music for major labels and being promoted by mainstream country radio was to remain vastly and overwhelmingly White until Darius Rucker hit the charts in 2008, eighty-one years after DeFord Bailey helped introduce the Grand Ole Opry to America.

There is a fascinating and peculiar architectural quirk that stands as a powerful metaphor of the thorough Whiteness of country music. Nashville's Ryman Auditorium is considered the mother church of country music. Between 1943 and 1974, it was the official home of the Grand Ole Opry, and the WSM radio broadcasts that beamed country music's greatest stars out to America originated from the Ryman. Literally—not figuratively but *literally*—every superstar, every influencer, every beloved and revered figure in the history of country music after 1943 played the Ryman stage. It is, without a doubt, one of the most justifiably famous concert venues in America, and today's country stars continue to perform there as an act of homage, even though the Opry has moved to a new home.

The Ryman was built in 1885, originally intended as a tabernacle for large religious services. In 1897, the United Confederate Veterans hired the Ryman for a meeting. While planning the gathering, they found that the venue was too small for their needs, so the Confederate Veterans paid for a balcony to be built into the Ryman. To commemorate their funding of the addition, at the very front and center of that balcony, visible from anywhere on the stage, the United Confederate Veterans placed a sign that said "CONFEDERATE GALLERY."

Although this sign was (sometimes) covered by a placard that read "1892 RYMAN AUDITORIUM," the Confederate Gallery sign remained in place until 2017. This means that when Darius Rucker first performed at the Ryman in 2008 (and many times thereafter), he was staring right up at a sign that honored the contributions of the veterans of the Confederacy.

But let's return to that meeting that halted one touring career and began another.

"Soni says in a meeting that he doesn't want to tour anymore," Darius Rucker explains, in a straightforward manner. "And ever since I heard Radney Foster back in the day, I would say, 'I'm going to make a country record someday, I'm going to make a country record someday.' It was like a mantra in my head. My original thought was that I was going to do this in my basement, or in some studio in South Carolina with my buddies, and I would have some fun doing it and that's all it was going to be. And I was totally fine with that."

"At some point, Doc becomes aware that I am saying this stuff about doing a country record," Darius continues, "And I get a phone call one night. And it's Doc. He says 'Whatcha doing?' I say, 'Oh, just hanging out.' And Doc says, 'I got ya a record deal in Nashville.' And my exact words to him were, 'With who?' Because I figured, oh, it'll probably be with Joe Schmoe records, in which case, forget that, I'll do it and release it myself. I said that on the phone. 'I don't want to sign with some indie label. If that's the case, Doc, I can just do it myself.'"

"And he pauses," Darius says, "and he builds up the moment, and then Doc says, 'No . . . it's with Capitol Records and you are signing with the president of the label.' And I said, '*Bullshit, Doc.*' And I didn't say it in a funny way, I said it in a 'don't fuck with me' kind of way. And then he hands the phone over to Mike Dungan [EMI/Capitol Nashville President]. And Dungan says, 'I'm going to give you a record deal, why don't you come see me in a few days?'"

Over a decade later and millions of records sold, Darius remains surprised. "I tell people all the time," Darius says, "if I was president of a record label, and I was looking at someone who had the exact same career arc as I did, I would not have given me a record deal. First of all, I am a *Black guy,* coming from pop, who has already had this huge career that is basically *over,* and now you're going to come to country music and you're gonna carpetbag? Never gonna work."

Darius makes it clear that race was not the only reason why much of the Nashville establishment thought his country career would be a nonstarter. "It was the race thing *and* the pop thing," Darius states. "Look at everyone from pop who tries to come over and break into country—from Jewel to Bon Jovi—and it just doesn't work. You might have a hit, but you don't have a career."

Doc McGhee: "So, Tim, let me ask you a question. Before we had Darius go country, you know how many people had a no. 1 single in country from any format outside of country?"

I tell Doc I have no idea.

"Zero," Doc emphatically states. "Nobody who came from another format had a no. 1 in country. Not Kid Rock, not Bon Jovi, not anyone. They had collaborations that did well, but not a song, and that's because country was very protective of country. And they didn't want this thing called carpetbaggers who thought 'Well, I'm having a tough time in pop and rock so I'm just gonna go do a country record because that's easy and I can have a newfound career in country.' Nobody did it but Darius Rucker."

Regardless of the fact that Nashville traditionally distrusted musicians from other genres attempting to break into country, Darius has no illusions about the primary obstacle he faced when he entered the country marketplace. "*Of course* the Black thing," Darius says, firmly.

"There hadn't been a Black guy on country radio at that time in twenty-five years. Before I got a record deal, I knew that would be a challenge. It's not hard to know when it's always right in your face. Until I came around twelve years ago, there were no Black faces on country radio. None. What makes me think that I'm going to change that?"

Learn to Live, Darius Rucker's second solo album and his first record in the country music genre, was released on September 16, 2008. Unbelievably, Darius had put out an album that actually shook up the music industry more than *cracked rear view* had. He had struck lightning twice. He had a hit record in a brand new genre when he was in his forties, and he had not just broken country's color line but trampled it. Today—and this is true—if you Google "Who is the Black guy who sings country music?" you get, "Darius Rucker."

Rather than detail *Learn to Live* in any deep musical context, it is more startling, more *important,* just to list everything Darius Rucker achieved with his first country record. *Learn to Live* became a no. 1 country album, and reached no. 5 on the *Billboard* charts (making it Darius's most successful "pop" release since *Musical Chairs*). It yielded three no. 1 country singles ("Don't Think About It," "It Won't Be Like This For Long," and "Alright," each of which also made it to the pop Top 40). Darius became the first artist to score three country no. 1 hits on the first three releases since Wynonna Judd in 1992; and on November 11, 2009, Darius became the first African American to win the Country Music Association's New Artist of the Year Award.

Frank Rogers, one of the leading producers in the country music genre, produced *Learn to Live.* The relationship forged between Darius and Rogers was so strong that not only would Rogers go on to produce or coproduce four more hugely successful Darius Rucker albums (in fact, every one but 2017's *When Was the Last Time*), but Rogers would also coproduce Hootie & the Blowfish's 2019 *Imperfect Circle* album.

In the years since *Learn to Live,* Darius's extraordinary country hit streak continued (and continues), as he rose to superstar level. Darius Rucker's second country album, *Charleston, SC 1966,* was released on October 12, 2010. Not only did it reach no. 1 on the country charts, it climbed to no. 2 on *Billboard*'s Top 200 pop albums (behind Lil Wayne's *I Am Not a Human Being*). It also yielded two no. 1 country singles. Hootie's sales and chart performance had been historic, but Darius was making history. This was underlined, in a goosebump-inducing way, on October 2, 2012, when Darius Carlos Rucker became only the third African American (and the first in nineteen years) to be invited to become a member of the Grand Ole Opry.

Darius Rucker: "I was doing the country thing because I wanted to sing like Radney Foster. I wasn't doing it to succeed and I didn't expect any success because looking at the situation beforehand, there was nothing that was saying, 'This is gonna be big, you're gonna have no. 1 records and no. 1 songs.' Being Black, being in my forties—I won Best New Artist at 41! I did not expect this. So yes, I look at this and go *wow*."

With Hootie's hiatus continuing, Darius's remarkable success kept on rolling, rolling, rolling . . . right up and through "Wagon Wheel."

On May 21, 2013, Darius released his third country record, *True Believers*. Once again, it reached no. 1 on the country charts and, for the second straight time, no. 2 on the all-genre top *Billboard* Top 200 charts (behind Daft Punk's *Random Access Memories*). The first single from *True Believers* became one of Darius Rucker's signature songs. There was a wonderful symmetry to "Wagon Wheel," and here's why: Both Hootie & the Blowfish's "Only Wanna Be With You" and Darius's "Wagon Wheel" had roots in songs composed by Bob Dylan.

In 1973, Bob Dylan was commissioned to record a soundtrack for director Sam Peckinpah's neo-realist western, *Pat Garrett & Billy the Kid*. Although it contains one of his most famous 1970s compositions, "Knockin' on Heaven's Door," for the most part Dylan's soundtrack is made up of loose, simple acoustic sketches. Even though much of the completed soundtrack album sounds like, well, outtakes (and I'm saying that as a fan of the record), there were tracks recorded for *Pat Garrett & Billy the Kid* that didn't make the final cut. One of these was a very rough, almost ghostly, partial sketch of a song. In essence, Dylan's sketch (which was released on multiple bootleg recordings from the 1970s onward) was really just a chorus, and Dylan is singing so far off microphone that he almost sounds like a wind, whistling through the misshapen windows or loose floorboards of an old wooden house. This outtake was the basis for "Wagon Wheel."

Fast-forward twenty-seven years. Keith Secor, of the much-acclaimed Americana string/folk/old-time country act Old Crow Medicine Show, decided to finish Dylan's sketch and released it on both the Old Crow Medicine Show's 2001 indie EP, *Troubles Up and Down the Road*, and the group's 2004 major label debut, *O.C.M.S.* From there, fans of Americana music all over the world, including Darius Rucker, picked up the song.

Frank Rogers: "Darius is the one who brought 'Wagon Wheel' to our attention. I had first heard the song when I was in college. I remember hearing it on a late-night PBS special, and I'm pretty sure it was Gillian Welch and Dave Rawlings doing a version of it. And I just went 'man, that is cool.' And I never could find the song. And then I would hear it in a bar every now and then. It was in my consciousness, but I didn't really know it that well. And then Darius texts me one day and says he had been to his daughter's school recital, and the faculty band played it. And he called me and said, 'Man do you know this song, 'Wagon Wheel'? I really didn't know it and they just played it and I love it. I wanna cut it!' And I said, 'Okay. I don't know if it's ever been a hit. It seems like a lot of people have recorded it.' Sure enough, I went back and looked, and a lot of people had recorded it, but no one's ever had a single with it. As soon as we started recording it, first, second take, you just knew that there was some magic in it."

So once again, Bob Dylan had (unknowingly) made a major contribution to Darius Rucker's career and bank account. And at the Fifty-Sixth annual Grammy Awards on January 26, 2014, Darius and "Wagon Wheel" won the Grammy for Best Country Solo Performance. Darius became only the third African American artist in Grammy history to win a vocal performance award in the country music category. Darius Rucker's country career continued to steam roll from there. *Home for the Holidays* in 2014, *Southern Style* in 2015, and *When Was the Last Time* in 2017 all were top three country albums, and each scored significantly high in the *Billboard* Top 200 charts.

And Darius didn't just have hits. He gave hope. His success means that a person of color who might never dream of having a country music career could now see Darius on stage or on TV and they will go, "I can do that, too."

Journalist Sara Rodman: "As somebody who was a huge country music fan and knew that, just like rock and roll, that there was so much African-American heritage in country music that had been overlooked, forgotten, and unsung, to see Darius succeed in that way gave me a great sense of pride. It was like, *here's somebody*. Charley Pride is pretty much all we've got in a mainstream, household name fashion. There are other people along the way, people in the Opry, people that if you are a true student that you can name. But Charley Pride's our guy. So the fact that Darius was able to be *the next guy* gave me so much hope that this door would be opening."

Rodman emphasizes that it wasn't that country artists of color just didn't exist for seventy-five years; it's that they weren't able to find their way into the system. "Those musicians of color were always there and working. They were turned away by people who thought that's not country music, that's not what you're supposed to be doing, why don't you go sing an R&B song? Why don't you go rap somewhere else? And of course, that's ridiculous and insulting. It's statistically impossible there weren't fantastic African American or Latino or gay or any other kind of marginalized group person making great country music. But no door was opened for them. Darius was already through the door, it was just a matter of what he did once he got through the door, and he did everything right. He's also incredibly charming, and that voice and he had so much going for him that a brand new artist wouldn't have. But it could have, should have happened before."

This gift of empowerment is perhaps the apotheosis of the ordinary and extraordinary magic of Hootie & the Blowfish. It led to Darius Rucker giving people the ability to believe in something that they once thought was impossible.

"You get a lot of notes from fans," Darius says, "and one of my favorite ones that I get with some frequency—and every time I get it, it gives me chills—is when I get something from an African American woman or African American man, and it says, 'Thank you, because I have always loved country music, and now I don't have to hide it, because there's somebody up there doing it who looks like me.'"

Sarah Rodman: "There are people that we have not yet heard from who will one day tell us that they saw Darius, and when they did they said, 'I wanna do that and now I know I can.' I don't think that was his point at all, or his goal. And that's what's so beautiful about organic representation. There's no reason that there can't be fifty other Charley Prides, fifty other Darius Ruckers."

-37-

COVERING YOURSELF

During these years of Darius's stunning success as a solo artist, the four members of Hootie & the Blowfish reassembled on a regular basis to perform at the two annual high-profile charity events they had long been closely associated with: Monday After the Masters and the HomeGrown Concert.

In the meantime, both Mark Bryan and Soni Sonefeld also released notable solo music.

Mark's first album, *30 On the Rail*, is actually the very first Hootie & the Blowfish solo album, released in 2000 (before Darius's *Back to Then*) and distributed by Atlantic. His second LP, *End of the Front*, came in 2008, and the third, *Songs of the Fortnight*, came in 2017, followed by *Midlife Priceless* in 2021. Suffice it to say that if you like Hootie & the Blowfish, you will like Mark Bryan's work. Deliciously warm and inviting, it presents a more intimate, you're-right-in-the-room-with-him take on the roaring, chiming Mellencamp-meets-college radio rock/good-time bluegrass you hear on every Hootie album. Drop your needle—figuratively, or, who knows, literally—anywhere on any of Mark's three albums, and you'll find yourself smiling, especially if you're a fan of 1980s and '90s guitar-based indie pop. Considering how uniformly melodic and welcoming these albums are, it seems slightly odd that Mark has never really tried to bring his solo music up to a "mainstream" level of visibility.

Mark Bryan: "I have never felt a strong desire to be a solo artist. I am a songwriter who likes to document his work and enjoys that process. I work, occasionally, as a solo artist, but I wouldn't say I pursue a solo career. I document the songs I write that mean something to me, and I share that with the world. I know I have something to say, and I don't need to get famous doing it, but I do want people to *connect* to this music that inspires me. This feeling still drives me."

Likewise, the solo releases of "Soni" Sonefeld will make a great deal of sense to fans of Hootie, many of whom are already long familiar with his extraordinary ability to mix melody, emotion, and drama in an extremely adept package. Since 2012, Soni has released three mini-albums—sixteen songs altogether—titled *Found* (2012), *In* (2014), and *Love* (2015). These document, with enormous grace and skill, Soni's unfolding, powerful, and multidimensional relationship with his faith. A song like "The Cross Before the Crown" (from *Love*) is very clearly composed by the same person who wrote all those big arm-waving Hootie ballads. In addition (as anyone who has seen a Hootie show can testify), Soni is a lead-singer-quality vocalist, and this is clearly on display in his recordings. Whatever your thoughts about music with overtly religious or faith-based content, pretty much everything Soni has released as a solo artist is flat-out terrific and showcases a singer, songwriter, and producer who probably would have been successful even if he had never met Darius, Dean, and Mark.

Toward the end of the formal Hootie & the Blowfish hiatus, Darius, Dean, Mark, and Soni reconvened in the recording studio for the first time in thirteen years. However, these sessions were not publicized, and even some of the band's most avid fans aren't aware they took place.

On March 17, 2017, Hootie & the Blowfish and producer Don Gehman came to Blackbird Studios in Nashville to re-record five of their best known hits (all from *cracked rear view*, which, of course, is not a surprise). These were never intended to be commercially released and probably never will be. However, they served an important purpose.

When an artist signs a contract, the label usually owns the master recording in perpetuity. However, after the expiration of the standard "re-recording clause"—usually seven years after the initial release—an artist is free to re-record their compositions. They can then sell these new versions without asking the original label for permission, and they don't need to give the original record label a cut of the profits. Sometimes, artists release these re-recorded versions (as Taylor Swift has famously done), but often they just use them for licensing to film, TV, and advertising, which can be an extremely lucrative business.

Re-recording is a win-win for most bands, and a lot of major acts have re-recorded their hits so they can control their usage and maximize their profit from that usage. Listen closely next time you hear hits by Devo, Electric Light Orchestra, Twisted Sister, or Modern English in a commercial or film, and you'll note that these are often not the versions of the song you grew up with, but very close replicas.

So, on St. Patrick's Day 2017, Mark, Dean, Soni, Darius, and Don, the original team who cut those ginormous Hootie hits back in the '90s, came together to cut new versions of some of those songs, with the intention of sounding as much like the original versions as possible.

"It's rare that a band can get some monetary leverage on their art," says Soni. "That's what these re-records were all about for me, pure and simple. Though it did raise this question: Are you selling out if you record cover versions of your own songs? I think not. It was great to be in the studio with the guys again, though. I think we did a respectable job of sounding like Hootie & the Blowfish."

Even if the re-records were a bit of a secret, Hootie's next move would be very, very public. America was about to fall in love with Hootie & the Blowfish all over again.

PART VI

2019-2020

The Soundtrack
of Your Life

–38–

THIRTEEN THOUSAND KEGS

By the time Dean Felber, Mark Bryan, Darius Rucker, and Soni Sonefeld reassembled in March of 2017 to re-record a handful of their hits, discussions were already underway regarding a full-scale Hootie & the Blowfish tour.

According to attorney Gus Gusler, there had been some consideration of staging a tour in 2014 to celebrate the twentieth anniversary of the release of *cracked rear view*. But the enormous success of "Wagon Wheel" put an end to even the most preliminary chatter about that possibility. In 2017, discussions regarding the possibility of a full-scale Hootie tour resumed.

The band did not have an official manager at the time, so Gus, in coordination with Darius's manager, Chris Parr, reached out to Rob Light, the head of Darius's booking agency, CAA. Light thought that the demand for a Hootie tour marking the twenty-fifth anniversary of *cracked rear view* would be enormous. Once he had Light's opinion, Gus went back to the band members to discuss the idea.

It wasn't just a matter of sending everyone a text and telling them when to stand outside their houses and wait to be picked up by the bus. An entire year had to be set aside, with all the resultant planning and rearrangement of business and familial priorities. In addition, even though there was still two years to go before the actual event, there wasn't much time for waffling or maybes. Major venues have to be booked years in advance. Of course, Mark was raring to go. That was the no-brainer. Dean and Soni, whose step off of the touring carousel had precipitated the decision to go on hiatus in 2008, also gave the thumbs up.

Next was Darius. He had the most at stake. He would have to set aside his lucrative solo recording and touring career for an entire year (which meant, essentially, taking a pay cut to do a Hootie tour). In addition, if the shows didn't sell well, it could reflect badly on his star power. Regardless of his affection for his bandmates and Hootie's legacy, Darius had his doubts.

Enter Rob Light. Light is one of the most powerful people in the music industry today. He is the head of the music division at Creative Artists Agency, one of the largest management and booking agencies for artists, musicians, filmmakers, and athletes in the world. As a booking agent and advisor, he was fundamental both in the emergence of Darius Rucker as a country artist and the return to the road in 2019 of Hootie & the Blowfish.

"The last time the band toured [in 2008], it didn't do very well," Light says. "It was theaters and ballrooms, and it didn't impact in any real way that people are gonna remember. And this sort of discussion and worry went on for a while, but at the end, Darius called me up. He said, 'Tell me what you're telling everybody else. Why do you believe in this so much?' And this is what I told him—it's the same thing I said to the promoters, to my agents, to the managers, to Gus, and then inevitably to the band, which is very simple—"

"Music defines your youth," Light states. "It always has, it always will. Your favorite bands when you are seventeen to twenty-five become the soundtrack of your life. Now, that doesn't mean that you won't like music when you're thirty, or you won't find new things when you're thirty. And it doesn't mean you didn't like music when you were twelve. But that junior year of high school to the end of college is the soundtrack of your life, and that music has an impact that is indefinable. You can't put it into words. Twenty years later, twenty years after college, when you're now in your forties, when you've had a couple of kids, when everything about your life has taken on a different look, good, bad, or indifferent, all you want is to *feel* what you felt when you were eighteen, and the only thing that really takes you back there is music."

"And I said to Darius," Light continues, "'There is a generation, and they all wanna be frat brothers again. Every one of them. And they all wanna wear jeans that are too tight and T-shirts that don't fit. And they all want to drink one extra beer and laugh and smile.' And if you were that frat guy, Hootie & the Blowfish represent that more than any band. This was the soundtrack of your life. I said to Darius, 'I have no doubt that they're gonna come out in *waves*. They're gonna call their buddies and say, 'Come on, we have to go see this.' If they could've brought a keg to these gigs, they would have. And I knew that before we even booked the first show. There were a lot of bands from that era that had big records and hits, but *cracked rear view* defined the moment. And if you were seventeen to twenty-two or twenty-three years old, you wore that record out. There are very few albums that do it. So I was *certain* it was going to work."

Darius still was not 100 percent convinced, but he signed on anyway. "My *real* thoughts—and I said this in the first meeting—if it's not going to be big, I'm not interested. I said it, just like that. When the idea of the twenty-fifth anniversary tour came up, I wasn't thinking about 1994, or 1995, or 1997, I was thinking about 2005, or 2008, when we were playing the rotating stage at the Melody Tent in Cape Cod! And I was, like, I don't want to go out to do that, I am out playing arenas by myself, so if we are not going to go out and do something big, I don't want to do it. And the day tickets went on sale, I called Rob Light and said, 'I was wrong.'"

In 2019, Hootie & the Blowfish staged one of the biggest comebacks in music history. This is one of those instances where the numbers say *a lot*, so I'm going to pile a whole bunch of them into the next few paragraphs.

The Group Therapy Tour (the name, a shoutout to one of Hootie's favorite Columbia venues of the 1980s), Hootie & the Blowfish's first tour in eleven years, began on May 30, 2019, at Veterans United Home Loans Amphitheater in Virginia Beach, Virginia. That night, Darius Rucker, Dean Felber, Soni Sonefeld, and Mark Bryan, ably assisted onstage by Peter Holsapple, Gary Greene, and Garry Murray, played a sold-out show in front of 14,865 people. That's more than the combined audience for the final six shows Hootie played at the end of their last tour in 2008. The opening date grossed $863,872, which is, uh, *a lot of effing money*—actually, more than the band made performing live during entire *years* in the dark days of the early 2000s. And that was one of the smallest grosses of the entire tour.

The North American leg of the Group Therapy Tour officially ended fourteen weeks later with three shows at the Colonial Life Arena in the band's hometown of Columbia, South Carolina. The tour played exclusively in arenas and sheds, ranging from nine thousand seats to twenty-five (the average was fifteen thousand to eighteen thousand seats). Hootie & the Blowfish sold out forty-five of the tour's forty-seven shows, and played in front of over 650,000 people. It was a virtually unprecedented comeback. Lightning had struck for the third time.

The North American Group Therapy dates grossed forty-two million dollars. That was *twice* as much as the band's biggest touring year in the 1990s. According to *Billboard*'s calculations, even when adjusted for inflation, in 2019, the band did 43 percent *bigger* business than they did in 1996, previously their best year for touring. And the higher grosses weren't just because of the higher ticket prices; in 2019, Hootie were selling an average of three thousand more tickets per show than they were in 1996.

In 1985, the Wolf Brothers would play Pappy's and get paid in a keg, which Darius and Mark would roll up the hill to their dorm, where the party—and the gig—would continue. With what they made on an average night on the Group Therapy Tour, Darius and Mark could have bought thirteen thousand kegs. And if you returned thirteen thousand kegs (ask Paul Graham to do it), with your deposit return *alone* you could send your kid to the University of South Carolina for fifty-four years (only slightly longer than it took Soni to graduate).

This wasn't a comeback. This was a legitimate American phenomenon.

"I felt deep in my soul that we could have a successful tour, and that we could *probably* do amphitheaters," says Dean, long the most pragmatic and business minded of the band. "I wasn't thinking sellouts—maybe here, maybe there—I figured the Midwest would be strong; the numbers in the Midwest had never really gone down for us, for whatever reason, we had always continued to play amphitheaters in Midwest. So we remained strong in some territories, but in other places, back in the first decade of the 2000s, we had reached the point where a promoter might not even offer us a gig. I didn't have a lot of expectations because I didn't want to have a lot of expectations, I just wanted to have fun, and have my family come out and enjoy it. Different promoters had said that they thought it would do well, but I took that with a grain of salt."

"But they were right," says Dean. "I think it ended up blowing everyone away, even the promoters. It was the same feeling as when we sold out amphitheaters back in the day, so flattering that so many people want to spend their money and their time to come out and see us."

For me, there were some dramatic differences between the shows in 2019 and the many earlier Hootie performances I had seen. First and foremost was the emergence of Darius as a *true* frontman, as opposed to the lead singer in a band of equals who had formerly spent most of the set with a guitar strapped on. The strutting, dancing, hip-shaking, catwalk-prowling Darius Rucker you all saw on the Group Therapy Tour dates would have only been evident for five or ten minutes back in 1996 or '97. It did seem like a logical progression, however, and in some ways, it allowed Darius—always a somewhat restrained, almost shy live performer—to *finally* hold his own against the band's long-time stage extrovert, the leaping, stomping, running, windmilling, grinning Mark Bryan. In many ways, the "new" Darius gave Hootie what it always was missing: the classic guitarist–lead singer dynamic, where two hugely competent and outgoing performers challenge each other for the spotlight.

One other consistent difference was the addition of Garry Murray, Darius Rucker's longtime sideman, to the onstage lineup (alongside Peter Holsapple and Gary Greene, both of whom had been playing with the band since Bill Clinton was in the White House). Unlike Gary and Peter, both of whom largely stayed on the risers to the rear of the stage, Garry spent most of the set on or near the Dean/Darius/Mark frontline. In addition to Garry's stellar playing (especially on fiddle, which was a new and welcome addition to the onstage sound arsenal), his presence on stage further contributed to the "classic" rock band dynamic to the group.

And that "classic" live rock dynamic was the biggest difference between 2019 and the 1990s. In the 1990s, Hootie & the Blowfish were still, essentially, just a college rock band doing their thing in larger venues. But on the Group Therapy Tour, by consistently working from a set list that was coordinated with an extensive yet not overwhelming video backdrop that complimented the content of the songs, they had finally taken the logical steps to being an arena band, without sacrificing any of their joy or subtlety.

Rob Light: "The brilliance of the tour was not how well it did 'cause that's great, they deserve to do well. And not the shock that they played so well, 'cause they're a great band. It's that when you got there, it didn't feel nostalgic, it didn't feel dated. It felt fresh and vibrant, Sure, the room is full of forty-year-old frat bros, but it didn't feel old. It was so organically fresh, I think the audience had even a better time 'cause it was more than they thought it was gonna be."

"It's the coolest thing," says former South Carolina governor, Ambassador Nikki Haley. "When you start singing 'Hold My Hand' or 'Time' and people go back to that moment. And they celebrate. It says so much about the band and the guys and who they are and what they've done. I love that they're still relevant. And I think that the reason they're relevant is because they're genuine."

For me the best moments during the Group Therapy Tour was when you saw Mark, Dean, Soni, and Darius interacting again as friends, as people who shared a dream. For one hundred or so minutes every night, these four middle-aged men could once again relate to each other with the same spirit, joy, and love they had thirty years earlier, when the adventure began. I truly believe that the main reason these guys agreed to do the twenty-fifth anniversary tour wasn't the money, nor the desire to readdress history, or even the urge to reconnect with the audience who so dearly loved them. Watching them on stage, it was easy to believe that the primary reason Darius Rucker, Dean Felber, Mark Bryan, and Jim Sonefeld were on the road in the summer of 2019 was because, for a few minutes each night, they were best friends again.

"I wanted us to do it again and go out and be who we were when we were kids," says Darius. "And we did, we had a blast."

"People ask me all the time," Darius continues, "'Do you miss when you were the biggest band in the world?' And I say, not at all. I miss when we were playing in clubs, and it was us against the world. That's the one thing about us that is so real. When the four of us get up there to do that, even if we hadn't played in forever, we could get up there right now and we would have that camaraderie. We'd have that laughter. We'd have that love of doing what we do together."

Another extraordinary thing happened to Hootie & the Blowfish in 2019, something I would never, ever have anticipated. The press started to like them.

One of the fascinating things about this phenomenon was that the 2019 pieces had the feel of a mea culpa. The writers weren't just saying, "Hey, I may have gotten this wrong back in the day, I've listened to *cracked rear view* again, and it's actually not so bad." The journalists were taking big gulps of breath and releasing great sobs of sorrow and pleas for forgiveness. The two most interesting and articulate of these articles was a whopper of a piece in *Esquire* by Dave Holmes (from January 2, 2019) and an even more gigantic overview in the *New York Times* by Jon Caramanica (published on June 6, 2019).

Caramanica's piece was, tellingly, headlined, "Hootie & the Blowfish, Great American Rock Band (Yes, Really)" and sub-headed "Twenty-five years after the group's pop supernova 'Cracked Rear View,' it's time for a reassessment." Now, that headline would have been enough, but Caramanica (who was nineteen when *cracked rear view* was released) did something most music journalists had been reluctant to do for a quarter of a century: He saw the depth in *cracked rear view*: "The first thing you notice when you return to 'Cracked Rear View' now is how ramshackle and loose at the edges it feels," Caramanica writes. "Even though the songs are sturdy, it feels remarkably hand spun. And it offered a tonic: Optimistic harmonies drive it from the very beginning. But this joy wasn't uncritically ebullient—beneath each of its healing lyrics was something broken." Caramanica also refers to the rest of *cracked rear view* as "underappreciated," and he picks up on the very solid and prevalent political content of *cracked rear view*, noting, somewhat sadly, "That Rucker was as much agitator as pacifier wasn't something critics took much note of."

Dave Holmes's article in *Esquire* took all this a bit further. The headline is, well, perfect: "How Our Cruelty Killed Hootie and the Blowfish—and Damaged Our Souls." Holmes goes on to note that America bullied and attacked Hootie with "performative viciousness" and that "We laughed them out of the game for no good reason, while we let Dave Matthews Band continue kicking around the same hacky sack for their next few albums." Holmes then writes one of the most accurate things I've ever read about the band and the warped public perception of these smart, sensitive, and even musically hip four men: "We thought that our neighbors thought that Hootie was no longer cool and, afraid of appearing uncool ourselves, we threw them overboard . . . We began a long slow slide in 1996, and we didn't even notice it. We got mean, then we got meaner . . . then we got social media, now Donald Trump is the president of the United States. . . . We have late-stage disease of the soul, and the first 1990s hipster to make an easy crack about Hootie and the Blowfish was patient zero." Holmes concludes with this: "We left our sincere, hopeful, big-hearted selves back in the middle of the Clinton administration, and we're going to have to reach all the way back there to retrieve them. Admit it: the world looks better in your cracked rear view. Welcome back, Hootie, and may all be forgiven."

And a new Hootie & the Blowfish album was coming down the turnpike, too.

-39-

WHERE'S OUR COUNTRY SONG?

In 2018, while the Group Therapy Tour was coming into focus, the band started making plans for their sixth studio album. It would be their first release of new material in fourteen years and their first record for a new label, Capitol Nashville.

"It started out the same as always," Mark says. "Soni, Dean, and I, throwing a bunch of our ideas out there. We began by collecting these ideas and making reasonable laptop/GarageBand demos, and we'd give it to Darius. He would spend some time with them, then we'd all get together, and the ones he liked, we would try to play together as a band."

"It did feel a little different," the Hootie guitarist continues, "because we hadn't done it in over ten years, so we were so disconnected stylistically at that point that it was harder to find that 'center.' We were not immediately on the same wavelength. That's to be expected when you haven't jammed on anything but old songs for over a decade. But that was also cool, in a certain way, because we were all coming from different places, and in typically Hootie fashion, we ended up with these really eclectic ideas."

Enter Jeff Trott. Like Hootie & the Blowfish, Trott (who was suggested to the band by Hootie co-manager Chris Parr) began his career working with (slightly) left-of-the-dial bands who mixed Americana with an R.E.M.-influenced jangle rock. This led to him playing very prominent roles, both onstage and as a songwriter, with

Wire Train, Sheryl Crow (he co-wrote some of Crow's biggest hits), and World Party. He also worked as a songwriter and producer with Stevie Nicks, Liz Phair, Counting Crows, Rob Thomas, and many others. All of this indicated that Trott was very much on the same wavelength as Dean, Soni, Mark, and Darius.

Recording for Hootie's "comeback" album proceeded relatively smoothly. It appeared that Trott, another fan of '80s college rock and roots music who could rattle off the names of obscure southern indie bands, was on his way to making a terrific twenty-first-century Hootie & the Blowfish album that would mix their twanging, jangly quirkiness with his undeniable hit-making credentials.

But about two thirds of the way through the recording process, a conscious decision was made by the band's management to gear the record more toward country radio. There were legitimate reasons behind this thinking: Since the last time Hootie had released a record, the album rock, adult rock, and adult alternative radio formats that had favored the band in the 1990s had lost much of their power. Undeniably, country had become the dominant radio format for a guitar-based act such as Hootie & the Blowfish. And it certainly didn't hurt that the band's lead vocalist had become a gigantic country star, and that many of Hootie's legacy fans had grown to love contemporary country music.

Frank Rogers, the super-acclaimed Nashville producer who had been behind the board for all of Darius's big country hits, had been involved in the Hootie album project early on to co-write some songs with Darius. But with the new mandate, his role expanded. "Towards the end of the record, I think they had made the decision that country radio was the bull's-eye," Rogers explains. "They felt like they had a great record, but they decided they need to pull someone from the country format to cut a few sides to aim it a little more at the radio. It was fun, it was a good experience, they're all good guys and talented guys. I recorded three songs, and Jeff did all the rest of them."

This was new territory for Hootie: They had never re-addressed the direction of a project during the actual recording of a record. "We wanted to make sure whatever we did, it was Hootie & the Blowfish," Mark states. "It had to be something different from what Darius was doing already, so that when he came back to his thing, it would be clear that he had made a departure. And from our standpoint, we needed to be unique and original and ourselves, and not just an extension of what Darius does solo. We all felt pretty strongly about that. It was even written into our record deal."

But, Mark states, "It made sense to work us through country radio, which was exactly Darius's territory, which, in theory, was going against everything we had intended. We had a band meeting, and we decided to move forward that way—make a country single, and go to country radio. I would have done this a different way, but we are a democratic band."

Imperfect Circle was a polished, modern, swinging but highly dynamic album that sounded, essentially, like Hootie & the Blowfish channeled through contemporary (2019) Nashville production values. To my ears, it is very different than any earlier Hootie & the Blowfish album. Arguably, it's the first time the band made an album where they sounded as if they were actively trying to fit into contemporary songwriting, recording, arrangement, and mixing structures.

I sometimes think that *Imperfect Circle* is what happens when you put too much thought into making a record and not enough thought into making a record with Darius Rucker, Dean Felber, Mark Bryan, and Jim Sonefeld. To me, it feels like a producer's record; and the one thing Hootie & the Blowfish had never done in thirty years of recording was make a producer's record. This is not to say that *Imperfect Circle* is, in any way, shape, or form, a bad or disappointing album. It's full of sass, rhythm, soul, and very sharp songwriting, and maybe it's exactly what a middle-aged Hootie & the Blowfish released by a top-tier Nashville major label should sound like. There is, without any doubt, wonderful stuff on *Imperfect Circle*. "Miss California" is a flat-out joy, "We Are One" is utterly delightful, and "Change" may be one of the twelve best Hootie songs ever recorded. The song I consider the very best from the *Imperfect Circle* sessions—a big, empowering, arm-waving, mid-tempo Soni song called "Unafraid"—didn't make it to the album, for reasons no one is entirely certain of. Here's hoping that it sees the light of day some time.

But for all that, perhaps the oddest thing about *Imperfect Circle* was the timing of its release. Because they re-addressed the album's direction midstream, it wasn't completed in time for the Group Therapy Tour. That meant that *Imperfect Circle* came out on November 1, 2019, just as the embers of the tour's enormous bonfire of good publicity and visibility were burning out. *Imperfect Circle* entered the *Billboard* Top 200 charts at no. 26 on November 16, 2019. Although this was Hootie & the Blowfish's highest placing on the album charts in 21 years, the record dropped out of the Top 200 in just two weeks. The album had a slightly more impactful performance in the country charts, where it debuted at no. 3. And, after the extraordinary numbers of the tour, no one could remotely consider 2019 and 2020 anything but a triumph for Dean, Darius, Mark, and Soni.

-40-

AN UNFINISHED STORY

Because the Hootie story is unfinished, this story must remain unfinished.

I can, however, say this: I am quite damn sure we have not heard the last of Hootie & the Blowfish. These four men are family, and there has been nothing to date that has even come close to breaking that union. They have watched one of their members achieve superstardom as a solo artist, without any tension or jealousy. In addition, they have survived one member marrying another's ex-wife, and that's the kind of thing that very, very few acts can get past . . . but Hootie did. There is also, of course, extraordinary financial incentive for Hootie to consider performing and recording again in the future.

But I don't think that's as important as these two simple facts:

First, they are friends. And one of the greatest expressions of that friendship occurs when Dean Felber, Mark Bryan, Jim Sonefeld, and Darius Rucker are on the same stage, making music together.

Second, they remain a part of *your* lives. They will never cease to be the soundtrack for some of your most powerful memories, regardless of whether those memories were tragic or trivial, serious or silly, romantic or merely drunken. More than anything, I say this: Hootie & the Blowfish belong to you. Darius, Dean, Mark, and Soni have proven time and time again that they are kind enough and giving enough to embrace that obligation. Because you will want Hootie & the Blowfish in your life, Hootie & the Blowfish will want to be in your life.

"The way we left it after 2019 is that we would always do it again when the time is right," says Mark. "2019 was right this time, and we did it, and it was great. When the time feels right again, we'll do it again."

To my mind, it would seem logical that we could expect a tour to mark the thirtieth anniversary of *cracked rear view* in 2024, but no one is even remotely making plans for such a thing. We also must remember that (barring an unforeseen tragedy or the kind of personal rift that the band has utterly and completely avoided for the past thirty-four years), Dean, Mark, Soni, and Darius will all come together to perform at least once every year for Monday After the Masters; probably each year for the annual HomeGrown Concert held on Daniel Island; and in addition, for special destination concert events such as Hootiefest in Cancun, Mexico, January 2022.

At the time of this writing—the end of the utterly unprecedented, fear-filled, pause-button of a year that was 2020 and early 2021—I do know this: Both Soni and Dean are comfortable at home and spending time with their families. Darius loves being on the road, in the spotlight, and discovering the extraordinary dimensions involved with being the biggest African American country star in history. And Mark is always chomping at the bit to move, record, play, tune more guitars, and follow the Johnny Quest Playbook.

I truly don't think Hootie & the Blowfish are done yet, and they never will be, because they are yours. They are your memories. They are the night you met your husband. The day your first child walked for the first time. The day you heard you got your first job. The afternoon you packed to move to your first apartment in a different city. They are that amazing night you raced down college-town sidewalks, full of cheap vodka and tobacco and the illusion that you would always be twenty-one, and "Only Wanna Be With You" would play endlessly, out of every bar doorway and through every rolled-down car window.

DISCOGRAPHY
1990-2020

Discographies are a necessary evil of music biographies.

They are necessary because it's informative to have a rundown of everything a band has released, and every discography will contain at least one "Oh wow, I never even heard of that!" moment. They are evil because, well, these things are usually really boring, hard to visually track, and annoyingly comprehensive. Often, reading a discography is like listening to a friend at a bar talk about lesser known baseball players from the 1960s when you can't even name better known baseball players from the 2020s.

Therefore, in this discography, I have consciously tried to include the interesting and informative stuff and avoid the boring and marginal stuff. For instance, I do not run down each and every release in each and every territory, nor do I list the matrix numbers of German promo pressings. Instead, this is your basic rundown of everything Hootie & the Blowfish have released in the United States, along with a fairly comprehensive listing of the compilations and soundtracks the band appeared on and especially interesting non-American releases (like unique English and Japanese live releases and the Australian double CD packaging of the first two albums). Unlike most discographies, which are organized by release format—album, single, compilation, etcetera—this one is chronological.

I have opted to restrict this discography to the band and not include solo releases from Darius Rucker, Mark Bryan, and Jim "Soni" Sonefeld, despite the consistently high quality of this work. (As of 2021, Dean Felber has not released anything under his own name, aside from one mysterious country pop track on a relatively obscure compilation album in 2002.) Here's why I am sidestepping the solo stuff: I can be fairly certain that between the time this book goes to the printer and when it reaches your eager hands, there probably will *not* be any new Hootie & the Blowfish releases. However, Darius, Mark, and Soni are prolific solo artists, and it's likely that any solo discography I would include would be out of date before this book is even published. Who knows? While this book is getting set, sealed, and delivered, Dean might even explode in a tsunami of solo creativity. It could happen.

Many thanks to Layne Montgomery and Christie Crone for their significant help with this discography.

1990

EXTENDED PLAY (EP)
Hootie & The Blowfish

April 1990, Rustyfish Management/Fischco (cassette). (Rustyfish was the early name for the band's management company, soon to be renamed Fishco.)

Produced by Dick Hodgin. All songs written by Mark Bryan, Dean Felber, Darius Rucker, and Jim Sonefeld.

1. I Don't Understand
2. Little Girl
3. Look Away
4. Let My People Go
5. Hold My Hand

1991

EP
Time

February 1991, Fishco (cassette)

Produced by Dick Hodgin (except "Let Her Cry," produced by Gary Bolton). All songs written by Mark Bryan, Dean Felber, Darius Rucker, and Jim Sonefeld.

1. Running From an Angel
2. Time
3. Let Her Cry
4. Drowning

COMPILATION APPEARANCE

"I Don't Understand" (*Hootie & the Blowfish* version) on *Snickers New Music Search 1990-1991 Presented By Campus Voice Semi Finalists.* Thirsty Ear (vinyl). (This is Hootie & the Blowfish's first appearance on vinyl.)

1992
COMPILATION APPEARANCE

"Drowning" (*Time* version) on *Please No Profanity.* Closet Normal Records. (CD to benefit South Carolina college radio stations WUSC in Columbia and WSBF in Clemson.)

1993
EP
Kootchypop

July 1993, Fishco (CD, cassette)
Produced by Hootie and the Blowfish and Mark Williams. All songs written by Mark Bryan, Dean Felber, Darius Rucker, and Jim Sonefeld. (Only band release credited to Hootie and the Blowfish, as opposed to Hootie & the Blowfish.)

1. The Old Man and Me
2. Hold My Hand
3. If You're Going My Way
4. Sorry's Not Enough
5. Only Wanna Be With You
6. Hold My Hand (edited)

1994
FULL-LENGTH ALBUM
cracked rear view

July 5, 1994, Atlantic Records (CD, vinyl, cassette)
Produced by Don Gehman. All songs written by Mark Bryan, Dean Felber, Darius Rucker, and Jim Sonefeld, except where noted.

1. Hannah Jane
2. Hold My Hand
3. Let Her Cry
4. Only Wanna Be With You
5. Running From an Angel
6. I'm Goin' Home
7. Drowning

8. Time
9. Look Away
10. Not Even the Trees
11. Goodbye
    Hidden track: "Motherless Child" (Traditional)

SINGLES

"Hold My Hand" b/w "I Go Blind." July 1994. (CD, vinyl, cassette) ("b/w" connotes the other songs on the single, an archaic usage that alludes to the days when singles were vinyl only, and "b/w" stood for "backed with.")

"The Christmas Song" (by Robert Wells and Mel Torme). November 1994. (CD; promo only)

"Let Her Cry" b/w "Fine Line" and "Where Were You." December 1994. (CD, vinyl; cassette in Australasia)

———

1995

FULL-LENGTH LIVE ALBUM
Hootie & the Blowfish in Concert

Recorded live at the Wulfrun Hall, Wolverhampton, England, May 26, 1995. (Released only for BBC radio broadcast and promo use, no general distribution on CD.)

1. 10' Applause Faded In
2. Hannah Jane
3. I Go Blind
4. Not Even the Trees
5. Motherless Child
6. I'm Going Home
7. Fine Line
8. Look Away
9. Let Her Cry
10. Running From an Angel
11. Time
12. Only Wanna Be With You
13. Drowning
14. Hold My Hand

SINGLES

"Hannah Jane" b/w "Hannah Jane" (live). January 1995. (Europe-only promo)

"Only Wanna Be With You" b/w "Use Me" (live) and "Only Wanna Be With You" (live). July 1995. (CD, vinyl)

"Time" b/w "Use Me" (live) and "The Ballad of John & Yoko" (live). October 1995. (CD, vinyl, cassette)

"Drowning." November 1995. (promo only)

COMPILATION APPEARANCES

"The Old Man and Me" (*Kootchypop* version) on *Aware 2: The Compilation*. Madaket Records (CD).

"Hey Hey What Can I Do" on *Encomium: A Tribute to Led Zeppelin*. Atlantic Records (CD; cassette in some European territories).

"Dream Baby" on *Music For The Motion Picture White Man's Burden* (film soundtrack). Atlantic Records (CD, cassette).

"I Go Blind" on *Friends* (TV show soundtrack). Reprise/Warner Bros (CD, LP, cassette).

LONG-FORM VIDEO
Summer Camp With Trucks
(live concert with backstage and tour footage)

Recorded in West Homestead, Pennsylvania, June 27, 1995, and released October 24, 1995. Warner Vision Entertainment (DVD, VHS, NTSC, PAL, Laserdisc).

Directed by Adolfo Doring.

1. Hannah Jane
2. Not Even The Trees
3. I'm Goin' Home
4. The Ballad Of John & Yoko
5. Let Her Cry
6. Running From An Angel
7. Time
8. Only Wanna Be With You
9. Drowning
10. Hold My Hand
11. Goodbye
12. Love The One You're With - Medley
13. Mustang Sally

1996
FULL-LENGTH ALBUM
Fairweather Johnson

April 23, 1996, Atlantic Records (CD, vinyl, cassette). (A double CD release featuring both *cracked rear view* and *Fairweather Johnson* was released in Australia in 1998.)

Produced by Don Gehman. All songs written by Mark Bryan, Dean Felber, Darius Rucker, and Jim Sonefeld.

1. Be the One
2. Sad Caper
3. Tucker's Town
4. She Crawls Away
5. So Strange
6. Old Man & Me (When I Get to Heaven)
7. Earth Stopped Cold at Dawn
8. Fairweather Johnson
9. Honeyscrew
10. Let It Breathe
11. Silly Little Pop Song
12. Fool
13. Tootie
14. When I'm Lonely

SINGLES

"Old Man & Me (When I Get to Heaven)" b/w "Before the Heartache Rolls In." April 1996. (CD, vinyl, cassette)

"Tucker's Town" b/w "Araby." July 1996. (CD, vinyl)

"Sad Caper" b/w "Renaissance Eyes" and "I'm Over You." November 1996. (CD)

EPS
The Live Singles

March 10, 1996 (Japan-only CD)

1. Hannah Jane
2. Hold My Hand
3. Only Wanna Be With You
4. Time

Tucker's Town

July 1, 1996 (Germany-only CD)

1. Tucker's Town
2. Araby
3. Not Even The Trees (live)
4. Hannah Jane (live)

LONG-FORM VIDEO

A Series of Short Trips (video compilation plus some documentary plus some live)
October 29, 1996, Warner Home Video (VHS, DVD)

1. Hold My Hand
2. Let Her Cry
3. Only Wanna Be With You
4. Time
5. Old Man And Me
6. Tucker's Town
7. Sad Caper
8. Honeyscrew
9. She Crawls Away
10. Be The One
11. Before The Heartache Rolls In
12. Araby
13. I'm Over You
14. 16 Runners And No Jim Beam

COMPILATION APPEARANCES

"The Christmas Song" (1993 version) on *A Very Special Christmas 3.* A&M Records (CD, vinyl, cassette in some territories).

"She Crawls Away" (*Fairweather Johnson* version) on *Mad About You - The Final Frontier (Music From And Inspired By The Television Series).* Atlantic records (CD).

1998

FULL-LENGTH ALBUM
Musical Chairs

September 15, 1998, Atlantic Records (CD, vinyl; Poland-only cassette)
Produced by Don Gehman. All songs written by Mark Bryan, Dean Felber, Darius Rucker, and Jim Sonefeld

1. I Will Wait
2. Wishing
3. Las Vegas Nights
4. Only Lonely
5. Answer Man
6. Michelle Post
7. Bluesy Revolution
8. Home Again
9. One By One
10. Desert Mountain Showdown
11. What's Going On Here
12. What Do You Want From Me Now
    Hidden track: Closet Full of Fears

SINGLES

"I Will Wait" b/w "Driver 8." September 1998.
"Only Lonely" b/w "Michelle Post" and "Frances." October 1998.

1999

SINGLE

"Wishing." May 1999 (promo-only CD)

COMPILATION APPEARANCES

"The Ballad of Hollis Brown" (by Bob Dylan) on *The Times They Are A Changin'—A Tribute to Bob Dylan Volume 3*. Sister Ruby Records.

"Freedom's Child" (song by Frank Wildhorn and Jack Murphy, from the concept album/musical *The Civil War*) on *The Civil War: The Complete Work*. Atlantic Theatre (CD).

"Only Lonely" on *Music From And Inspired By The Motion Picture Message In A Bottle* (film soundtrack). 143/Atlantic Records (CD).

2000

COMPILATION ALBUM
Scattered, Smothered and Covered

October 24, 2000, Atlantic (CD)
Produced by Don Gehman, Don Dixon, and Mark Williams.
(The Japanese version of this album contains "Freedom's Child." A cassette version of the album was released in Malaysia and Indonesia.)

1. Fine Line (Radney Foster)
2. I Go Blind (Neil Osborne, Phil Comparelli, Brad Merritt, Darryl Neudorf)
3. Almost Home (John Croslin)
4. Hey Hey What Can I Do (John Bonham, John Paul Jones, Jimmy Page, Robert Plant)
5. Renaissance Eyes (Don Dixon)
6. Before the Heartache Rolls In (Radney Foster, Bill Lloyd)
7. Araby (John Croslin)
8. I'm Over You (Bob Rupe)
9. Gravity of the Situation (Rob Veal)
10. I Hope That I Don't Fall In Love With You (Tom Waits)
11. Dream Baby (Cindy Walker)
12. Driver 8 (Bill Berry, Peter Buck, Mike Mills, Michael Stipe)
13. Let Me Be Your Man (Gregory Ritchey)
14. Please, Please, Please Let Me Get What I Want (Johnny Marr, Morrissey)
15. Use Me (Bill Withers)

SINGLE

"Use Me" (live version featuring Edwin McCain and Don Dixon) b/w "I Go Blind." December 2000 (vinyl).

COMPILATION APPEARANCES

"Hold My Hand" (live) on *The Best of Hard Rock Live*. Sire Records (CD).

"Hold My Hand" (live) on *Today Presents: The Best Of The Summer Concert Series, Volume One*. NBC Records (CD).

"Lovely Day" (by Bill Withers) on *Stop Handgun Violence*. Rounder Records. (This track appears nowhere else.)

"City By a River" on *Music From And Inspired By Jesus: The Epic Mini-Series*. Capitol/EMI/Sparrow (CD; this track appears nowhere else).

"Can't Find the Time to Tell You" on *Me, Myself & Irene (Music From The Motion Picture)*. Elektra Records (CD; cassette in some territories; This track appears nowhere else.)

2001 AND 2002

No new or previously unreleased music released

2003
FULL-LENGTH ALBUM
Hootie and the Blowfish

March 4, 2003, Atlantic Records (CD, vinyl)
Produced by Don Was. All songs written by Mark Bryan, Dean Felber, Darius Rucker, and Jim Sonefeld, except as noted.

1. Deeper Side
2. Little Brother
3. Innocence (Bryan, Felber, Pete Masitti, Rucker, Sonefeld)
4. Space
5. I'll Come Runnin'
6. Tears Fall Down
7. The Rain Song
8. Show Me Your Heart
9. When She's Gone
10. Little Darlin'
11. Woody
12. Go and Tell Him (Soup Song)
    Hidden track: Alright

SINGLES

"Space." August 2003. (promo-only CD)

EP
The Attachment

January 2003 (EP).

1. Ebb and Flow
2. Goodbye Girl (David Gates)
3. Ford Econoline (Nanci Griffith)
4. Inner Coastal Liquor Store

COMPILATION APPEARANCE

"Hold My Hand" (Sesame Street version) on *Songs From The Street: 35 Years Of Music (The Ultimate Sesame Street Music Collection)*. Sony Wonder label (CD; this track appears nowhere else).

2004

COMPILATION ALBUM
The Best of Hootie and the Blowfish (1993 thru 2003)

March 2, 2004, Atlantic (CD)
Produced by Don Gehman and Don Was. All songs written by Mark Bryan, Dean Felber, Darius Rucker, and Jim Sonefeld, except where noted.

1. Hold My Hand
2. Only Wanna Be With You
3. Time
4. Let Her Cry
5. Not Even the Trees
6. Old Man & Me (When I Get to Heaven)
7. Hey, Hey What Can I Do (John Bonham, John Paul Jones, Jimmy Page, Robert Plant)
8. Tucker's Town
9. I Go Blind (Neil Osborne, Phil Comparelli, Brad Merritt, Darryl Neudorf)
10. Sad Caper
11. Be the One
12. Use Me (Bill Withers)
13. I Will Wait
14. Innocence
15. Space
16. Only Lonely
17. Goodbye Girl (David Gates)

2005

FULL-LENGTH ALBUM
Looking for Lucky

August 5, 2005, Sneaky Long/Vanguard (CD, vinyl)
Produced by Don Gehman. All songs written by Mark Bryan, Dean Felber, Darius Rucker, and Jim Sonefeld, except where additional songwriters noted.

1. State Your Peace
2. Hey Sister Pretty (Nick Brophy, Bryan, Felber, Rucker, Sonefeld)

3. The Killing Stone (Matraca Berg, Bryan, Felber, Rucker, Sonefeld)
4. Get Out of My Mind (Nick Brophy, Bryan, Felber, Rucker, Sonefeld)
5. Another Year's Gone By (Bryan, Felber, Radney Foster, Rucker, Sonefeld)
6. Can I See You (Bryan, Felber, Derek George, Rucker, Sonefeld)
7. A Smile
8. One Love (Bryan, Felber, Phillip Lammonds, Rucker, Sonefeld)
9. Leaving
10. Autumn Jones (Bryan, Keith Burns, Felber, Rucker, Sonefeld)
11. Free to Everyone
12. Waltz Into Me (Bryan, Felber, Hank Futch, Rucker, Sonefeld)

EP
Looking For Lucky B-Sides

July 2005, Vanguard/Sneaky Long (CD)

1. I Deal
2. I Deal Conversation
3. Ride Along
4. Ride Along Chatter

2006
FULL-LENGTH LIVE ALBUM
Live in Charleston - The Homegrown Tour

Recorded August 12, 2005, and released August 8, 2006, Sneaky Long/ Vanguard (CD, LP)
Recorded and mixed by Gary Lux.

1. State Your Peace
2. Time
3. Space
4. Hannah Jane
5. Hey Sister Pretty
6. Running From an Angel
7. One Love
8. Look Away
9. Leaving
10. I Hope That I Don't Fall in Love With You (Tom Waits)
11. Desert Mountain Showdown

12. Let Her Cry
13. I Go Blind (Neil Osborne, Phil Comparelli, Brad Merritt, Darryl Neudorf)
14. Old Man & Me
15. Drowning
16. Get Out of My Mind
17. Hold My Hand
18. Go and Tell Him (Soup Song)
19. The Killing Stone
20. Only Wanna Be With You

SINGLE

"Get Out of My Mind" (with Callout Hook). January 2006. Vanguard/ Sneaky Long (promo-only CD).

2007-2018

No new or previously unreleased music released

2019
ALBUM REISSUE WITH BONUS TRACKS
cracked rear view
Deluxe Edition, Remastered, 25th Anniversary

May 31, 2019, Rhino Records (CD, vinyl, cassette)
(First release on CD of complete *Hootie & the Blowfish, Time*, and *Kootchy-pop* material. Liner notes by Tim Sommer and Peter Holsapple.)

1. Hannah Jane
2. Hold My Hand
3. Let Her Cry
4. Only Wanna Be With You
5. Running From an Angel
6. I'm Goin' Home
7. Drowning
8. Time
9. Look Away
10. Not Even the Trees
11. Goodbye (with hidden track "Motherless Child"

Disc 2 - B-Sides, Outtakes, Pre-LP Independent Recordings

1. All That I Believe
2. I Go Blind (Neil Osborne, Phil Comparelli, Brad Merritt, Darryl Neudorf)
3. Almost Home (John Croslin)
4. Fine Line (Radney Foster)
5. Where Were You
6. Hey, Hey What Can I Do (John Bonham, John Paul Jones, Jimmy Page, Robert Plant)
7. The Old Man and Me - *Kootchypop Version*
8. Hold My Hand - *Kootchypop Version*
9. If You're Going My Way - *Kootchypop Version*
10. Sorry's Not Enough - *Kootchypop Version*
11. Only Wanna Be With You - *Kootchypop Version*
12. Running From an Angel - *1991 Version*
13. Time - *1991 Version*
14. Let Her Cry - *1991 Version*
15. Drowning - *1991 Version*
16. I Don't Understand
17. Little Girl
18. Look Away - *1990 Version*
19. Let My People Go
20. Hold My Hand - *1990 Version*

Disc 3 - Live at Nick's Fat City, Pittsburgh, PA, February 3rd, 1995

1. Hannah Jane
2. I Go Blind
3. Not Even the Trees
4. If You're Going My Way
5. Look Away
6. Fine Line
7. Let Her Cry
8. Motherless Child
9. I'm Goin' Home
10. Use Me (Bill Withers)
11. Running From An Angel
12. Sorry's Not Enough
13. Drowning
14. Old Man & Me
15. Only Wanna Be With You

16. Time
17. Goodbye
18. The Ballad of John and Yoko (Lennon-McCartney)
19. Hold My Hand
20. Love The One You're With (Stephen Stills)

FULL-LENGTH ALBUM
Imperfect Circle

November 1, 2019, Capitol Records Nashville (CD, vinyl)
Produced by Frank Rogers and Jeff Trott. (2020 Digital Reissue included
 "Losing My Religion" [Bill Berry, Peter Buck, Mike Mills, Michael Stipe]
 and "Turn It Up - Walshy Fire of Major Lazer Remix.")

1. New Year's Day (Tofer Brown, Bryan, Felber, Eric Paslay,
   Rucker, Sonefeld, Jeff Trott)
2. Miss California (Bryan, Andrew DeRoberts, Felber, David Ryan
   Harris, Rucker, Sonefeld)
3. Wildfire Love (Bryan, Joel Crouse, Dean Felber, Darius Rucker,
   Kyle Rife, Ed Sheeran, Sonefeld)
4. Hold On (Jim Beavers, Chris Stapleton)
5. Turn It Up (Bryan, Felber, Rucker, Sonefeld, Jeff Trott)
6. Not Tonight (Bryan, Andrew DeRoberts, Felber, David Ryan
   Harris, Rucker, Sonefeld)
7. We Are One (Bryan, Felber, Rucker, Sonefeld)
8. Everybody But You (Bryan, Felber, Frank Rogers, Rucker,
   Sonefeld)
9. Lonely On A Saturday Night (Chris August, Bryan, Felber,
   Rucker, James Slater, Sonefeld)
10. Why (Chris August, Bryan, Felber, Rucker, James Slater,
    Sonefeld)
11. Rollin' (Bryan, Adam Doleac, Felber, Zach Kale, John King,
    Rucker, Sonefeld)
12. Half A Day Ahead (Bryan, Felber, Rucker, Sonefeld)
13. Change (Bryan, Felber, Rucker, Sonefeld)

SINGLES

"Rollin'.'" September 2019.
"Miss California" b/w "Half a Day Ahead." September 2019. (vinyl)
"Hold On." October 2019.
"Lonely On A Saturday Night." October 2019.
"Turn It Up." October 2019.

2020

FULL-LENGTH LIVE ALBUM
Live At Nick's Fat City, 1995

September 26, 2020, Rhino Records (vinyl; limited edition of 5,000)

- A1. Hannah Jane
- A2. I Go Blind
- A3. Not Even The Trees
- 4A. If You're Going My Way
- A5. Look Away
- B1. Fine Line
- B2. Let Her Cry
- B3. Motherless Child
- B4. I'm Goin' Home
- B5. Use Me
- C1. Running From An Angel
- C2. Sorry's Not Enough
- C3. Drowning
- C4. The Old Man And Me
- C5. Only Wanna Be With You
- D1. Time
- D2. Goodbye
- D3. The Ballad Of John And Yoko
- D4. Hold My Hand
- D5. Love The One You're With

SINGLES

"Losing My Religion" b/w "Turn It Up (Walshy Fire Of Major Lazer Remix)." April 2020. (vinyl)

"Won't Be Home For Christmas (feat Abigail Hodges)" October 2020. (Originally recorded in 2006, with Hodges added in 2020.)

ACKNOWLEDGMENTS

The list of those who made this book possible is largely synchronous with the list of those who made the story of Hootie & the Blowfish possible. This is a testimony to the consistent willingness of the actors in this amazing drama/dream to share their time, memories, memorabilia, and experience.

Sometime late in the past decade when my agent, Rick Richter, and I first discussed the idea that I might attempt to write the story of Hootie & the Blowfish, my very next calls were to Darius, Dean, Mark, and Soni. I reached out to them within minutes. I would not even begin to consider undertaking the project without their blessing and cooperation. I was flattered that they not only readily agreed to assist me but also actively encouraged me. From that moment forward, each one of these gentlemen made themselves available for hours upon hours of interviews, not to mention dozens of email and text conversations—sometimes quite lengthy—to clarify points or direct me toward friends and associates who might be of assistance. If any of them ever got tired of hearing from me—and I am damn sure they did—they never showed it. Therefore, first and foremost, let me thank (alphabetically) Mark Bryan, Dean Felber, Darius Rucker, and Jim "Soni" Sonefeld, not just for their music but also for their willingness to allow me to tell the story of their music.

Rusty Harmon, Gus Gusler, and Brantley Smith also made themselves available whenever I needed them, regardless of how small, large, or completely inane my questions were. Because of this generosity of time and memories, I was able to hear the story of this band, in profound depth, from the seven people who actually lived every moment of it.

Kevin Oliver, Chip Latham, and Dick Hodgin offered indispensable insight into the band's life and career before 1993. In the very earliest days of this project, these same three individuals gave me an enormous amount of help and direction and were always there to tell me when I was—and wasn't—chasing the right trail of donut crumbs. Paul Graham, who was present for so very many of the events detailed here, was also extremely generous with his memories. His datebooks, calendars, and tour books were essential in reconstructing the band's (mostly) happy grind as a touring act in the days before they signed with Atlantic and the furious and magical salad days that came after the release of *cracked rear view*. One of the true pleasures of this book was reconnecting with Paul, a great friend from the days when both our lives were all Hootie, all the time.

Stan Shuster, the A&R person who signed Hootie & the Blowfish to their first (doomed) record deal, helped me make sense of one of the least-understood and least discussed chapters in the band's life. It would have been impossible to render an accurate account of the JRS saga without him.

The band's manager during the first decade of this century, the legendary Doc McGhee, could not have been more pleasant to speak with, and the time I spent on the phone with him was one of the unexpected pleasures of this whole endeavor. His frank and abundant memories and insight helped fill many gaps.

So very many people quickly and enthusiastically responded to my inquiries and helped shape the book you have in your hands. From Atlantic Records (that is, the people who were at the label during the Hootie era), let me thank Danny Goldberg (without whom there would be no *cracked rear view*); Val Azzoli; Linda Ferrando; my mentor at Atlantic, Tom Carolan; Tracy Zamot; and Jean Cawley. I would like to single out one of the prime forces behind Hootie's success, Kim Kaiman. Kim should write her own book; between her work with Hootie and her similar efforts shaping the early career and marketing of Britney Spears, she has a helluva story to tell. Scott Schiff was truly *the* person who brought the band to the attention of Atlantic Records, and I am so happy I have been able to reveal, for the first time in print, his fundamental role in this story. Micheal McLaughlin, who took the pictures that appeared on the cover of *cracked rear view*, graciously shared not only his experiences working with the band on one very important day in their life and career but also the photos he took at the time. From MTV and (especially) VH-1 (as it was known at the time), I would like to thank David Weir, Rick Krim, Patti Galuzzi, and Michael Simon. Over a quarter of a century later, the VH-1 vets still take great pride in the role their network had in breaking Hootie.

Like Kim Kaiman and myself, Evan Lamberg put his young career on the line to get an underdog band out to the world, and Evan unhesitatingly spoke with me multiple times about his substantial role in this story. There were also some very significant music industry movers, shakers, and music makers who made time in their busy schedules to speak with me, but none more so than Rob Light of CAA.

A who's who of highly respected journalists added light, shade, and detail to the story of Hootie & the Blowfish. I would like to especially thank David Menconi, Sarah Rodman, Jim DeRogatis, Jon Caramanica, the legendary Chris Berman, and the great Dan Patrick (the sportscaster, not the politician). Dan has spent so much time with Darius, Dean, Mark, and Soni and had so many experiences with the band he should write his own Hootie book. Also, the very talented and prescient Michael Miller's earlier work and research into Hootie & the Blowfish was an enormous help. Additionally, Richard F. Thomas from Harvard University shared his voluminous knowledge of the life and work of Bob Dylan, and Professor Jon Hale of the University of South Carolina contributed significantly to my understanding of the troubled and complex story of race in South Carolina, and how it impacted the biggest recording artist to ever come from that state.

Many musicians who shared studios and stages with Hootie & the Blowfish eagerly shared their memories with me. These people included John Hiatt, Jon Wurster, Gerald Duncan, Todd Nichols, Frank Rogers, Jeff Trott, Mike Mills, and the greatest utility player of all time and one of the unsung heroes of rock 'n' roll, Peter Holsapple. Record producer Don Gehman's constant and legendary qualities of kindness, patience, and frankness not only helped guide Hootie & the Blowfish through four album projects but also were on full display when he spoke with me about his work on *cracked rear view*, *Fairweather Johnson*, *Musical Chairs*, and *Looking for Lucky*.

The band's friends and associates from their time at the University of South Carolina were a terrific font of information. I would like to thank Chuck Denton, Jeff Rutstein, and Coach Mark Berson for their time and wisdom. Let me also thank Chris Carney and Hannah Jane Carney for sharing their time and very valuable memories. Going a little further back in time, Jan Smoak and Kelly Ann Sharpe eagerly spoke with me about their experiences in high school and middle school with Darius Rucker, and Steve Lipton shared valuable information about Mark's and Dean's musical endeavors in high school back in Maryland. Gary Greene, Jeff Poland, Billy Huelin, and any other Hootie associates and old friends I have failed to name—you were very much in my hearts as I wrote this; even if the stars didn't align for us to speak, you were a big part of this story, and I treasure not only the time we spent together in the past but also the time we will spend together in the future.

Ambassador Nikki Haley spoke with me, at great length and with great joy, about her deep affection for the most famous band from her home state and the exceptional charity work Hootie and Darius have done. She also contributed significantly to my understanding of the arcane (former) liquor laws of South Carolina.

At every stage of this project, a large and loving peanut gallery was there to chew over ideas and cheer me on. Although there are surely names that I left out, let me thank Bertis Downs, Cary Baker, Matthew Goodman, Geoff Edgars, Kevin Hogan, Doug Herzog, Paul Sherman, Matthew Barton, Mick Hargreaves, Alec Cumming, Alyssia and Scott Totten, Justin Joffe, Louis Maistros, Kay Kasperhauser Goldberg, Peter Sommer, Cathy Iselin, and especially Cole Garner Hill, Ron Hart, Ken Kurson, and Robert Kurson. Ken and Robert supplied some very helpful early guidance on this project. Many of these people had been rooting for me to write a book for decades, and I am so proud I can show them this. In addition, Samantha Weiner provided some enthusiasm for this project at a very, very early point, and I remember her kindly for this. The women and men in the various Hootie & the Blowfish fan groups on social media made their singular insight into and experiences with the band readily available to me. None of these people was of more assistance than Christie Crone, who rolled up her sleeves and went above and beyond the call of duty whenever asked.

A few weeks after I turned sixteen, I cold-called the offices of *Trouser Press* magazine. The person who normally answered the phones and screened out annoying callers like me had momentarily stepped out, so the magazine's editor-in-chief, Ira Robbins, picked up the phone. For some very strange reason, Ira not only hired me as an office boy, but he also gave me the chance to write about rock music. I'm not sure anyone else would have taken such a risk on a skinny eleventh grader who had more nerves than sense. If I have a godfather in this business, his name is Ira Robbins.

This book would not have been possible without the cooperation and resources offered by Chris Parr and Jason Hauser at Maverick, Darius and Hootie's current management. At every step, they encouraged this project and assisted in any way requested. I thank them—as well as publicist Ebie McFarland—hugely.

Layne Montgomery helped significantly with many factors of this project; most notably, research, fact checking, confirming dates, and the hugely thankless task of interview transcription.

There could be no more appropriate home for this book than the University of South Carolina Press, and I thank Richard Brown, MacKenzie Collier, Kerri Tolan, and Aurora Bell for their patronage, encouragement, and particularly their patience during this strange time when the story of these artists was changing almost daily and the entire world was shuddering with uncertainty. Aurora has been a skilled, patient, kind, and utterly on-point editor. It has been an absolute pleasure to work with her.

Brilliant, literate, poetic, provocative, scientific, and musical, the Brouts—Jennifer, Emily, Madeline, and Bo—were a constant source of inspiration during the long gestation of this project. They were always available for feedback, course correction, positivity, and positive digression, not to mention inspiring discussions about Dylan, World War II, "The Match Game," the potentiality of hot Chipwichs, and all the best sorts of distraction, support, and love. I cannot thank them enough for their tolerance, wit, company, love, and support.

Finally, I am not sure any of this would have happened without two extraordinary people who are no longer with us, Mia Zapata and John Loscalzo. In 2013, I had been effectively retired from music journalism for about twenty-nine years when a random street encounter in Brooklyn Heights with an old college-radio friend, the dear and much-loved John Loscalzo, led to my contributing to an arts and culture blog he was running. This, in turn, led to other major and minor publications seeking me out and, not so circuitously, to Rick Richter at the Aevitas Creative Management literary agency contacting me and asking if I had any ideas for a book. It is entirely possible that I would not have reactivated my writing career if it wasn't for John, whom we lost suddenly in 2014. Mia Zapata was simply the greatest female rock singer of her generation; she was taken from us in a senseless act of violence in early July of 1993, before most of the world had the chance to hear her. Not only was I one of those fortunate enough to know and be awed by Mia, it was also my intention to sign her to Atlantic. Tragedy took her, but the power of her work opened my heart in a way that would allow Darius, Dean, Mark, and Soni to step into it.